MW01100927

Bill 'Swampy' Marsh is an award-winning writer and performer of stories, songs and plays. He spent most of his youth in rural south-western New South Wales. Swampy was forced to give up any idea he had of a 'career' as a cricketer after a stint at agricultural college was curtailed because of illness, and so began his hobby of writing. After he had backpacked through three continents and worked in the wine industry, his writing hobby blossomed into a career.

Swampy runs writing workshops throughout schools and communities, and is employed part-time through the Adelaide Institute of TAFE's professional writing unit. He has won and judged many nationwide short story writing competitions, and performs his stories and songs regularly on radio, television and stage. His plays have been performed across Australia.

To discover more about Swampy's work, visit www.billswampymarsh.com

Other books by this author

Beckom Pop. 64
Old Yanconian Daze
Looking For Dad
Great Australian Flying Doctor Stories
Great Australian Shearing Stories
Great Australian Droving Stories
Great Australian Railway Stories
More Great Australian Flying Doctor Stories

BILL 'SWAMPY' MARSH

GOLDIE

ADVENTURES IN A VANISHING AUSTRALIA

ABC
Books

Published by ABC Books for the
AUSTRALIAN BROADCASTING CORPORATION
GPO Box 9994 Sydney NSW 2001

First published in July 2008

Marsh, Bill, 1950–
  Goldie: adventures in a vanishing Australia/
  Bill "Swampy" Marsh.
  1st ed.
  Sydney: ABC Books, 2008
  ISBN 978 0 7333 2260 0 (pbk.)
  Goldsmith, Jack, 1933–
  Drovers – Australia – Biography.
  Korean War, 1950–1953 – Personal narratives, Australian
  Cattle droving – Australia – History.
  Australia – Social conditions – 20th century.
636.213092

Cover designed by Christabella Designs
Typeset in 11.5/15pt Granjon by Kirby Jones
Printed and bound in Australia by Griffin Press Pty Ltd, Adelaide

5 4 3 2 1

Bill 'Swampy' Marsh would like to dedicate this book to David and Christine Harris in appreciation of their many years of love, support and friendship.

Goldie would like to dedicate his story to the packhorse drovers, in memory of the vast distances and the sound of horse bells in the night, sounds that only a drover would understand. And to the ringers from the cattle camps. Though those days are now a memory, it was a great privilege to have lived through them.

Introduction

Through my work and travels as a story collector, storyteller and writer I meet many fascinating characters. A true gem among them is Jack 'Goldie' Goldsmith. After a troubled childhood he took off bush and began his many adventures, always moving on, sometimes being knocked down but always getting back up on his feet again to face another round or another challenge.

Over the years, Goldie has been an enthusiastic contributor to my many books about the Australian outback and its people. Like me, he doesn't view life as a sequence of events: more like a string of stories. And what stories they are. Many times we were sitting at his kitchen table and he'd be telling a story so vividly that I could feel the pain of a child being thrashed, sense the panic of a mob of cattle the moment before they rushed, smell the waft of smoke from some time-distant campfire, or break out into a nervous thrill as if I was riding beside him as we went over into Glenore to duff some cleanskins. It is in Goldie's voice that I have tried to tell his story.

Something beyond a book has come out of our sessions together. I was able to experience a life that I could only dream of living, and to learn that age might have wearied Goldie but it has in no way diminished his vitality or spirit. But more importantly the writing of *Goldie* has nourished a great friendship and mateship between us.

I hope you enjoy reading *Goldie* as much as I've enjoyed writing it, and as much as Goldie has loved telling it.

Bill 'Swampy' Marsh
Adelaide 2008

Goldie

1

To tell you the truth, when I was thinking about this early part of me life, it stirred up things and it wasn't too nice, aye. Like, a few years ago I bought this big old railway clock. It's in the house here and it's got a very loud ticking sound to it and last night I dreamed that the ticking sounds was the footsteps of me stepmother walking round, looking for me – you know, to give me a flogging. I woke up singing out: 'Why're yer doin' this to me? Why're yer doin' this ter me?'

So, yeah, and I was only a kid when all that was going on and now I'm into me seventies. So it must've made a big impression, aye. But it was the ticking sounds of the old railway clock that got into the dream and it sounded like the clicking steps of the stepmother.

Anyway, okay, here goes. Before all that started, my mother and father lived up in the Blue Mountains at a place called Springwood. Springwood, in them days, was just a little country town. There was even bullock teams, would you believe. Now, my mother didn't go into the hospital to have me. I was born at home because on the birth certificate it's got 'Born in Short Street'. That was on 4 December 1933 and back then there was only three houses in Short Street.

I was born – delivered – by a woman who was a nurse. These days she'd be called a midwife. My father told me later that this nurse held a lot of very strange superstitions. One of them was that the placenta and all the stuff that was wrapped around me had to be burned because, if it wasn't, I'd be cursed for the rest of me life. You know, that type of thinking was what they had back in the medieval times, aye. So my old man – well, I shouldn't call him 'my old man' – so my father told me that this nurse made him light a fire out the back of our house and he burnt all the placenta and that himself.

My father worked in the post office in Springwood. He was behind the counter and he also did the mail delivery twice a day. At the start he used to deliver the mail on a horse but then, later on, he got a pushbike, and I still remember him riding round on that thing. And those real early memories are very precious to me, especially of my mother because, see, my mother was gorgeous and I can only remember she had a lot of love. In fact, after the stepmother come along and started belting me, when I went to bed at night, I used to try and get a bit of relief by thinking about the love of my mother and how close I felt to her. But then my mother died. I was three and a half years old at that time and me brother, David, he was only

Goldie aged 3

five months old. Actually, I can remember looking at him one day and he was asleep, with a mosquito net or a veil over the top of the bassinet.

Well, what happened with my mother was that a cyst grew on her wrist, see, and she went to the doctor in Springwood. Now, this doctor was apparently very highly thought of but he lanced the cyst before it should've been lanced and somehow my mother got blood poisoning and five days later she died in Royal South Sydney Women's Hospital. One of me aunties gave me some photos of me and my mother where you can see the bandage wrapped around her wrist. So they must've been taken just before she died, aye. In one of them we're in the garden and she's holding my hand. I like that one. Then I sort of half-remember them taking her away in the ambulance, to go to the hospital. Well, the ambulance fellers come and they was taking her out, down the hall, on a stretcher, and the feller at the back of the stretcher, he was walking frontwards and the feller at the front of the stretcher was walking backwards, if you catch my drift. Then, when they gets to the front doorstep, they put the stretcher down so that the feller at the front could turn around and walk forwards, out to the ambulance. And that's the last I saw of her.

After my mother died I went to live with Aunty Millie and Uncle Frank, up at Katoomba, for nearly four years. Frank Bushby his name was. They was childless for some reason or other. Uncle Frank worked on the railway and Aunty Millie, I tell you, she was so good to me, aye. She reared me up with love but with discipline. Then with me brother David, some people from a dairy farm looked after him. I forget their name just now but, when they eventually sold the farm and subdivided it, those people who'd looked after him had it in their will that one of the streets in the subdivision be named David Street, after him. That street's still there today. But I can only remember

Goldie and his mother just before she died

seeing David about twice when we was living in separate homes, over that four-year period.

Now, I heard somewhere later, and I'm not sure where, but I heard that before my father married my mother he'd been courting the stepmother-to-be. Yeah. That was back when my mother's family was living in Sydney. But see, my mother's father had been gassed over in France, in World War I, and he had some sort of breathing problem so the doctor in Sydney told him, 'You've gotta go up to the mountains 'n' get some good fresh mountain air.'

And that's the reason why my mother's family come up to Springwood to live. So they comes up and, of course, my mother's the talk of the town, aye. Like, here's this beautiful woman who's just arrived in town. So then my father drops me stepmother-to-be and he starts courting my mother-to-be, you see, and then he marries her. That's when she had me and David. So that's apparently what happened there and that could've been where the deep cause of all the trouble come from. But as far as I know, I only saw the stepmother for the first time, just a week or so before my father took me out of Aunty Millie's home and back down to Springwood to live with them. Well, I think she come up to Katoomba to talk to Aunty about something. So then, yeah, they come up and they took me back in a car but, no, I don't know how long before that they'd gotten married or anything.

So then it started, aye. In fact, on the very first day it started. My father had gone to work at the post office and me and David, we're sitting in the lounge room. It must've been about ten o'clock in the morning and she's still in bed, reading or something. Anyhow, I calls out, 'I'm hungry.'

And out she came, aye. 'You insolent pup.' It's as clear as yesterday. She always called me an insolent pup. 'You insolent pup,' she shouted and she went on shouting at me and I don't know what we got for breakfast; maybe just bread and milk with water and sugar because that's all we got, summer, winter, all year round. In our house in Springwood there was only a water tank and a wood fuel stove and an old-fashioned copper, where she done the washing. Anyhow, they was renting the house, so then she says to me, 'Go up ter the wood heap 'n' get some wood 'n' light this fire 'n' be quick about it.'

But, see, I was only about six and I'd never lit a fire in me whole life before. So I goes up the wood heap and I picks up all this sawdust and a few sticks and I brings it all back down, then she roars at me for being stupid for not getting the proper wood to light the fire. Anyhow, she never flogged me for that. But that's when I first remember when all the fear of her came in – you know, because that's when all the misery began, on that first day.

And every day from then on it was like a life sentence because then the floggings started with the feather duster. I tell you, the things she done to me, she should've been locked up and had the key thrown away. Like, sometimes I'd get a belting and I'd hardly know what it was for. But, no, she never belted David as much as me because, see, what I reckon got into her craw was how I was almost identical to my mother, in looks. So we'd be up town and someone would come over and say, 'Oh, isn't he just like his mother?'

And when that happened I knew that I'd only have do the slightest thing wrong, when I got home, like spill something, and I'd get a flogging. And she never spent money on us so I always had colds and everything because we'd go to school in summer clothes, even in winter. And the clothes, I'd outgrow them and they'd be all tight on me and I'd have to be careful how I bent over because I was always worried that me shorts would split at the back, aye, and then I'd be in trouble again when I got home. Yeah, another belting. So it was that sort of drama I went through.

Of course, while all this was going on so was the war. I'd just come down from Aunty Millie's when it started and I was about twelve when it was coming to an end. My father didn't go to war because he was called 'Essential Service'. That's for people who worked in government departments and other jobs they said was very essential in helping the war effort. But I give him credit because he apparently did try and go but they knocked him back because they said, 'No, you're needed on the home front.'

So I don't know what would've happened if my father had gone off to fight. I'd hate to think. But, yes, I was very much aware that the war going on. Like, all we did at school was draw dog-fights with aeroplanes. Sometimes even army tanks went through Springwood and we had an air-raid shelter at the back of the house and we had blackout paper.

Anyhow, I was quick to learn how to chop wood and light the fire and I'd get up early of a morning to get my father a cup of tea and some toast and, of course, then I had to take her in a drink of tea and some toast. But there was never a 'thank you' or nothing. In fact, she never ever spoke to me or David. The only time she ever said anything was when she roared abuse at us and told us off and what-not. That's the only time. And, now here's a strange thing – see, all this time she was a very staunch Roman Catholic. Like, we lived a couple of miles out of town and she'd walk to church every Sunday. She'd never ever miss mass. And her strict instructions before she left was, 'Have the fire alight when I get back 'n' don't go off the concrete.'

See, we had a great big slab of concrete off the back of the house and she forbade us to go off that concrete, which we did, of course. But from the backyard we could see her coming home from church, down through the town pound, and we knew then that it was time to get off the concrete and get things done. Yeah, that's how it was. Always that fear of her. So she didn't really care for us, aye. And when I'd go to school, all the other kids had nice little lunch boxes which had cheese and lettuce or corned beef and tomato sandwiches all wrapped up real nice in a tea towel or greaseproof paper and they'd have a piece of cake and some fruit and all I'd have was a couple of slices of bread with a bit of sugar sprinkled over it, wrapped up in old newspaper. Even the black ink from the newspaper got into the bread. And I remember one day the schoolteacher calls out, 'Goldsmith, come out here to the front.' So I goes out the front and I stands there and she looks down at me like I'm disgusting and she shouts out, 'Look at you, you always look so dirty. Dirty. How often do you have a bath?'

I says, 'Oh, 'bout once a week, Miss.'

And the whole class started laughing, you know. And that was horrible. But, see, what happened was that on Sundays David and me, we'd have a proper bath in the water my father and she had used, then during the week nights we'd wash ourselves in the basin. So they all laughed at me. What I should've done was just put me back to the class and lift me shirt up to let them see all the scars and the welts from all the floggings. That's what I should've done, but I didn't think about that till afterwards.

Well, mainly the feather duster was what she belted us with. It had a cane about three foot long with the duster bit on the other end. Then after it wore out, which didn't take long, when she was going to flog me she'd get David to go up to the apple tree and get a switch off that and bring it back. And, oh boy, I tell you, it stung like all heck. And if she was going to give David a flogging she'd get me to go up and get the apple stick. And as hard as you might, you'd try to pick one you don't think was going to hurt so much on your little brother, aye.

Then another time I remember with fear was when I was playing with some kids down the bush and, before I realised it, I was late coming back home and I got frightened to go back because I knew I'd get a belting. I knew I had to go back because the longer I left it the worse the flogging would be. So by the time I arrived home I was scared stiff, aye, of what she was going to do. Then, when I come down, she was splitting wood, with a tomahawk, at the back step. So there was all these sticks about a foot long and about an inch thick, to start the fire going, and she belted me and she belted me with one of them sticks and, oh, the splinters in them, oh, they just ripped me to pieces, you know.

So she loved flogging us, aye, and the welts came up, about four inches long. Not only on our backs, sometimes she went for the legs too. Then, of course, you'd put your arms down to protect yourself from the hit and so you'd get lots of scars around the arms. But here's the thing: for the life of me I don't know why the teachers didn't say nothing. And why my father didn't know or he didn't do nothing, that's got me beat, too. She just got away with it, well, for a good while, anyway, because I think it eventually got rumoured what was going on. See, a woman who lived near us, Mrs Kilduff, she woke up to it all because every time the stepmother took to us she'd turn the wireless up real loud so the neighbours wouldn't hear us screaming.

But when the rumours was starting to fly around Springwood, what did my father do? Well, he gets a transfer into Sydney, doesn't he? Gets us out of there. And to this day I'm still stumped as to if he knew anything about it or not. I mean, you'd reckon he must have, aye? What I should've done was to have fronted him with it. I should've fronted him with it and asked him straight out, 'Why is it we left Springwood?' That's what I should've done. I should've said, 'I know why you left Springwood but I want you to tell me why we left Springwood.' Because surely he would've seen the welts on me back and on me legs and on me arms. Surely. You'd have to be blind not to have, aye. Only once did he ever come to our defence. She was giving me a good walloping there one day and he says, 'Oh, lay off him, Mollie.'

That's the only time he ever came to my defence. The only time. And she'd always stare out the kitchen window, looking at the bush, and she'd stand there for ages thinking to herself and I'd be hoping she was feeling guilty about all the things she done to us and she'd stop flogging us and start being kind. But that never happened.

Anyway, that's how it was and it got so bad, I once had tuppence ha'penny. I think someone we visited give it to me. Usually, if anyone gave us some money she'd take it straight back off us when we got back home. But this time I still had it and I was walking to school with this tuppence ha'penny in me pocket and I thought how if I gave it all to God, then He'd get her to stop belting us. So I was going past this telegraph pole, you know, like a light pole, and I dug a little hole and I put the

Goldie's father and stepmother on their wedding day 1940

money there and I said, 'There yer go God, that's fer you. Help her stop beltin' me.' Then a week or so later I'm going past the light pole on me way to school and I thinks, I wonder if God's taken that money up ter heaven. And the curiosity got the best of me so I goes over and I dug around and the money's still there and, you know, I was just so disappointed that God never took it to heaven. So I just took the money then and I spent it on lollies. But, oh, I was so disappointed, aye.

But, I mean, we had a bit of a laugh on her too, sometimes. See, very reluctantly, of a Saturday afternoon, she might say, 'You boys can go ter the pictures. Here's sixpence each ter get in 'n' there's a penny ter spend on lollies. But I want some of the lollies you buy.'

So what we done was, we'd go round to the back of the picture theatre to where they burnt the tickets from the week before and we'd fish out the tickets that wasn't burnt so bad and we'd pass them over to get in. Now we had sevenpence for ourselves. So we'd have a good time on that and then, when we're walking out after the pictures, we'd pick up the lollies that people had left behind or had dropped and we'd take them home and give them to her. So we got a bit back there, aye.

2

Well, I was about twelve by the time we moved down to Sydney. We lived in Croydon. But things didn't get any better and what still gets me is how I had opportunities to tell people about what was going on, but I didn't. And you mightn't believe this, but I know a person who's a psychiatrist, and I must ask him this – see, she used to bath me right up till I was fourteen. True, right up until I was fourteen. Not only that, and I'm ashamed to say this, but she used to take a bit longer in places, you know, like down there and all that. Yeah, because by now I'm starting to mature, like, you know, and so I'm growing hair. So there was really something wrong with her, aye. And what upset me was that, sometimes, my father was right there in the bathroom, shaving or that. Now wouldn't you think he'd say something? Wouldn't you think he'd notice something's wrong? But, no, he never said a thing. Not one thing.

And she still wouldn't buy us any clothes so, of course, I'm always having bad colds and things. In dead winter, one time, when I went down the shop to get the paper, I still had summer clothes on, see, and the neighbour from up the street says to me, 'Geez, aren't you cold?'

'No,' I said, but, in fact, I was freezing. And even when I went to high school at Ashfield Tech I still only had two shirts and two pairs of trousers. That's all. And the clothes got so tight on me that, in the end, I'd wag school because I was too ashamed to turn up there because all the kids called me names and laughed at me and things.

But I had a mate and we'd wag school together. Like,

sometimes we'd go to Taronga Park Zoo. And this feller, me mate, in my opinion he was heading for disaster, aye, because he'd always be thieving and that. And because I never had any money, well, maybe it was him who shouted me on the ferry over to the zoo. Anyway, when we'd get there we'd climb over the wall so we'd get in for nothing. One time he climbed over a railing and pinched a little tortoise. So he was no good, aye. And he also showed me how to get into one of the picture theatres without paying. See, down this lane there was a door that went to the back of a restaurant and the restaurant shared a toilet with the picture theatre so you'd go up the lane and duck in through the back of the restaurant, into the toilet, then you'd sneak into the pictures for free.

Yeah, I used to do a lot of that because I just loved the cowboy films. And, oh, the cowboy books, I loved them, too. I'd read them all the time and imagine I was the cowboy – you know, to get on a horse and just ride, and all that openness and have no one to abuse you all the time. I reckon that's where I got the idea of going west or up north, into the outback places, and working with cattle and all that. Just the freedom of it. I loved that. Of course, I didn't know the terms of 'ringer' instead of 'cowboy', and 'station' instead of 'ranch', or 'a rush' instead of a 'stampede', and those sorts of things. Not then I didn't. I just wanted to be a cowboy and get away.

But I must say, about my father, one thing he'd do was he'd take me and David up to the Megalong Valley, out from Katoomba, and we'd go shooting rabbits and camping out and that sort of thing. One time we even went up to a timber place out of Kempsey. But even if it was only for a few days, we'd be away from her, aye. So that was good. Then I would've been near on fourteen when my father got me my first rifle. He bought it from one of those hock shops in Bathurst Street. It was a .22 pump-action Winchester, and he got me brother a single-shot Belgian rifle. And he taught us how to fire a gun and how to set up a camp and catch and skin rabbits and all that. That was me first taste of freedom. Oh, I just loved the bush – you know, making dampers and flapjacks and that, and shooting. And we'd just camp out in a swag sort of thing. All we had was just a fly, which is a basic sort of tent. It was a cowboy's sort of living and I thought, Well, this's the life for me.

But oh, I dreaded going home after those trips because, by then, even though I was too old to belt, what did she do? She started to tell lies about me to my father, about how I was doing horrible things like stealing money from her and all that. But they was deliberate lies, see, because she could see that every now and then my father and me, we had a good time together, and she just wanted to turn him against me. Anyhow, all this was no good, so one day when I did turn up at Ashfield Tech I says to another kid there – Harold somebody or other, his name was – I says, 'I'm gonna run away from home.'

'I'll go with yer then,' Harold says.

See, my idea was to go right up into Queensland. I was starting to feel me oats, you could say, and with going to all the films and reading all the American westerns, you know, I just wanted to go west and be a cowboy. I mean, back then, even Dubbo seemed like it was the end of the world. Anyrate, this Harold feller was stuck on going to Wallerawang, which is only just out from Lithgow, so I says, 'Well alright, we'll go ter Wallerawang first 'n' then we'll just keep goin'.'

'Okay,' he says.

So we starts hitchhiking and we only slept one night out in the bush and when we gets to Wallerawang it turns out that Harold had a grandmother who lived just up the road. By then he was starting to get homesick anyway, so he went up to his grandmother's place and he rang his father and then my father come up with his father and I was dragged back home and, boy, didn't I get into some strife over that? But, see, it was me first little taste of a getaway, and I liked it, so I thought, Okay, next time I go it'll be fer good 'n' I won't make a mess of it.

But, what I needed, of course, was money. By now I'm about fifteen, which was the minimum age you could leave school. So I gets a job. That was in a factory where they made tools. It was in walking distance from home. Now I can't remember what happened but I soon finished up working there and I ends up down at the Government Printing Office. No, I don't remember what the actual wages was but, as plain as day, the stepmother took all me pay, then she'd give me two shillings and tenpence back, which was exactly the weekly juvenile travel fare. That's all, just enough for the fare. No pocket money. Nothing.

At the Government Printing Office, they wanted to apprentice me as a paper ruler. The paper ruler was the machine that makes the red lines going down and red lines going across, in accounts books. Then, like on writing-pad paper, where the blue lines go across, I was also learning how to do that. So that's what I done. Nowadays, of course, it's all done by computers so the trade's died. Anyhow, after I'd been working there for a while, I got a rise. But I never told her, see. I started saving the balance, aye, so I could get away, and that was going well till she found a pay packet under the cushion of the lounge and, oh boy, didn't I suffer for that?

But, see, by then I'd saved up twenty-seven shillings – yeah, exactly twenty-seven shillings. There was another feller who worked with me in the printing office. His name was Frank Yateman. Frank was apprenticed to be a linotype worker. Well, a linotype is like a typewriter but where you have to press lead letters and numbers into it when they set it up for printing. And Frank had gotten to know me stepmother too because he used to come round and we'd go bush and that, on weekends. So I says to Frank one day, I says, 'I'm gonna clear out. How's about comin' with me?'

He says, 'Yeah, okay.'

We didn't tell no one but we booked our seats on the train to Brisbane. I don't remember the finer details but I do know we somehow got away with only having to pay a child's fare. Maybe it was because we was under sixteen or whatever it was. And here's something else, and it's got me thinking if my father might've got wind how something was going on because, not long before I left, he comes and says to me, 'One day, son, when you go out in the world there's two things I want you to remember. First of all, I want you to promise me that you'll never join the police force.' So he must've had something against coppers, aye. No, I never found out what it was but when he'd come out of a hotel, the first thing he done was to look out for coppers. And later in me life, a feller was telling me that, one time, he was standing with my father in the main street of Katoomba and they saw these two coppers walking down the street and this mate said to my father, 'Look out George; here comes two coppers. They might be comin' ter get yer.'

And my father said back to this feller, he said, 'Oh no they're not. They'll have ter send a lot more than two coppers when they come after me.'

So there was something going on there, aye. But I never found out just what it was. And the other thing, the second thing he said to me was, 'When you get older you'll have a lot to do with women, son.' Then he said, 'Remember this, a woman's tears is her greatest weapon.'

Yeah – 'a woman's tears is her greatest weapon' – and that was just before I left. But, no, there wasn't a big fight or nothing. I just left a note on the kitchen table which roughly said 'I'm leaving and you'll never see me again', and that was it.

All I left with was an old air-force kitbag with all me stuff in that. Like, I hadn't learned how to roll a swag, not back then. And I took the Winchester pump-action .22. You could break it in half and stick it down in the kitbag and you couldn't see it. I loved that rifle. But you could walk around in those days with a gun and no one much minded.

Anyhow, so Frank and me, we catches the train up to Brisbane and then we heads out west on the motor rail. And in Queensland, back then, you weren't allowed to go into a hotel till you was twenty-one. In New South Wales the legal age was eighteen. And I remember this rail motor, it pulled up at some place on the way out to Toowoomba. It was night time and everyone went to the Railways Refreshment Room for something to eat and drink and in them days you could get alcohol in them refreshment rooms, so Frank and me we asked for a beer and they gave us one and that was my first taste of Queensland beer. But I always thought it was a funny thing because I was still only fifteen or sixteen when I left home and I got a child's railway fare on the train up to Brisbane and then I had me first taste of Queensland beer and I was supposed to be twenty-one.

Anyhow, by the time we gets to Toowoomba we'd run out of money and so we goes to the great big Southern Cross windmill factory there and asks for a job. But there was nothing going. Then we tried some other places and that didn't turn out either, so that's when I sold me rifle. I didn't want to but we'd gone a couple of days without a feed and a bloke picked us up and he asked me what I had in the bag and I told him I had the gun.

'I'll buy it off yer,' he said.

'Okay then,' I says and so I sold it to him.

I forget how much I got for it but it was practically nothing. But by then I didn't care, just as long as it was enough for a feed, aye. So things weren't working out too well and in the end

I says to Frank, I said, 'Let's go further out inta the cattle stations.'

But by then Frank was homesick and he wanted to go back home so I says, 'Oh well, I'll tag along with yer.' So I finished up back down in Sydney. But the last thing I wanted was to end up going back home with me tail between me legs so I camped up in the bush for a week or so, then I thought, Well this's gettin' me nowhere. I'm gonna go out west.

Anyhow, while I was in Sydney, I got back in contact with an old mate of mine, Bluey Flannigan. Well, I'd first met Bluey when we lived in Croydon. We was always wandering round together and I was always round at his place because of me stepmother. So I got to be very good friends with him and his family – he had two sisters – and they sort of half-adopted me, like. Oh, they was a real lovely family, actually, the Flannigans, and Bluey had a good home life, other than his father. Well, he had a bad father. In fact, his father once tried to kill him. True. See, Bluey used to always ride his pushbike and one day his father put vaseline on its brakes. So Bluey's racing down Parramatta Road and he goes to pull up at a stop light and the pushbike just keeps on going. Fair dinkum. His own father did that. But Bluey was alright. Nothing hit him. So he was lucky, aye. But he couldn't understand what was going on till he took a look and there's all this vaseline wrapped around the brakes.

But, oh, they hated each other, Bluey and his father. The father owned a truck or something so he was away a lot of the time, which was good. And I don't think his mother got on that well with the father neither, because I was around there one time when the dad come home and Bluey and him had this great big fight and Bluey's mum took to his dad with a frying pan. Oh, I remember that real well, I do, because I was wishing my father would've done something like that with me stepmother. You know, not to hit her with a frying pan but just stick up for me. So yeah, I remember that real well. But as I said, other than his father, Bluey had a good home life.

Anyhow, so I gets in touch with Bluey and I tells him how I'm going out west to Dubbo and he says he'll come along too but he'd have to wait for a week or so. So we agreed to leave each other a message at the first barber shop as you go into Dubbo. Okay, so I'm heading north again and, anyway, I gets out to Hornsby and I'm standing at the edge of town, hitchhiking, and this car pulls up. It's an unmarked police car. So they gets out and there's this other feller with them and before I know it they're going through me kitbag and, see, I had an old hessian blanket where the wool was somehow sprayed onto hessian. So this blanket had all these, sort of, patches of hessian on it and when the police pulled it out of me kitbag this other feller says, 'Yeah, that's it, that's the one. That's my blanket, alright.'

Now, apparently, what'd happened was that, earlier that night, this other feller's car had been broken into and the thieves stole a blanket like mine that was wrapped around his tools. So now they think that I stole this feller's tools. So they takes me back to the police station and they asks me lots of questions about who I am and where I live and I sort of had to tell them. Then I says to the sergeant, 'Look, if this blanket had tools wrapped in it, where's the grease from the tools? Where's all the dirty marks?'

Anyhow, I must've convinced them that I wasn't the thief, aye, because after that I could hear them talking to this feller in the next room – the one who'd had his tools stolen – and they was saying to him, 'No, that's not the thief. He never took yer blanket. That's not yer blanket.'

But apparently – and I didn't know anything about this till a long time after – when I'd told them where I lived, the police from Hornsby rang up the police from Burwood and the police from Burwood, they goes down and wakes up my father and says, 'Yer son's been booked fer stealin' out at Hornsby Police Station.'

My father had an Indian side-car motorbike, back then, so he jumps on the bike and he goes and gets a workmate from up the street and they rushes out to Hornsby. I'm supposing now that he just wanted to see I was alright because he would've known full well that the last thing I was going to do was to go back home and see her gloat at the way I was. No fear. That would've been a win for her, aye. But, in the meantime, while my father was on the way up to Hornsby, the Hornsby coppers had let me go. So I goes back out on the road again to hitchhike and, apparently, I missed my father by just a few minutes.

3

So I gets to Dubbo and I'm camped out under the bridge to Nyngan, waiting for Bluey to turn up. Now I don't know how long I was camped under the bridge for but then I went potato picking-up for a Jewish feller called Schibble. I haven't got the foggiest idea how I got the job but he lived three mile out of Dubbo, right alongside the Macquarie River, and when I started picking spuds for him I camped out at his place, under a tree, just sleeping on the ground, basically. So, yeah, I roughed it out there and I'd light a bit of a fire and I'd cook spuds in a quart pot, for a feed. You know what a quart pot is, don't you? It's a tin container that's sort of flattened on one side so it doesn't roll around when you carry it. Anyhow, there was plenty of spuds to eat and also Schibble's daughter sometimes brung sandwiches and things down to me. I'd say she'd have been about fifteen or sixteen. But oh, this Schibble, he had acres and acres of spuds. He had a tractor with a plough sort of thing behind it and as it went along it'd turn the soil over and the potatoes would come up to the top of the ground. I'd say there was about three or four of us working for him and we'd go along behind the tractor, picking up the spuds, then we'd bag them. And we got three shillings and sixpence per bag. Schibble was the highest payer round there and he was a Jew, aye. So how's about that?

Anyrate, I'd left a message for Bluey at the first barber's shop on the way into town but he hadn't turned up. Actually, I decided to give up on him and go me own way; then, just after I'd finished working for Schibble, I ran into him in town. That was down near an old jail they had there, a touristy thing. I ran into him down there and I said, 'What kept yer so long? I thought yer woulda been here weeks ago.'

So then we stuck around Dubbo for a few days because, see, it was summer time and there was a shop there and the heat had melted all the chocolate and so the owner feller, he refroze it and he was selling it for something like tuppence for a great big slab of chocolate. Real cheap. So that's what we ate, aye, till we heard that there might be some work going up at Gulargambone. So we hitchhiked up there and the feller at the shop told us to go to the local stock and station agent. See, stock and station agents are the places to go and ask if there's any rural work because they're always in contact with the local farmers. You know, a sheep cocky or someone might say, 'Look, can yer find me a fencer or some fellers ter do some dam sinking or whatever?'

So we goes to the stock and station agent at Gulargambone and he took us out onto the street and he says, 'Look, see that house over there?' It was a sheep station but the homestead was right in town. He says, 'Go over there 'n' see Mr Christie. I reckon he'll have some work fer yers.'

See, this was back when wool was at its highest price, when it was fetching a pound a pound. The only trouble was that the rabbit plague was on and the rabbits was eating all the grass, aye, and apparently he wanted some fellers to help get the rabbit population down on his farm. So we goes over there. We knocks on the back door and, would you believe it, the rabbits was so bad that there was even a rabbit burrow right under his back doorstep. Yeah, under his back doorstep. Anyrate, we ask Mr Christie if there's any work and he says he'll take us on as rabbit trappers. Nothing was said about wages. Then he says, 'Alright then, go down ter the hotel. I'll book yers in there fer the night 'n' I'll meet yers back here early tomorra mornin'.'

Good, at least we had a job. So we goes down the pub and we're late for a feed so we goes into the kitchen and helps ourselves. They didn't worry about that. Then, next morning, Bluey and me, we'd somehow missed breakfast but we had our gear packed up and we're just mucking around in our room, having a pillow fight and one thing and another, and we was just about to go over to Mr Christie's place when this girl comes up and says, 'Oh, Mr Christie just rang 'n' said don't bother comin'.'

So we'd got the sack before we even started. Yeah. See, he expected us to be there at the crack of dawn and now it was about eight o'clock. So we goes back to the stock and station agent and he says, 'What happened?'

Anyway, so then he sends us out to a place called Brightling Station. The sheep cocky out there also wanted to get the rabbit population down. So the stock and station agent, he pays for the taxi fare and, when we arrive, the overseer's sitting alongside this massive big pile of rabbit traps. All brand new Lanes-aces, they were. They was the most common of the traps. They had a big factory in Newcastle. Anyhow, the overseer had a file and he's going through every one of them traps, making the triggers more touchy to set off. So Bluey and me, we're standing there and he says to me, 'How many can yer skin in an hour, boy?'

Now, my father had taught me how to skin a rabbit, back when we used to go out bush. So I knew what to do but I didn't want to lose us the job by saying something too low and I wasn't too sure how many a good rabbit skinner could do in an hour, so I says, 'Oh, 'bout sixty.' That's one a minute.

'Oh sixty, aye?'

He's got a small fire there and he kept looking into this fire and saying to himself, 'Sixty an hour. Sixty an hour', and by the way he was saying it I started thinking that maybe sixty an hour wasn't good enough and perhaps I should've said 'Eighty'. I was already smoking by then – I'd started when I was fourteen – so anyway, I rolls a smoke and I'm watching him do all this, then he says, 'Boy,' he says, 'sixty an hour's pretty fast fer a smoker.'

But we got the job. He said he'd pay us a pound a day and he'd provide a bit of tucker, which was pretty good, plus we could keep all the rabbit skins to sell for ourselves. As I said, basically, he just wanted to keep the rabbits down on his property. So he took us from Brightling homestead out to a camp in his sulky and he drops us off, away out in the middle of this black soil plain, with about sixty traps. That was the maximum you could work, really. Then he gives us a bit of meat and some flour – you know, the basics. And there was only two trees out there, so he gives us a fly – a tarpaulin – and we put a ridge pole up between these two trees and we pegged the fly out. But the only trouble was that we planted this thing right over a rabbit warren, aye, and these poor rabbits, they'd come out of a night to have a feed and they'd get the fright of their lives because there we'd be, trying to get some sleep. So they'd shoot back down the warren. Then after three or four nights they got so hungry, they started jumping out all over us, which didn't do much for our sleeping, I can tell you.

Anyhow, I showed Bluey how to trap and skin a rabbit and all that. Now with rabbit trapping, the idea is to set the trap at the front of the burrow so you catch him when he comes out for a feed. I think it's been banned these days because of the cruelty of it but, if you can imagine, the whole contraption's made of steel, about fifteen or so inches long. The back part's the handle and the front part's a spring trap with jaws on it. A lot of trappers don't like the jaws too sharp. They file them off a bit because if they're too sharp they'll cut the leg of rabbit clean off and it'll get away. Then, when you squeeze the handle on the trap, that opens up the jaws. Now, the old Lanes-aces, you can open them by hand, and under the jaws you've got a flat plate and you put your finger under the plate – not on top or you'll lose it – and you carefully set the trigger before you release the handle very lightly. Very lightly, yes. If you do it too quick, the trap'll go off.

Then at the handle end of the trap there's a chain attached, which has a peg on the end and you push the peg into the ground so that when the rabbit gets caught in the jaws it won't take off with your trap. After you've done that, you remove some of the top soil from in front of the burrow and you place the trap in there and put newspaper or something over the plate. Some trappers just roll toilet paper across. Then you sprinkle a little bit of dirt over the top with some grass around it to hide the trap and, when the rabbit comes out of the burrow, it puts its paw on the plate and the trap goes off and the jaws snap shut on its leg, and you've got him.

Yeah, well, most trappers go round and check their traps at about nine o'clock of a night because that's when all the rabbits have come out for their first meal. So around then or a bit later, we'd go out and check the traps and take what we'd caught and reset the trap. And we'd do the same thing in the early morning. Then every three days or so you'd generally move your traps to another area, like. But, oh, the rabbits. There was so many rabbits out there, we'd be laying under the fly of a night and we'd hear them all squealing as they was being caught.

Okay, with the skinning, what you done was, when you get him out of the trap he's still alive, see, so first you knock him on the head – rabbit-kill him – then you lay him on the ground, on his back, and you open his back legs out and you run the knife down on the inside of both of the legs and you sort of poke the legs through where you split both sides. Then you put your foot on his head and you pull the whole skin off. It sort of comes straight off, up to his front legs, and then you have to poke his front legs through the skin and you run the knife around his neck so the skin comes off nice and clean. Then, after you've done that, you grab a bit of no. 8 fencing wire and you work it into a U-shape and you slip the skin over it and you stick the two ends of the wire in the ground so the skin dries. Now, most buyers didn't like the skins being dried in the sun because, apparently, they're harder to tan. Then, with the carcass, carcass buyers was paying something like one and six a pair. But we was too far from the buyers. We didn't even have our own transport and we're stuck out in the bush, with no refrigeration to keep them fresh. So after we'd skin them we'd just burn the carcass.

And, after we'd done all that, we'd just lay down for the rest of the day. Like, there was basically nothing else to do, you know. So that's what we was doing, and the overseer, he'd come down every two or three days to check on how we're going and he'd say, 'Here's a wee bit 'a meat fer yers,' and he'd give us a bit of mutton or something. So we got free meat and, of course, there was plenty of rabbit to eat.

But, see, I'd told this feller that I could do sixty an hour when, actually, I could only do about thirty. That was the truth of it and every time he'd come out in his sulky he'd say, 'How many did yer catch terday, boys?' And we'd say whatever we caught. 'Oh, is that all? Yers should be doin' a lot better than that.' That's all we got out of him; 'Yers should be doin' a lot better than that.'

Then one day he arrives and he's brung this empty wool bale out. 'Oh look,' he says, 'yer should be doin' better than what yer doin' so I think yers better move on.' He said, 'Here's a wool bale ter put yer skins in.'

The wool bale was all nice and dry and everything, and we had a huge pile of skins like this. Actually, I think he was surprised just how many we really had. But by then I could see Bluey's getting homesick, aye. Like I said, other than his father, he had a real good home life so he was missing his mum and that. But, no, I was really enjoying it out there. I wasn't missing my home at all, and I didn't mind being on me own. You get used of it, see. So really, thinking now, what I should've done was say to the overseer, 'Look, I'll stay on 'n' work fer ten bob a day 'n' you tucker me.'

But anyway, I didn't say that and so Bluey and me, we packed up all these skins and we put them on the sulky and the overseer took us to this little railway siding. The platform was only about fifty feet long, if that. I don't think it even had a name. It was so bare out there, we couldn't even see a tree. Not a one. So he drops us off and we stood about on this platform with our stack of skins, for I don't know how long before we seen this thin bit of smoke coming from over on the horizon. So we're standing there, waiting and waiting with our big bale of rabbit skins and the train eventually comes along and we're waving it down, hitchhiking the train. It was a goods train. But when the thing arrived, it just seemed to keep on going on. 'You rotten mongrel, why don't yer pull up?' I called out. But he did. See, being a goods train, there was only the one passenger carriage, away down at the back end and the train driver pulled the train up right in front of the carriage. So we got on with the wool bale full of skins and we heads off to a place called Gular, where there was a skin buyer.

When we gets to Gular the skin buyer sorts all the skins out. Like, big bucks, you get better money for because they're heavier; round six skins to the pound. Then you get kitten rabbits; they'd be the seconds. And you get milky does; they're rabbits that's got kittens. But, see, there was a big export market in rabbit skins to America and that same year, when the myxomatosis come in, first-class bucks went from a pound a pound down to ninepence a pound. Incredible, aye? Anyhow, after we got paid whatever it was, I says to Bluey, 'Mate, let's not go back ter Sydney, let's go up ter Queensland.'

But he said, 'Nah, I wanta go home.'

So I says, 'Oh, okay, then, I'll come with yer.' Which was something I shouldn't never have done.

4

So Bluey and me, I'd say we was only away for maybe six months or something. But he was like that, aye. Like, he'd be busting to come along. 'Yeah, yeah, I'll go with yer. I'll go with yer.' But then, when he got away, after a bit, he'd want to go back home again. And now here's a funny thing; see, Bluey couldn't read or write, yet his brother was a Qantas pilot – you know, the old propeller jobs. And, oh, it'd be annoying; you'd be at the pictures and Bluey'd be forever asking: 'What does it read? What does it say?' That sort of thing and, of course, all the people are turning around gawking at you. It was embarrassing really. But look at the difference between one brother and another, aye; one couldn't read or write and the other was a Qantas pilot, aye.

Anyway, when we gets back to Sydney, Bluey goes back home and I camp out in the bush in some open paddocks at Rydalmere. Well, I could've gone to Bluey's place, yeah, but, I don't know, I just didn't. And I certainly wasn't going back home because she would've gloated – you know, with me arriving on the doorstep with the backsides out of me strides. She just would've loved that, aye, to have seen me beat, to have seen me as a failure, to see me as if I needed her help. So, I just went and camped out bush.

But it was a mistake to go back to Sydney. And what made it worse was, one afternoon I come back to camp and all me gear was scattered all over the place. Hoons or young kids had gone through it all. I had a whip. It was gone, and there was other stuff missing. All I had left was a bit of shaving gear and that old moth-eaten blanket I took with me in the first place. It was still there, but not much else. That was the last straw, aye, because I never felt so destitute in all me life. So I says, 'I'm going back ter Queensland.'

Of course, by then, all the money I'd got off the rabbits is gone. So I hitchhiked up the coast to Newcastle, then onto the New England Highway, till I finally gets to Tamworth. It's in the middle of winter so it's freezing cold, aye. Then I thought, I'll go across ter Kempsey. See, I might've told you, back when I was still in school, in Sydney, our father took David and me up to a timber town just out of Kempsey, to go shooting. I think the name of the place was Carri or something like that. It was a timber camp about forty mile west of Kempsey. There's a lot of red cedar there and there's these big timber jinkers. I forget exactly how long we was up there for but I even went to school for a couple of days so it must've been for a week or more, aye. It was a one-teacher school with kids from kindergarten up to twelve or something. Anyhow, I could use an axe pretty well because the stepmother always sent me out to cut wood so I thought, I'll go there 'n' get a job timber cuttin'.

So from Tamworth, I hitchhikes up to where the Oxley Highway turn-off is, then I heads down towards the coast till I gets to Walcha, and when I arrived in Walcha there's a bloke cutting his hedge, see. It was just on dark and I says to the feller, 'Look mate, can I leave me things here? I wanta get round town 'cause I'm lookin' fer work.'

'Oh, yer lookin' fer work, are yer?' he says.

'Yeah.'

Then he points and he says, 'Just go up that hill ter where that light is. There's a feller up there who's always lookin' fer labourers.'

'Thanks,' I said and I put me kitbag down behind the hedge and I goes up the hill to see this feller. It was just on tea time and I hadn't eaten for a couple of days and, oh, I can smell this roast coming out of the kitchen, aye. Beautiful. I can just about smell it now. Anyhow, I knocks on the door and this feller appears and I says, 'I heard yer want some men, mate?'

He looks me up and down. 'Oh yeah.' He says, 'How long do yer want work for?'

I says, 'Don't know. Whatever, three months, maybe.'

'So yer want a job fer three months, do yer?'

I says, 'Yeah.'

'Hmm, three months,' he says. Then he thinks for a bit and he says, 'No, I can't give yer a job fer three months.'

I says, 'Well, how's about two months, then?'

'Oh, two months.' And he's going through all his business like he knows I'm real hungry and I'm desperate and it's like he's liking what's going on. And I'm trying to look past him, down to the kitchen, and me mouth's watering, aye. Anyhow, we goes from two months down to one month, then he gets me down to a week.

'Yeah,' I says, 'just a week'll do, mate. Anything.'

'Oh, no,' he says, 'I can't put yer on for a week.'

I says, 'Look mate, can yer just give me a job so I can get some money ter buy a feed?'

So he's standing there looking down at me and I can smell this beautiful roast cooking and then his little daughter comes along, 'Ah, Daddy, Mummy said ter come in fer tea, now.'

And the mongrel turned around and he shut the door in me face. True. Not even saying, 'Come in mate 'n' have a feed.' No. He just says, 'Nah, sorry, can't help yer.' And that was it. He shut the door on me.

Oh, he had a blue-metal quarry or something like that. Trucks was parked up there in his yard, everywhere. So then I goes back down to town and gets me kitbag and it's getting on dark and I'm broke and I haven't got anywhere to go. But I'd seen this church, see, so I decides to go round to the church. The door was open so I goes in and I'm laying on a wooden pew and I'm not only starving but I'm freezing cold too. So I goes behind the vestry thing and I pulls all the priest's gowns down from off a hook behind the door and I wrap myself up in them and I sleeps in the church for the night.

Then, when it's getting near morning, I could see the clock at the back of the church. Like, most churches have the clock on the back wall so that, when the priest's talking, he knows what the time is. So it's just on morning and I don't want to get caught in the church, wrapped up in the priest's cloaks. But the wind's blowing outside, aye, and it's freezing cold, and – I'll never forget it – I'm lying there on this pew looking at the clock and there's this little mouse only a foot away, on the floor, looking at me and cleaning himself. Anyway, I gets up and puts the priest's things back and when I opened the front door there's a foot of snow outside. True. That's dinky-di. There was a foot of snow outside, aye, and it's blowing a blizzard.

Anyway, here I am, cold, broke and hungry, so I makes me way down town. Nothing's opened yet. I'm standing in the doorway of a saddle shop, see, and I looks inside, shivering, and there's this feller inside, sitting round a potbelly stove, and I'm just staring at that potbelly stove, aye, and the feller sees me and he comes and opens the door and he says, 'Yer'd better come inside 'n' warm up.'

I says, 'Yeah. Thanks', and I was into that saddle shop in a shot, I can tell you, and I'm just about hugging this potbelly stove, aye. That's how cold I was. Anyrate, we're talking there for a while and I'm not sure what I told the feller or what he asked me about but he says, 'Look mate, here's three 'n' six, go over ter the Greek cafe 'n' get yerself a feed.'

And I just couldn't thank him enough, aye. 'Oh, thank you very much,' I said. 'Thanks very, very much, mate.'

So I goes over and has a good a feed and I just had enough left over to buy a packet of what they called Old Chum cigarettes. Cheap, horrible things, but I was tonguing for a smoke, see. Tailor-made, yeah. Anyway, so then I thought, Well, I'll go ter the stock and station agent 'n' see what's goin' on. But I hadn't had a bath for quite a while and I can smell meself. By now the pubs are opening up so I goes to a pub and I says to the feller there, 'Can I have a bath, mate?'

'Yeah,' he says.

So I got cleaned up, to a point, and I goes round to the stock and station agent and I asks if there's any work about and he says, 'The best thing fer you to do is go 'n' see the taxi driver. He's the feller in town who knows all about what's what.'

When I goes round and sees this taxi driver, he says, 'Yeah,' he says, 'the mail truck goes out ter Nowendoc.' Nowendoc's a little village about forty mile or something, south-east of Walcha. He says, 'Me brother-in-law, Bill Hicks, he's got a little place out there. He'll give yer a job.'

Anyhow, he gave me the fare for the mail truck, and this feller, Bill Hicks, he didn't even know I was coming, so when I arrives there's nobody home. It was a nice cottage but not flash. Then I'm looking around, wondering what to do when, next thing, this feller rides up on a grey mare.

I says, 'Are you Bill Hicks?'

'Yeah.'

'Oh,' I says, 'the taxi feller sent me out here fer a job.'

'Oh, yeah, all right then,' he says, 'but yer'd better come inside 'n' have somethin' ter eat.' Anyway, his wife wasn't there. She was away somewhere with the kids. 'Are yer hungry?' he asks me.

'Too right,' I says.

He says, 'We mostly eat stews – kangaroo meat with turnip 'n' spuds.'

'That's okay by me.'

Well, I soon found out that he had acres and acres of turnip and, of course, there was always plenty of 'roos around, and rabbits. Anyhow, he made his dampers in the coals of the big open fire he had going and he'd made a kangaroo stew with a lot of turnip. Always turnip – turnip or spuds. So we're talking away and he starts to yawn and he says, 'Oh, you'd better sleep in with me ternight.'

And I started to panic a bit, aye. I thought, Boy, I don't know about this. I'm not sure what's gonna happen here.

Anyhow, we go to bed and he's talking about this and that. But he was alright. I think he just wanted the company. So, next day, I starts working for him and about a week or so later his wife turns up with their daughter and a little feller. I don't know where she went or anything, but they was visiting somewhere. Then the wife, she gave me a room of me own to sleep in. She was good, very good. Oh, she'd go out and do cattle work and everything. But, oh, they was living real hard out there. That's where I first really learned how to handle a horse, you know, and I done a lot of fencing. It was a little cow cocky place. He had Hereford cattle and then he grew these turnips and spuds and the rabbit plague was still going on, so there's rabbits everywhere, and, of course, there was all the 'roos. But he wasn't paying me hardly nothing at all, see, and I remembered the mail truck bloke – the one who took me out there – saying, 'How much do yer expect ter get paid?'

I said, 'Don't know. What's the basic wage?'

'Not sure,' he'd said, 'but one thing's fer certain, yer won't get much outa Bill Hicks.'

And, I can tell you, he was right.

But anyway, I was made to feel almost part of the family. In fact, he even had plans for me to be with him forever and a day. Now, I may be jumping to conclusions here but, going from the flavour of all his talk, sometimes I thought, Oh, he's keepin' his daughter for me. I guess she would've only been about twelve at that stage so it might've only been some stupid thing that a young feller would think. I don't know. But I got that opinion. Like he'd say, 'I'll teach yer to be a bushman. I'll teach yer all about horses. I'll teach yer this. I'll teach yer that. I'll teach yer to butcher up a beast.'

But gee, he worked me hard. I tell you, there was times there when I never saw the fowls leave the roost. They was on the roost when we left the house to go out to work, and they was back on the roost when we come back home from work, you know. That's true; we'd go out a mile or something to do some fencing and by the time we got there it was just light enough to sight the posts up and when we left it was just too dark to sight the posts up.

So he certainly got his fair day's work out of me, aye. Even so, I liked it there, except he hardly gave me any money. And I never went to town. When he'd go to town I'd have to ask him to get me something. And he didn't like smokers. Oh no, he always reckoned that smokers take up too much time, rolling their cigarettes. Anyhow, he'd bring me back a bit of tobacco. Then I'd say I'd been there for about five months and one day I was digging these mulga trees out and he reckoned I wasn't digging them out deep enough. 'Oh,' he says, 'I was gonna put yer wages up till I seen the way yer left them mulga roots.' He said, 'But now I'm gonna put yer wages down.'

I said, 'What do yer mean "put me wages down"?'

'Oh,' he says, 'I'm gonna put your wages down 'cause yer not diggin' them mulga roots out right.'

I mean, I'd hardly seen any money anyway, so I wouldn't have known what me wages was in the first place. Anyrate, that's what started me thinking that I might as well pull the pin. Well, I was getting nowhere, aye. So when he went off to some other part of the property I just went back to the house and started packing me gear up. Then, when his missus seen me packing up, next thing Bill comes in. 'Oh, yer leavin', are yer?' he says.

'Yeah.'

He says, 'Look, stay here 'n' I'll really look after yer. Yer can trap rabbits 'n' make some extra money fer yerself.'

But I said, 'No thanks, I've made me mind up.'

I mean, if I'd stayed I would've been unsettled anyway. So he paid me out. Well, it wasn't much because he docked me for me tobacco and then, one time, when he was going to town, I'd said, 'Can yer get me a pair'a trousers, these ones are almost done.' And so he docked me six shillings for them.

So I just walked off the place and I went about two or three mile from their home and I camped out in the bush that night and I built a little fire because it was freezing cold. When I got back into Walcha, the first thing I done was I went around to the saddler feller who'd give me the three and six to have a feed that time. 'Here,' I said, 'here's yer money back 'n' thanks very much fer what yer done.'

5

Yeah, all me life I had this thing about 'Head west, go north'. I've never had a want to live out in the southern parts of New South Wales, you know, like Hay or any of them places. I just wanted to go north or west, so I says, 'I'll go back out ter Dubbo 'n' go potato pickin' again.'

Of course, what I didn't realise was that potato pickin's seasonal work. Well, I just had the idea you could go and pick potatoes any time of the year. But I didn't find that out till I got to Dubbo, aye. So then I'm back onto this thing of 'going west'. And that's what I done. I kept hitchhiking west with the aim of getting to Bourke. Now, this was in the days where the last of the fellers went round the bush like gypsies, in horse-drawn wagonettes. This was the time Prime Minister Menzies had put on a credit squeeze and it'd somehow got out of hand because there was massive unemployment. Now, whether Menzies wanted to stop inflation or what, I don't know. I'm not sure about the politics but I think the banks tightened things up.

So things was tough and when you're bagging it, like many fellers was, you'd do anything, see – rabbit trapping, fencing, putting up stockyards, general rural work. Oh, them fellers could turn their hand at anything. Like, they could even crutch and shear and all that as well. And so they'd travel around in their wagonette and, when they come to a place, lots of places had a town common where you could hobble your horses out and there was a water trough and all that there, and so fellers – sometimes even with their families – they'd stay there while they're looking for a bit of work.

Anyhow, when I gets to Nyngan, I'm going past the town common, carrying me kitbag, and there's these two fellers there who was travelling around in a three-in-hand wagonette and they called out, 'Yer trampin' it, mate?'

'Yeah.'

They said, 'Well yer'd better come over here 'n' wet yer whistle 'n' have a feed.'

'Thanks,' I says and so I go over to have a feed with them.

Now, I reckon their wagonette would've been about eighteen foot long, with the four big old wagon wheels. You know, the ones with the wooden spokes. I forget what the sides was made of. They might've even been of canvas, but there was a fuel stove inside the wagonette and underneath there was wire netting where they kept their spuds and onions and that.

Oh, that's right, it's all coming back to me now. See, I had a beautiful old Canberra two-shilling piece with me. Well, when they opened Parliament House in 1927 they put out a special two-shilling piece which was very heavy with silver and the Parliament House was beautifully embossed on it, so it bulges out. Like, it's not just flat. And I was determined to hang on to it for as long as I could and I remember these two fellers with the wagonette, they kept saying to me, 'When yer get a job young feller, yer'd better hang onta it 'cause things are gonna get a lot worse.'

Okay, so then after they'd given me a feed I thanked them very much and I went back out on the road to hitchhike to Bourke. And I would've only been a mile or so outside Nyngan, just out of town, when these other fellers stopped in an old Fargo truck. 'We're off ter Brewarrina,' they said. 'We're goin' out there shearin'. Come with us, yer'll earn some real good money.'

And I says, 'Okay, but where the heck's Brewarrina?'

Anyrate, there's four of them, see, three in the front of the truck and one feller on the back, sitting with all their gear. They said they come from Orange. So I threw me kitbag on the back and I climbs up there and off we go. Then when we gets to Byrock, which is the turn-off to Brewarrina, they pulls up there and went in for a beer. No, they never shouted me a beer or nothing. I sat outside, hanging on to me Canberra two-shilling piece because that's about all I had on me. And so, after they'd had their beers, they drove on and that night we camped out on the Bogan River and I remember distinctly, the next morning, one of the fellers caught a yellow belly and so they had fish for breakfast. Mind you, I missed out on that too. Anyway, if that's not bad enough, when we gets to Brewarrina me kitbag's gone missing. Yeah, it'd somehow fell off the truck. And, like, now I've lost all me gear. It's the last thing I need. So I goes over to the police station and I says, 'I lost me kitbag.'

Then the copper asks me what it looked like, aye, and so I tells him. Then he says, 'What was in it?'

So I told him what was in it, which wasn't much really, but it was all I had. Then he reaches down behind the counter and he lifts up me kitbag and he says, 'Yeah, here it is.'

And, oh boy, wasn't I relieved, aye? Somehow, someone must've picked it up along the road and they'd gotten to Brewarrina before us. Anyhow, I'm relieved and I'm hungry and that's when I spent me Canberra two-shilling piece. And the funny thing was, later that day, I'm walking past the Brewarrina Post Office and I heard the feller from behind the counter saying, 'Guess what I scored today? A Canberra two bob.'

So wherever I spent it, they must've taken it and bought something at the post office, aye. So then these shearers take me out to this Aboriginal settlement about nine mile out of town. It was right alongside the banks of the Barwon River, which ran into the Darling River. I guess there was twenty or so houses there with families and all that. Yeah, they was proper houses, nothing like the sheets of corrugated iron and the twenty or so dogs you see in other places. A feller called Summons, he was paid by the government to run it. Now, I'm not sure what the Aboriginals actually did – you know, whether they worked or not – but one of the blackfellas from there, he carted wood around town. Then some of them used to walk into town and walk back out again. But the conditions for the Aboriginals was good, really, and we stayed in an empty house which was also pretty good.

Now, to get an exact time on it, I was out there when King George VI died – Queen Elizabeth's father – because I remember this blackfella come along while I was doing something and he said, 'Hey, 'bin King died.'

And, you know, I thought he was on about some king of this Aboriginal tribe or something, so I answers, 'Oh yeah, big deal.' But it was King George VI. So that would've been sometime in early 1952, aye. But apparently, the owner of the sheep – a white feller – had these sheep on agistment on this Aboriginal settlement, because one of the shearer fellers said to me, 'Look, if this boss feller ever comes here, make yerself look busy 'n' I might be able ter get a few extra quid fer yer.'

Now, I didn't know anything about it at that time but this was when the big shearers' strike was on and these fellers from Orange was working non-union – you know, as scab labourers – and they had me doing everything. They was working nine or ten hours a day and I was roustabouting – sweeping the boards and picking up the fleeces. They was also doing the mustering, so I'd help out there, and they'd even send me down to get a feed going. Everything that was possible I done, and I liked it because I was working out bush, aye. Then after a month or so, when we finished the shearing, because we was scab labour, we even took all the wool bales into Brewarrina and loaded them onto the railway trucks ourselves.

But up until then I still hadn't been paid so when we finished up there these shearer fellers said, 'Come down ter Orange with us, we've got some more work 'n' we'll pay yer there.'

'Okay then.'

Then when we gets to Orange, they paid me a lousy two pound. True. That worked out to be less than six bob a week for all that time and all that hard work. So they used me up, aye, and then they just turned their backs on me. 'See yer later,' they said. 'We've got no more work.' And that was it. I don't know if the shearers' strike had come to an end and they was out of work or what, but that's what they did; 'See yer later' and they just dumped me there. I tell you, I was devastated, I was.

6

So there I was, stuck in Orange without a job, and with only a lousy two quid to me name. Anyway, it was north for me, aye. I wanted to get back to Queensland. So I hitchhiked all the way up to Warwick, just over the border into south-eastern Queensland. I don't remember too much about getting up there but back in them days hitchhiking was pretty easy and if I ever got stuck I'd just sleep out overnight. I liked doing that anyway. But by the time I gets to Warwick all me money's gone so I camps out in a wheat field. I remember that because there was all these little mouses running over me, all through the night. Yeah, field mice. Oh, they was everywhere.

Anyhow, I thought I might get a job in the big flour mills, there at Warwick. So next morning I left me kitbag down behind the flour mills and I'm walking through town and I sees this big blackboard saying: 'Fettlers wanted in Texas'. Fettlers are people who do maintenance work on the railway lines, and Texas is right down on the Queensland – New South Wales border. So I goes down to the railway station and I says to the station master, 'I see yer want some fettlers, mate.'

He goes, 'Yeah.'

'Good,' I says, 'because I'm lookin' fer work.'

'All right then,' he says, 'just go up ter the Government Employment place. They've got a special form yer have ter fill out. Then after yer done that bring a copy back to me. The train goes out ter where yer'll be fettlin' this arvo.'

So I goes up to this employment place and they gets me to fill out this form and I'm just about to turn around and take my copy back to the station master when the feller in the office takes one look at his copy and he calls out, 'Hey, come back 'ere. You should be doin' yer national service.' He says, 'I'll give yer a ticket ter go to Wacol', Wacol being the big army camp in Brisbane.

See, the Korean War was going on then. In fact it was escalating and the Menzies government reckoned that if the 'commos' – communists – won in Korea they'd soon be getting into Malaya and all over the place. That's why they brought the national service on, and I was just over the legal age of eighteen. So I said to the feller in the employment office, 'Yeah, righto mate. I'll join up.' I says, 'But first I'll have ter go down 'n' grab me gear.'

But that was only an excuse, see, because I wasn't too keen on joining the army. So I goes back down behind the flour mills and I grabs me kitbag and I heads straight back out onto the highway and jumps on the first truck that pulled up for me. No, I didn't care where I ended up. Well, the Government Employment feller had given me such a scare that if the truck would've had a Victorian number plate I would've gone there. If he would've been going to Perth I would've gone there. I just wanted to get out of Warwick, and quick, aye. Anyway, this feller pulls up in his truck and he's got a New South Wales number plate.

'Here we go again,' I says to meself, 'headin' south insteada north.'

It turned out that this feller had a big fruit shop in Narrabeen, down near Sydney, and he used to come to Queensland to pick up spuds. From what I could gather he'd made a fortune out of it because, at that time, spuds was as rare as gold in Sydney. So yeah, there I was, sitting in the truck with all these bags of spuds and the further we drove along the more I started thinking, geez, maybe this army business mightn't be too bad. At least I'll get a decent feed, aye.

So we kept going and something that's coming back to me now was that the nearer we got to Sydney the more fearful I got that I might run into someone who knew me. Well, because I didn't want me family to know where I was, especially the stepmother. I wanted to keep as far a distance from her as I could. And then I remembered the time when we was up in Springwood and, see, David and me, we was always hungry and I got up early one morning and I was looking in the cupboard for something to eat and, while I had me head in the cupboard, I hears her coming down the hall. So I shot into the bathroom and hides behind the door. Like, I was expecting she'd go straight past and go out to the outside dunny. But she didn't. Instead, she come into the bathroom and she squatted over the bath and she urinated in that. Then after she'd done her business she splashed a bit of water around and walked out. And there's me, still hiding behind the door. So it was lucky she didn't shut the door, aye. But then, after that, whenever we had our bath of a Sunday, David and me, we'd have to bath in the same water she'd just used and I always wondered if she'd urinated in it before we got in. I mean, you wouldn't put it past her, aye. That's how terrible it was. And the closer I got to Sydney, the more those sorts of bad moments come back to me.

Anyrate, we gets to Narrabeen and the fruit shop feller gives me a good feed and I thanks him and then I ended up camping out in the pine forest. See, I'd learned back when I was passing through Tamworth, on me way to Walcha that time, that, when there's a thick bed of pine needles between yourself and the ground it's nice and soft and dry and you don't get so cold. So that's where I camped, and I lost a good pocketknife there too, I did. But, see, I was still in two minds about this national service thing – you know, whether I should or whether I shouldn't. Then after a few days of roughing it I thought I might catch up with Bluey Flannigan and his family to see how they're going. So I went around to where Bluey lived and I was told that they'd moved to somewhere else. Then I went around to Frank Yateman's place. 'I'm lookin' fer Bluey,' I says. 'Do yer know where he is?'

Frank says, 'Oh, they've moved out ter Five Dock.'

So Frank gave me their address and I went out to see Bluey and, oh, they took me back under their wing again. Oh, I was welcomed with open arms because, see, they knew I was a good mate for their son. It was like I was one of theirs, you know. They was such a good family, when the old man wasn't there, like I said before. So I'm staying at the Flannigans' place and Bluey's working at Peek Frean's biscuit factory and so I gets a job there.

Okay, well, they put me on this machine that makes wafer biscuits and, see, all this liquid would pour onto a hot plate about a foot square and then the top of a revolving plate would come down onto it and, as the wafer's being cooked, it'd squeeze the liquid waste out the sides. So it was my job to sit there with a knife and just run around the edges of it, trimming off the stuff that was squeezed out. But, oh, it was boring, aye. I tell you, it was one after another, after another, after another, and it just didn't seem to stop, so before long I started going to sleep on the machine. Then the dayshift complained how the job wasn't being done properly, and they tracked it all down to me and my machine. So they put me off, aye. Well, actually, they sacked me.

So then I goes to the meat works at Homebush and I gets a job there. See, how the jobs worked in them days was they had what's called a 'pick-up'. That's when a company might want fifteen men for the day and there might be twenty waiting at the gates to get work. Of course, the ones who'd worked there before and was known to be good workers, they'd get picked up first and, if by then they'd got enough men, the rest would miss out. But sometimes they might want fifteen men and only ten'd turn up and, once you get your leg in, you're right. That's what happened to me, and that's how I ended up working on the brain table.

Well, with the brain table – see, first, they cut the heads off all the animals. I was doing sheep and so they'd have a big pile of sheep heads. Then they had this automatic knife machine, about twice the size of a meat cleaver. It went up and down. You couldn't stop it so, if you left your hand there, you'd lose it. So this big knife goes up and down and while it's up you put the head of a sheep under it, jaw bone up, and when it comes down it cuts the skull clean in half. That's how sharp it was. But it went pretty slow. Like it'd go down ... up ... down ... up ... down ... up ... down ... up.

There was four of us on a table about three square foot. One feller cut the skull in half, then there's two fellers standing each side of the table, one to take the gland out of the skull on that side and the other feller would take the gland out on the other side of the skull. These glands was only about half the size of the top of your little finger and they went into a special box, which went to the hospital or to Sydney Uni. I don't know what they was used for but it had something to do with medicine. So there was two doing that and then the fourth feller, he was taking the brains out of the skull and putting them into little punnets.

But, when I started there, I left Bluey's place to be closer to work. But, oh, I was roughing it, aye. In fact, I ended up camping out where they yarded up all the animals and I was getting me drinking water out of the troughs they drank out of. Like, I wasn't drinking straight out of the troughs. I'd go over to the float that was on the trough and I'd push that down and then the fresher water would come out and I had me tin quart pot which had a little cup. But it was rough, aye, and I was cooking and eating brains. That's what I was living on, more or less, till I got paid and then I'd shout meself a decent feed. I never drank much in them days, so I was saving good money with the idea of going back up north. But then, at the same time, I was also thinking about this national service business because at least I knew I'd get a decent feed in the army. Anyrate, one day I just turned up back at Bluey's place and when his mother seen me, oh, she took one look at me and she made me stay with them. And it's when I made me mind up: 'Blow this,' I says, 'I may as well go 'n' join up with the national service.'

So I goes round to the recruiting office and I had a medical and I signed up for national service. Then, next day, a whole heap of us gets on these buses out to Holsworthy Army Camp where we're all lined up to get our gear: trousers, boots, hat and all that. And, with the national service back then, how it worked was that you done your basic training for three months at some army camp or other, then you had to do another two and a half months in the Citizen Military Force – the CMF – living outside the camp. So Holsworthy was the start of the three months' basic training. The food was good and living conditions was also very good and we was looked after very well. We had huts just down from the big Holsworthy army boob – the army jail. It was like a dormitory.

And during basic training you learned to march and you learned how to pull a Bren gun to pieces and put it back together again and you run with it for a hundred yards, firing from the hip – the Bren gun's pretty heavy – then laying it down on a tripod, shooting. Same with a .303 rifle. They gave you a rifle and we had it with us the whole time we was there at Holsworthy. We done other things too. You know, we learned how to throw grenades and do the obstacle course, like climbing up nets and climbing through barbed wire – the whole set-up.

And I was in immaculate condition. The other blokes was from the city, see, so I could outrun them. I could carry a full pack, no troubles, and I used to love shooting. I even done some boxing for the division I was in and I won a few and I lost a few. But I enjoyed that as well, aye. Anyhow, no, I loved it. I didn't even mind the discipline. I only had to front the colonel once and got fined two pounds and that's because we went on leave and I didn't bother coming back for the night. That was nothing.

But I was in D Company, 12th Battalion. See, there's two hundred to a company, roughly, and there's two captains to a company. One of our captains was Captain Murphy, the other was Captain Noonan. Captain Murphy had a pencil-line moustache and oh, his brass would shine, aye. It would shine, and he was dressed immaculate. A real army sort of feller. Like, we'd march out to the parade ground and he'd call out: 'D Company. Atten-shun!' And we'd stand to attention. 'D Company. Stand at ease.' So we'd stand at ease. He'd say, 'The Korean War is escalating. Many of you will be reinforcements.' Then he looks us up and down like he's real superior. 'Tomorra, you'll embark in an orderly fashion – I repeat "an orderly fashion" – on the trucks to go to ANZAC rifle range where you'll be using the Bren gun. Get very, very familiar with the Bren gun.' Then he shouts out, 'D Company. Atten-shun! I'll now hand you over to Captain Noonan.'

So Captain Murphy hands us over to the other captain, yeah, this Captain Noonan. You always stand at attention when the next chap comes along. Anyhow, along comes Captain Noonan and he's the complete opposite to Captain Murphy. He's munching on chewing gum. Looks around. Scratches himself on the backside. Scratches himself under the arms. Makes sniffling sounds. Then, as flat as a tack, he says: 'Okay D Company. Stand at ease. As Murph says' – it's not Captain Murphy, it's plain old 'Murph' – 'as Murph says, yer'll be goin' out tomorra ter the ANZAC range. Pile on the trucks when they come.' So there's no 'in an orderly fashion' about it, it's just 'Pile on the trucks when they come'.

Anyhow, they put me in the artillery and I was a gunner and I went on a few bivouacs with the 75-pounders. They're the big heavy ones, for firing long distance. They used the 75-pounder in World War II for air raids, you know, because it could send the shells up a few mile. Well, you could set it to explode at whatever height you wanted. Like, say a plane's coming over and you judged it at 10,000 feet, you'd just set the shell to go off at that height. Then you'd put it in the bridge, fire it and when it got to 10,000 feet – boom! No, it didn't have to hit anything. Just the shrapnel, or flack as it's called, was enough to bring a plane down, because it'd rip it to pieces and go into the fuel tanks and all that.

Eventually we was to be part of the reinforcements for the 3rd Battalion who was already over there, in Korea. But anyway, try as I might, I couldn't get to Korea. I was just too young. See, the minimum age you had to be was eighteen and nine months. And after I'd done me three months basic training at Holsworthy, they gave me an honourable discharge. But I'm still only eighteen and seven months see, so I still had a couple of months to go before I could get to Korea. So then I thought, Now what am I gonna do?

They said, 'Join the Regular Army.' But if you joined the regular army you had to sign on for five years and because the Korean War had started to scale down a bit by then they was only taking the best of the crack shots out of the regular army to go over there as reinforcements. So I thinks, Will I join the regular army or will I not? No, it's too big a risk. I mightn't get chosen as a crack shot 'n' then I'm tied down fer five years.

By now I'm back at Bluey's doing the last two and a half months of me national service, in the CMF. See, we all went into different units that was attached with the army. Being artillery, I was going to lectures of a night – in uniform – down at Leichhardt. Other fellers went into transport, learning to drive trucks and all that. Some went into light machine gunners. I mean, I wouldn't have minded a career in the army but really, my first love was to go out into the back country, aye. I still hadn't had a real taste of it yet and I wanted to go and be a ringer. Anyhow, before I'd done me two and a half months with the CMF, I pulled the pin. Yeah, I just rolled me swag and I says to Bluey, 'Mate, I'm off ter Queensland.'

And he says, 'Yeah, well, I'll come with yer.'

'Okay,' I says. But then I starts thinking, Here we go again. He'll be all for us going somewhere 'n' then, like when we went rabbiting together that time, when we get there he'll get homesick 'n' want ter go back home. So I says, 'Now listen Blue, if yer comin' with me, we stick together forever 'n' a day till one of us marries. I'll help yer write home 'n' ring up yer family but none'a this gettin' homesick 'n'runnin' back home again, right?'

'Goldie,' he says, 'I'm with yer all the way.'

7

I'd gotten twenty-seven pounds in deferred pay after I'd finished the first three months of national service out at Holsworthy. I still had most of that, so the first thing I done when Bluey and me decided to take off was I went into Sydney and I bought a saddle in Bass Street. That's how keen I was to get up into the station properties in Queensland, aye. I'd even heard there was work out Charleville way. So me and Bluey, we set off from Sydney in the train and we heads north. All I had was the saddle and by then I had a swag with a couple of blankets and a change of clothes – all me worldly belongings, you could say. I don't remember too much about the trip apart from when we got to Armidale. See, we was broke by then, and even though Blue wasn't a Christian or nothing, he grew up in the Catholic Church and so he went around to the Catholic priest in Armidale and put the bite on him for some money. And it worked too.

Anyhow, we gets to Brisbane and we're heading out to Charleville and we end up at a place called Miles and we've run out of money again. Miles is about halfway between Charleville and Brisbane. About three hundred mile each way. So we jumped a rattler at Miles. 'Jumping a rattler' is an old term meaning that you jump on a goods train, like, for a free ride. There was still a lot of unemployment then because of the credit squeeze and everywhere we went you'd see fellers jumping rattlers and sleeping under bridges or in railway stations and that. But, jumping a rattler came from the Depression when unemployment was very high and it was the only way a lot of fellers could travel around, to try and find work.

Actually, that's where the story about Wingie, the railway cop come from. They called him that because he had one of his hands missing and in its place they'd put a big hook. Not too many people might know about this but I'm even sure that Buddy Williams sung a country and western song called 'Wingie the Railway Cop'. But, see, this Wingie, during the Depression he became one of the most feared and hated railway cops throughout Queensland. Oh, he was a tough, hard, vicious man. So these out-of-work fellers, they'd jump a rattler, because that's what they done – just rattled along – the trains that is, not the hard-up blokes – and when they jumped a rattler, if they couldn't get into one of the enclosed wagons, they'd try and hide under a railway's tarpaulin, covering the flat-top wagons, with goods on them. Of course, when that happened, sometimes the bulge of their head could be seen from under the tarp and this Wingie, the railway cop, he'd sneak up real quiet-like, and he'd smash them on the noggin with his hook. Crack! Yeah, true. And, other times, if he heard anyone talking in one of the enclosed wagons, he'd tap on its sliding door and call out in a down'n'out voice, 'Any room fer one more?' And as soon as they opened the door, he'd arrest them.

But anyway, this Wingie, he was so much hated that, one time, there was this train called the Sunshine Milk Train. It got that name because it done the milk pick-up run, out and back from Brisbane. Anyhow, one night some down'n'outs jumped Wingie and they tied him up to the railway line, just under a pedestrian bridge. And they tied him in that exact spot because it was right on a bend where a train driver wouldn't be able to see him till it was too late. So they really wanted to kill him, aye. Then, at about two o'clock in the morning, just before the Sunshine Milk Train was due through, a sixteen-year-old girl was walking across the bridge on her way home and she heard

Wingie crying out 'Help! Help!' So she climbs down the embankment and she unties him. So she saved his life, aye. And do you know what Wingie did in return? He arrested that girl for trespassing on railway property. And that's fair dinkum. He was a railway cop in the strictest terms of the word, right down to the marrow of his bones, aye.

Now, of course, a lot of those railway fellers weren't anywhere near as bad as that. And just as lucky because that night Blue and me jumped the rattler at Miles there was only one enclosed wagon and that was right next to the engine, where we'd be too easy seen. Next best thing was for us to go further down the train and climb under a tarp, which was covering a flat-wagon of bore casings. So that's what we did; we jumps aboard with our gear and makes ourselves as comfortable as we could under the tarp. By now it's the middle of the night and we didn't go very far before there was a lot of shunting going on, moving us up and down. So we sticks our heads out from under the tarp to see what's going on and they'd shunted our wagon off onto a little side-track, ready for the people to come and get these bore casings.

'This's no good,' I said, so we grabs our stuff and we races along trying to find a place to get on, in another part of the train that was still on the main branch line. Then we sees a drover's box. Now, a drover's box is where a drover stays when he's looking after cattle in the train. It's his own little camp, aye. Like, there's the guard's van right at the end of the train, then there's enough room for about twenty or thirty head of cattle, and then there's the drover's box. The actual box is only about a yard or so long by the width of the train. Just a little place where the drover can wash his hands and there's a bench thing he can fold down to get some sleep, and a seat. Then, if I remember correctly, there's a rack to put his gear on. A good little camp, it was.

Anyway, Bluey and me, we jumps into this drover's box and we just gets settled when this guard comes along with a hurricane lamp and he sees us. 'Hey, what're youse blokes doin'?'

I says, 'We heard there's work on the cattle properties, out Charleville way.'

'So yer wanta go ter Charleville, do yer?'

Then he put the lamp up to get a better look at us and I'll never forget what he said. He said, 'So where's the wife and kids?' I'll never forget that because I wasn't even nineteen, yet, aye.

I says, 'I got no wife 'n' kids, it's just me 'n' me mate, Blue.'

He says, 'Look, this train isn't goin' ter Charleville but there's goods trains goin' there all the time. I'll let yers jump on one'a them.'

So he was real good to us, aye, because a lot of them, oh yeah, they'd hunt you. So we jumps another rattler and we ends up out at Roma. We're still heading in the right direction, but Roma's still well short of Charleville. And when we gets to Roma we're getting a fair bit hungry, so we gets off the train and we goes around to the local baker's shop and I says to the baker, 'How's about we cut some wood up, if yer give us some old cake or bread?'

He says, 'Oh, don't worry about that', and he gives us a big bag of old cakes and things, yeah.

So that was good. Then we goes back to the railway station, looking for somewhere to stay. See, a railway station's the place to go because fellers who are down'n'out, the first place they'll head for is the railway station because, for starters, they've always got a coal fire, if it's cold; then there's always sheds and that for shelter. Anyhow, we struck it real lucky because the Queensland Railways Commissioner's carriage was there, and it was empty. Apparently, he kept one in Roma, one in Brisbane and one in Rockhampton. And inside this carriage, oh, you ought to have seen it! I tell you, it was luxury like Bluey and me, we'd never seen. It had a beautiful kitchen and beds with proper white sheets and a first aid kit with brandy in it. Oh, there was everything you could wish for.

Well, we couldn't let that go, aye, so we decided to live in luxury and we camped in the Queensland Railways Commissioner's carriage for about a week, just living on handouts from shops and that. The only trouble was, the carriage was parked alongside this little platform in Roma and, by using the toilet and that, we created a big mess, aye. So then I says to Bluey, 'I think we'd better get outa here before we gets found out.' Because, I mean, we could've ended up in jail or something for using all the Commissioner's stuff and drinking all his brandy and that. Anyrate, we still didn't have any money so I goes down to the saddle shop.

'What's up?' the feller down there asked me.

'I wanta sell me saddle,' I said.

He says, 'How much?'

See, I wanted twenty-four pound for it and he offered me twenty, so we tossed for it and I won the toss. So I got twenty-four pound for the saddle and then we jumps another rattler and we finish up out at a place, about eighty odd mile west of Roma, called Mungallala. Anyway, we sees a feller there who's looking for fettlers and I gets a job, fettling, just out of Mungallala and Bluey gets a job, fettling, at Dulbydilla, another fifteen mile further west. At the time, Bluey was a bit worried about us getting split up, so I says to him, 'Don't worry about it, Blue.' I said, 'We're in this together 'n' when we get a bit'a money, we'll pull the pin here 'n' go up the station country.'

'Oh, okay then,' he says, 'if you think so,' but he didn't sound none too keen on it.

But one funny thing – see, at the fettler camp where I was we had a section car, which is a motorised thing you put on the railway line and you all sit on it and you putt along, out to where you're working. Some camps didn't have a section car. They had the old type that's called a 'push-me-pull-me' where one feller pushes down on a T-bar while the other feller pulls up on the other end of it and you go along the track like that. But also, where I was working, they had a three-wheeler, like a tricycle-pushbike where two wheels ran on one rail line and the third one ran on the other line to balance it, see. Yeah, it was sort of shaped like a triangle. Anyway, one night I'd run out of tobacco, see, so I thinks, well, Blue'll have some. So I snuck down to the works shed where this bike thing was, gets it out, puts in on the line and off I goes. But, oh, it's all up these hills and mountains, aye. Anyhow, I finally gets to Dulbydilla and I walk in. All the fettlers are playing cards so I says, 'I'm lookin' fer Blue.'

And they say, 'Who the dickens are you? Where do you come from? What're yer doin' out at this time'a night?'

Then I sees Bluey and I says, 'Mate,' I says, 'gimme some tobacco. I'm tonguin' fer a smoke.'

So he gives me some tobacco and we yarns there for a while and one of the fellers goes out to the toilet and when he gets back he says, 'Did you get permission ter drive that thing up 'ere in the middle'a the night?'

I says, 'Who cares?' And as I was saying it, I was punching one fist into me empty hand as if to say, 'Well, if yer wanta make anythin' of it, I'm game.'

Okay, then I turns it around and starts back to camp. And every hundred yards or so there's a little platform on the side of the line, about eight foot by eight foot so, if a train comes along, you can just run your section car or whatever in there to let the train go past. Anyhow, I'm going along and I see the light of a train coming my way. But I'm only about two or three hundred yards from our camp so I starts panicking and I run this bike off onto one of these platforms and I hid under it so the engine driver wouldn't see me as he goes past. Then, when he's gone,

I takes it off and I puts it in the shed and I goes back to me tent and nobody knew the difference, aye. No, not even a word was said. So I don't know if they knew or not. But you'd do anything to get a cigarette, aye. That's how addicted people get. I even saw a feller the other day – no shame – picking up bumpers right in front of everybody in the street. So it gets to you, aye.

Anyhow, I'm working in the fettling camp, putting new sleepers in and all that to make the lines safe, and there was one part there, where there's three hills, and, over the years, the railway line had worked its way down the hill so that, up on top of the hill there's a gap of about six inches. And I just got there when they're pulling the lines back up again, aye. See, how we went about it was, we started at the top of the hill where the gap was and we worked our way back down to the bottom of the hill. Like, we'd undo the dogs – they're the spikes that keeps the rail line in – and then we'd grease the length of rail to make it slippery and we had, sort of like, a ramming pole and we'd all go 'One ... two ... three' and we'd push the line back up the track, about half an inch at a time. Then we'd put the dogs back in and then we'd do the same with the other side of the rail. And we done that all the way from the top of the hill, right down to the bottom of the hill and we got rid of the gap. It took us about ten days just to do that one hill, so imagine how hard that'd be, aye. Yeah, it was a gut-busting job, that one was. But I liked it. I like hard work, I do.

But, oh, the grasshoppers. One time a train come through and they was so thick they got squashed on the railway line and the train couldn't get any traction to get up the hill, not even when they put sand on them from the sand box. Another time, I was trying to roll a smoke and they was so thick that I had to turn me back on them and get me hat down and roll me cigarette that way, in me hat. Yeah, that's how thick they was.

And, well, out there at Mungallala, there was quite a few fettlers. Us single ones lived in tents and the married fellers, well, a lot of them had been there all their lives in the railway and they had married quarters. Then there was a feller looking after the bore – pumping the water up into a big overhead tank so the steam engines could get their water. And, when he was pumping the water up, he used to pour treacle over the belt to stop it from slipping. There was no kids there, no, so I don't know what the wives did all day; probably just yakked amongst themselves, I suppose.

Then, the camp, itself, was only about a mile out from Mungallala and so, when we got paid, we'd go up there to the pub. Two sisters had the pub, Mrs Clancy and Mrs Kerr. I remember them because, back then, you had to be twenty-one to drink in a pub in Queensland and I wasn't quite nineteen but they still let me drink, anyway. But, as I said, I wasn't seeing much of Bluey and that got to me a bit because we'd made all these big plans together, see. Then, when I got me first pay, I went into Roma to get some tucker and some rations. So I'd done all that and I was on me way back to the railway station to go back to Mungallala and, lo and behold, I runs into Bluey. I says, 'Oh, how're yer goin' mate? How's things out at Dulbydilla?' Gee, I was so pleased to see him, aye. I says, 'Look, don't worry about payin' fer yer rations. I'll pay. It's on me.' I says, 'I've heard there's a Harley Davidson fer sale fer ninety quid in Mungallala. It's got a side-car so I reckon if we save real hard we'll buy it 'n' learn to ride it, then we'll pull the pin here 'n' we'll go up ter the cattle country.'

But, see, he's looking real sheepish at me, aye. 'Goldie,' he says, 'I'm goin' home.'

I says, 'What?'

He says, 'I'm homesick so I'm goin' home.'

I said, 'Listen, you rotten mongrel, we made a deal. There was no quittin', not by me 'n' not by you. We stay together 'n' we travel together 'n' we get some experience on the cattle stations.'

'But I wanta go home.'

I says, 'Well, all right then Blue, but don't you ever, ever again ask me ter go knockin' around with yer again.'

So that was that and Bluey went back home. I didn't make the mistake of going with him this time but I kept in touch with his mother because I was very fond of his family. Yeah, real fond. Then it was only a couple of years later that she wrote and told me that poor Bluey had died. No, I'm not sure exactly what from but apparently, when he was young, he had rheumatic fever or something and then he died in about 1954, I think it was.

But, of course, I didn't know all that then so I was pretty sore on Bluey for breaking our promise to stay together and go up into the cattle station country. But, see, for some reason I've always had problems with fellers sticking with me. Like, we'd make all these big plans and they'd be all for it, then they'd pull out, all of a sudden. Anyrate, I stayed on fettling for a month or so and even though I enjoyed the work I still wanted to get up on the cattle stations, aye, even if Bluey wasn't coming with me. So one day I just told them I'm leaving and they still give me my pay, my holiday pay and everything.

8

Anyway, I goes back into Mungallala and I cash in me railway's cheque and I'm staying in the pub. I'm still shirty about Bluey pulling the pin on me, aye. Then on the weekend I gets talking to a few fellers who happen to have come into town from a cattle station called Taylors Plains, so I asks them if there's any work going out there and one of the fellers, the head stockman, he says, 'Oh yeah, I'll give yer a job. Be here tomorra mornin', at the pub, 'n' we'll take yer back out with us.'

'Yeah, righto,' I says, real enthusiastic-like, because now, at last, I've got the chance to go and work on a cattle station.

So next morning we met up at the pub and they're driving a Chev Blitz – you know, one of them old army ones, big square-nosed things where you can open the hatch in the cabin and stand up in the seat and look out over the top of the bonnet. During the war they put a machine gun up there. Anyway, we're all ready to go and the head stockman, he gets me to crank the Blitz, right in the main street, see. Now, they didn't say nothing about it but, apparently, them old Blitzes was notorious for having their timing out and something else they didn't tell me was that there's a special way of holding the crank handle so, when it backfires, it slips out of your hand. Anyrate, I had me thumb in the wrong place and when the Blitz backfired the crank handle shot right back around and – crack! – onto me wrist and straightaway I knew something was wrong because there was this terrible pain and me wrist swole up and I felt like vomiting.

Anyway, they went over to the store to get some tobacco and things and someone there bandaged me wrist up. And, well, I didn't know it at the time, but apparently I'd broke the wrist in about three places. Okay, so we goes out to Taylors Plains and the owner of the place wasn't there. In actual fact, the head stockman had no right to put me on in the first place really because he'd hired me without the boss knowing. But me wrist, oh, it was playing up something terrible, and I was struggling with doing any work. But there was this gin there, see, what they called a kitchen girl. She was about thirty or so and she done the housekeeping – like peeling the spuds, sweeping the floor, helping in the kitchen and all that. A real skinny thing she was. Anyhow they said, 'You'd better go 'n' see her. She'll fix it.'

So I goes over to this gin and she takes a look and she says, 'Me brodder-in-law, him 'bin breakin' arm when him ride'um bullock so I can fix 'em up all same along 'em doctor.' Then she bandaged it up real tight in some sort of cloth, like an old torn dress or something, and she told me to walk around with me wrist tucked in me shirt. So I couldn't really use it, aye. Then every second day or third day she'd call out to me, 'Goldie, come on now, you 'bin come 'n' I 'bin change 'em bandage.'

So I'd go back and she'd undo the bandage and she'd do it up again, real tight, and also someone gave me a leather wristband that you can tighten up, to support it. Oh, I even wore that wristband for years after the wrist had mended and when that one wore out I got a new one. And I'll tell you this, a couple of years later me thumb popped out from when I was brawling. It's that one there, see. Even though I don't brawl no more it still sometimes pops out. Anyway, I went to the hospital about it and when they X-rayed me hand, this doctor feller come out and he said, 'So you've had an accident with your wrist.'

I says, 'Yeah.'

And he looked over the X-ray real close and he said, 'Well, that'd be the best lot of setting I've ever seen on carpal bones.'

See, that's what I'd broke when the crank handle got me. See, there's heaps of little bones there in your wrist. They're what's called carpal bones, and I didn't tell the doctor feller that it was a gin that'd done it. He didn't know that, aye. So yeah, he's looking at this X-ray, saying, 'That's a beautiful set.'

Anyhow, I was only there at Taylors Plains for about six weeks. You know, I was really looking forward to getting on a horse and going out into the stock camp and working the cattle, but all we done was go out in the truck, cutting cypress pine to do some fencing. And we also built these new five-rail stockyards. But I just couldn't pull me weight properly, aye, not with one arm. Anyrate, finally the boss turns up – Rowland Staynem, his name was – and he says, 'Look, yer no good ter me. Yer can't use that arm.'

And his wife felt that sorry for me, like, she's telling me how I could get some sort of sickness benefits from the government, with not being able to work properly. Anyway, I didn't worry about that because, even though me wrist was just starting to come a bit good, in one way I didn't mind getting the shove from Taylors Plains. I just wanted to go out and work the cattle, aye. So the boss, he gave me me marching orders and I gets on the mail truck and I goes back into Mungallala. Then the next day or something, lo and behold, this drover feller, Mat Thomas, comes through town with a big mob of 4500 wethers. He's walking them to Muckadilla. Anyway, he comes up the pub asking if anybody'll go with him and I said, 'Boy, this'll do me. At last I'll be on a horse 'n' doin' somethin' I want ter do.'

So I set off on me first ever real droving trip. Mat Thomas had a three-in-hand wagonette. That's three horses pulling a wagonette, with all the gear on it and that. There was just him and me and about ten dogs and the cook, who was in the wagonette. And, see, because the stock route out there was fenced both sides, you could lock the sheep in along the fence line so there's no need for two fellers out on each side of them. We done six mile a day. That was the law of the overland – six mile a day with sheep, eight mile a day with cattle. But the idea with all stock is not to push them too hard or else they'll lose condition. That's the last thing you want because, when you present them for sale, naturally they'll get a better price if they're in top condition, aye. And one time we camped at a place where there was real good feed so Mat Thomas wanted to hold them there for as long as possible to build them up and the stock inspector arrived and said, 'Hey, yer've been here fer three days, what's the trouble?'

And Mat Thomas said, 'Oh, some'a the sheep aren't too well.' But really, he just wanted them to stay on the good feed for a bit longer.

Anyhow, the stock inspector didn't bite because he said, 'Well I want yer off here tomorra.' So he hunts us along, aye, because he don't want us to hang around and eat the place out.

But it was pretty easy sort of droving. At night I'd just roll me swag out under the wagon and I'd sleep there. And it was basic sort of droving food – you know, mutton and damper, though the cook feller was a bit inventive with his desserts because he'd make a bit of custard in one pot and he'd cook a bit of spaghetti in another pot, then he'd put them both together, pour a bit of sugar in, and that was our pudding. Anyhow, we delivered the sheep at Muckadilla a couple of weeks later. But, see, I'm not keen on sheep. They're a bit slow and boring for me, and quite dumb.

Then when I gets paid off I thinks, Well, I'll get a job round here somewhere. By now me wrist's pretty good, though me arm's still all bandaged up. So I'm hanging round the Muckadilla pub – see, in small country towns, if you wanted a job, you just went to the pub and asked around there because as sure as eggs somebody would know if there's work about. So

I'm boarding there at the pub and eating me tucker there – three good meals a day – and I was talking to a feller, one of the locals, and I said, 'Do yer know if there's any work around the place, mate?'

And he says, 'Look, mate, the musterin' season's finished now. If yer want work, go up ter a place just south of Townsville called Ayr because tobacco pickin's on now.'

And I thought to meself, Geez, at least I'll be headin' north.

9

I had a bit of money from the droving trip, aye, so I catches the train from Muckadilla back to Brisbane. Then, when I got to Brisbane, I only had enough left to pay for a ticket up to Mackay. Yeah, that was all. So in Brisbane I had to sleep overnight in Roma Street Station, and I ran into a feller at the pub there. I'll never forget his name – Snowy Lingard. Snowy was a World War II digger and he still wore his uniform. Anyhow, Snowy and me got talking about this and that and I must've mentioned how I wanted to be a ringer because he said, 'When yer get ter Mackay go ter so-and-so's place. They're Italians. Tell 'em I sent yer 'n' they'll get yer a ringin' job.'

Okay, so I gets to Mackay and I goes round to this place and I tells one of the fellers there that Snowy had sent me and I wanted to get a job as a ringer. So the feller says, 'Where did you work last?'

Well, see, this was always the problem because I hadn't really worked anywhere as a ringer. I'm still as green as next year's corn, aye. Like, I could ride a horse because I'd learned that when I was with Bill Hicks, out of Walcha. But, see, I couldn't ride a rough horse – you know, I didn't know how to saddle up a bad horse or anything like that, not at that time, and I hadn't had any real experience with stock and that. See, you've got to get into a proper cattle camp to learn all that sort of stuff, and I hadn't done that. I just wanted to get there. So nothing eventuated and I'm out of money, so now I'm walking out of town hitchhiking and this bloke pulls up. He's a well-dressed feller. He says, 'Jump in. I can't take yer very far.' He says, 'Where're yer goin'?'

I says, 'I'm off ter Ayr, hopin' ter go tobacco pickin'.'

'Oh,' he says, 'maybe I can get yer some type of work around here.'

'That's all right by me,' I says.

Anyhow, we stops at a little pub about eight mile north of Mackay – a place called Farleigh, I think it was – and I says, 'Look mate, I can't shout yer a beer or nothin'. I'm skint.'

He says, 'Oh that's all right. I'll shout yer.'

See, this's back when they're still cutting sugar cane by hand, and there's all these blokes in the bar and they're black from the soot, from the burnt cane. Dead black. Now, apparently this well-dressed feller was well known around the place and he says to one of the cane cutters, 'Do yer need any help?'

And the feller says, 'No mate, we're the last gang 'n' we've only got another five days to go 'n' it's all finished.'

Anyway, he tried his best to get me work but nothing came from it. Then, lo and behold, he takes me to his house and he introduces me to his wife. She'd just cooked a nice dinner, aye, so he asks me to stay for dinner and we sat down and she gave me a real good feed. And all this time, this feller, he's apologising because he can't put me up for the night because he had to go out somewhere.

I says, 'No, that's okay, mate. Don't worry about it. I just appreciate all yer've done for me, anyway.' So after dinner I thanked them again and I grabbed me swag and I went and camped out in the rainforest. Then, next morning, I'm walking along and I'm collecting all this sugar cane and I'm sticking it in me swag because I'm planning to keep some to chew on for a feed.

Then I gets to Farleigh Siding and I'm sitting there and a train arrives. It's heading north, so I'm on it, aye. And nobody asked me for a ticket so I just gets on and makes meself comfortable and I'm sitting there in the carriage trying to look like I've got money. Anyrate, we pulls up at a siding further up the track – I forget the name of the place, just now – and the guard comes along and I'm thinking, He's gonna ask fer me ticket. But he doesn't. Instead, he says, 'Alright, we'll be here fer about 'n hour so yer can go over there to the pub 'n' have a drink if yer like.'

But, see, I haven't got a brass razoo, aye, so I says to him, 'Oh,' I says, 'what're you doin'? Come over the pub 'n' I'll shout yer a beer.'

But, like, I was bluffing it, aye, just to make the impression I had money and I had a ticket. But I had nothing. So if he had've said 'Yes' I don't know what I would've done. Anyhow, he says, 'No, mate. Thanks all the same but I can't, 'cause I'm on the job.'

I says, 'Oh, okay, I may as well stay here, also, then', and I tried to look disappointed. Anyhow, he didn't say nothing more about it so I just sat there in the carriage till we choofed off again. But after we got a bit further on, the guard came around again and I sensed he was thinking, Hang on a tick, I don't think I've seen that bloke's ticket. Like, that's what I was thinking, he was thinking, see. Anyrate, before he gets to say anything, I says, 'Oh, I was lookin' forward ter shoutin' yer a beer, mate.'

'Were yer?' he said and we started to have a chat about this and that and, you know, he never asked to see me ticket. Now, I don't know if he forgot or he knew I was tramping it and I didn't have one, or maybe he just liked me. But, no, he never asked me for a ticket.

Okay, we gets to Bowen. I don't know how far Bowen is from Mackay – maybe 150 mile or something – and the train pulls up there and I'm thinking, well, he's gonna have ter ask fer a ticket some time or other. So I decide to get out here and hitchhike up to Ayr, otherwise this guard feller, he'll end up putting me off and there could be trouble.

So I'm back out on the road again, aye, to hitchhike further north and these fellers come along and the driver feller, he says, 'Look, I can only take yer up ter Guthalungra.'

Guthalungra – what a name, aye. I mean, I didn't even know where it was, but I said 'That's okay' and I gets in with them.

As it turned out, Guthalungra was only about forty mile up the road and they was going up there to get some firewood. They was driving an old '28 Chev they'd made into a ute and they're telling me how, whenever they got a good load of wood on, the old Chev couldn't make it up some of the hills, even in low gear, so they had to turn it around and reverse it up because, apparently, the reverse gear had a smaller cog. Anyhow, we goes up the road a bit and they drops me off just short of Guthalungra and they heads off into the bush to get their wood. So I'm hitchhiking again and oh, I'm hungry, aye. Broke and hungry, so I'm chewing on this sugar cane I'd collected back near Farleigh, and these other couple of fellers come along and the driver says, 'Where're yer goin'?'

I says, 'Ayr. They reckon there's work up there tobacco pickin.'

'Jump in,' they said, 'we're just goin' up the road a bit. We'll drop yer there.'

By now, Ayr's only about sixty mile further north. So I'm getting closer, aye. Anyway, the story goes that the passenger feller in this car had been in a Main Roads gang, building a bridge at Guthalungra, but he'd pulled the pin and he'd gone back down to Bowen. So now he's got his mate to drive him back to Guthalungra to pick up his swag and all his cooking gear. So we're driving along and the driver says, 'So yer lookin' fer work, are yer?'

I says, 'Yeah.'

'Can yer use a shovel?' he says.

'Yeah.'

He says, 'Well, they want men down at the salt mines in Bowen.'

I says, 'Okay, I'll have a go at that.'

Anyway, when we arrives at this Main Roads camp, his mate had a bottle of lager in with his gear. The only trouble is that it'd been laying in the sun for about three days and when he said to me, 'Do yer want a drink, mate?' I did and I tell you, oh, never drink hot beer, aye.

So then I went back down south to Bowen with them fellers and they got me into the Commercial Hotel and, oh, the people there really looked after me, they did. They even cut me lunch and everything. Oh, they looked after me real good. And I didn't have any problems getting work because it was October '52 by now, see, so the salt season's just started. Yeah, they have seasons, because after you dig up all the salt, then you have to wait another nine months or something for the next lot to settle. See, they have these one-acre and two-acre salt pans and they have a little wooden gate at the end where they let the salty seawater in from the tides. Then, when the saltwater's all in they shut the gate and let the water evaporate and after they've done that a few times, in the end, there's about a four-inch crust of salt all over the pans.

Then, when the season starts, you grab a pick and a shovel and you dig up the crust of salt and you put it in these little railway truck-type things. Like, if you can imagine, they're about four or five foot high and about six foot long. There's about ten trucks on each set of tracks and when all the trucks are loaded, a little train takes them away and you move the railway lines to another place and start all over again. But, oh, it was hard yakka, all right, out there in the glaring heat with your eyes always squinting. And because you're tonguing for a drink all the time from the heat and the glare off the salt and all that, they had this canvas bag of water. But there's only the one cup that everyone had to share and blokes are rushing down there all the time to get a drink of water and the sweat's pouring off them and they're dipping this cup into the canvas bag and by the time ten or twelve blokes have been in there, oh, you're drinking everybody else's sweat, aye.

So, okay; now the salt company, they didn't supply boots or nothing but, on top of your pay, they gave you three and six a week for what they called 'boot money'. Well, that's because the salt's real coarse and it gets into your boots and it cuts into your skin, then the brine of it somehow gets into your system – I don't know how – and you end up with what's called a running sore. And, even after you've left the mines, these running sores just wont heal up till they're treated properly. Anyrate, I got a running sore, aye. But I stuck the whole season out, right up till the wet started, around January or February '53. So I was there a good four months – October, November, December, January. And I can tell you, not too many stuck the season out. I tell you, work like that sorts out the men from the boys.

Originally, I was thinking about buying a vehicle but I couldn't because I didn't really end up saving that much money. Oh well, you know, staying in a pub, and it was boring, you had nothing else to do, so you'd have a drink and things like that, aye. Anyhow, I didn't know how to drive. I was nineteen by then. Actually, I think I might've even spent my nineteenth birthday in the salt mines, on afternoon shift.

10

But, see, I still had this thing in me head about going out into the
back country, you know, ringing and all that. So I catches a train
from Bowen up to Townsville, then out to Cloncurry. Anyhow, I
gets to Cloncurry – The Curry, as it's known – and I'm skint again
so I goes to the line inspector. 'Have yer got any work?' I says.

'Done any fettlin'?' he asked.

'Yeah.' And so I gets a job fettling, out at a place called
Oorindi. Oorindi's about forty mile each way, between Julia
Creek and Cloncurry. So now I'm out there fettling in the
middle of this big, black soil plain and there's these two Polish
fellers in the camp, see, and I see how they're saving and saving
and saving. Like, they'd order their rations from The Curry just
so they could stay in the camp most weekends and they'd only
go into town once a month to have a bit of a blow-out. That's
all. Once a month, aye. And, see, with wanting to buy me own
vehicle and get up into the stock camps, I thought I'd do the
same as these Polish fellers.

And that was good. Yeah, while I stayed out at the fettling
camp I was saving money. Then I met two fellers, about my age,
Vincent and Benny Smith. They was fettling at the next little
siding down from Oorindi. I forget the name of the place, just
now, but their brother-in-law, Kenny McKyber, he was the
ganger out there. Kenny was married to one of the Smith boys'
sisters, Tootsie. Anyhow, when the Smith boys went into town
after paydays they'd come by Oorindi and come over and have
a yarn to me. Actually, they come from Normanton. They was
ringers up there in the Gulf but they was fettling down at this

little place because the mustering season had finished. But I was determined now not to go to town, aye. I was going to save all me money, see. Then the Smith boys said, 'Hey, Goldie, why don't yer come inta The Curry with us?'

I says, 'Oh, no.' I says, 'I got no clean clothes.'

'Oh, we'll lend yer some.'

So Benny gives me a lend of a shirt and trousers and we went into Cloncurry and we had a good time. Then after that I used to go to town with them after every payday. See, a train would go down on the Friday night and we'd go to the pub and things, then we'd get the train back to the fettling camp on Sunday evening. I mean, we never got real drunk or went looking for fights or anything like that, but I got to know both the Smith boys pretty well. And with their other sister, Lois, being a barmaid at the Central Hotel in The Curry, I got to know her, too. Like, I wasn't going out with her or nothing, even though I would've liked to have had a girlfriend. But, see, when you've got no money and you've got no car, it's a bit hard. And Lois was a pretty good sort. Oh, all the fellers was after her. But no one could catch her, aye. That's why they called her 'Bernborough', after that famous racehorse. So yeah, that was Lois.

Actually, a woman named Phyllis Hawes used to own the Central and oh, she really stuck to me, that lady. She really liked me, she did. Whenever I was broke she'd always stand me. Now here's a story. See, Phyllis nearly lost her liquor licence a few times for selling grog on a Sunday. So she sort of had a thing about coppers and what broke her heart was that her only daughter up and married a copper. But the thing is, see, the daughter and the mother was so close that when Phyllis died the daughter actually fretted to death. True. That's a known thing around The Curry. She just mourned and mourned after her mother. She'd sit out there at the cemetery and weep and go on at the gravesite and, yeah, she just fretted; wasted away.

But, see, all the times we went into The Curry, Benny and Vincent was on to me about how great Normanton was and how I could get a job ringing up there, real easy, and I'd tell them, 'Look,' I'd say, 'I'd really love ter but I've got no experience.'

Anyhow, to save me a bit of money, when I went into town I'd camp in one of the train carriages up at the railway station. And I was camped up there one weekend and there's another feller also sleeping in this carriage. He was a returned serviceman from World War II – I think he'd had some sort of rank – but it turns out, he's now a carpenter and he says, 'Look, I've got a contract out on Canobie Station. Would yer like ter work fer me?'

But I liked it out there fettling. It was good. But, see, since I'd met the Smith boys, I was coming into town after every payday and I wasn't getting to save much money, and I knew if I was stuck out on Canobie I wouldn't be able to get into town. So I thinks about it and I says, 'Okay then, it might be better than wrestlin' crowbars 'n' dodgin' snakes all day.'

So I went back out on the mixed goods train that Sunday evening and I pulls the pin and gets me gear and I comes back into The Curry on the next train to meet up with this carpenter feller. Now, because he had work out on Canobie, his credit was good and so we went around to a big store and he booked up a saw and carpenter's tools and this and that, then we caught the mail plane out to Canobie Station.

Canobie was about ninety mile north of Cloncurry. About a thousand square mile, it was. Back then it belonged to a company called Australian Estates. They had a lot of property in Australia. Now, with a lot of them stations in them days, the manager had his own big homestead and the workers' camp was separate, and our job was to build new quarters and a new kitchen for the ringers. And I was making good money. When I say good money, I was getting around two pound ten a day. And because I wasn't getting into town, after a couple of months, I'd built up quite a good cheque, aye. Then one time they sent me into The Curry for some reason or other and I goes round to the Oasis Hotel and the publican there, Sam Thurleigh, he says, 'Goldie, yer wanta watch that carpenter feller.' He says, 'When he was workin' on the railways here, he was goin' about of a night wantin' ter have sex with the other fellers.'

Well, I thought he was pretty straight, so I says, 'Are you fair dinkum?'

He says, 'Yes, I am, so yer'd better watch him.'

'Yeah, okay,' I says, 'I will.'

Anyhow, after Sam said what he'd said, I started thinking there was some things that did seem a bit suspicious. Like, I'd have a bag with nails in it – you know those nail bags carpenters wear on a belt that hang down your front – well, he'd grab one of the nails out of my bag and he'd keep his hand down there too long. You know, that sort of stuff. So I says to meself, 'Now, what am I gonna do here?' Because, see, this carpenter feller, he reckoned I was a pretty good slave and he kept saying, 'Look, I need somebody like you because yer such a good worker. I'll teach yer all about the building game.' Like he wanted to apprentice me in a sort of a way. And I didn't mind the work, actually, but the thing was, it was still me lifelong dream to be a ringer, you know, and every chance I got on Canobie, when the ringers was drafting cattle in the yards, I'd be over there to be among the cattle. I just loved the cattle, aye – the cattle and the horses.

Anyrate, so I goes back out to Canobie and it's coming to the time when me and this carpenter feller are to go and camp out together while we build some boundary riders' huts. And I noticed how he was starting to store all this grog up. Like, every week, when the mail truck come out from The Curry, there'd be another three or four cartons of grog for him and he was stacking it all up behind his door at our quarters. Then it struck me, Oh, I know what this bloke's up to. He's gonna get me drunk 'n' have his way with me.

So I had to get away from him, aye. Well, first, I tried to get him to sack me. Like, when we nailed the three-ply lining up in the rooms of the new ringers' quarters I'd put some tools behind it so he couldn't find them and whenever he'd get me to cut a bit of timber on the wooden horse I'd not only saw through the timber but I'd also, purposely, saw through the wooden horse as well. But he still wouldn't sack me so, in the end, I wrote to that mate of mine in Sydney I told you about, Frank Yateman, and I said to Frank, 'Send me a telegram telling me to meet you in Bourke for a droving trip.'

But it was all a big excuse, aye, so when this telegram comes back to Canobie from Frank Yateman, I says, 'Oh, look at this. I can't miss out on this.' I said, 'I'm outa here.'

So I just told him I was leaving, aye. And he didn't argue much about it. Well, he couldn't really because nothing was going to change me mind. And also that running sore I got from when I was up in Bowen, it was still playing up and I needed it seen to. So he paid me off and I left Canobie with a few quid and I went back into The Curry. That's right, I remember I had eighty pounds because I could've bought a vehicle in Cloncurry with that exact money. But, in the end, I decided not to because I would've had no spending money left over.

11

Okay, so I'm back in Cloncurry, aye. I think the Korean War was just finishing up. I still would've only been nineteen, going on twenty. Well, I was born in December 1933 and I turned twenty-one in December 1954. But because the salt from when I was up in Bowen had got into me system, I still had this running sore so, when I got back into The Curry, I went up to the Outpatients at the hospital. Harvey Sutton was the name of the doctor and Harvey took one look at it and he says 'You've got a running sore', and when he lanced it open, inside, it was all black, about the size of a shilling or ten cents, so he stuck some stuff in it and, believe it or not, it healed, pretty much, straightaway. And after all them months, aye.

Oh, incidentally, in '53, they caught a three-foot grey nurse shark at The Curry, three hundred mile from the ocean. Fair dinkum. It'd somehow worked its way all the way up the Cloncurry River. And in that same year, during the wet season, it rained fish. True. There was little two-inch fellers flapping like this, down the gutter in the Post Office Hotel. Ridgy didge. I was there.

Anyhow, after I gets the running sore sorted out, I met a bloke called Arthur Reid. I forget exactly how. Maybe I just heard he was after a worker or something. But he gave me a job and we went cutting wood around town, for pubs and that. He had a truck and he'd jack this truck up, then the back wheel had what's called a floating axle, so he'd put a belt onto that and attach it to a circular saw. But old Arthur and me, we got on real well. I suppose he could see I was a good slave, aye.

Like, I could use an axe, of course, from when I was a kid in Springwood and the stepmother had me chopping wood up. So, yeah, you could say I'd been well trained. So old Arthur and me, we worked around town for a bit, then he offered me a job, yard building, at a station out of The Curry. Now, I won't mention the name of the place because I'm about to tell you a story about the owners and it's fair dinkum.

See, what happened in The Curry was that, on a Sunday, everyone would go down the weir and go swimming and have picnics and talk to friends and one thing or another. And the bank manager feller – I think he might've been from the old Bank of New South Wales – well, the manager, he was down there this time and he got into his togs and went for a swim and he left his clothes on the bank. And in among his clothes was all his keys – like, not only his house and car keys but also the keys to the bank vault and all that. So the owners of the station old Arthur and me went to work on, they got a cake of soap and they made impressions of all the bank keys into the soap. Then, from the impressions, they made a mould of them and they used that mould to make some keys. Then one night, shortly after, they knocked the bank over, and 40,000 pound went missing.

A few months later the Taxation Department decided to make a spot raid and check their books because they thought that the amount of tax they paid was pitiful to the amount of cattle they'd sold. Yeah, a pittance. So a big taxation accountant come up there and he went through the books. Then he said to the old man owner, he said, 'By the records of your transactions you owe the Taxation Department in excess of 40,000 pound so we'll have to go to a court, and if you're found guilty, which you will be, because we've got the proof here, you could be in for a hefty jail term.'

So the old man owner said, 'Forty thousand pounds, aye?'

'That's right,' said the taxation accountant. 'In excess of.'

'But, just as a bottom line, you reckon it's around 40,000 pounds?' says the old man.

'Yes.'

'So if we paid you 40,000 pounds, would you be happy with that?'

And the taxation accountant, he thought about it for a while, then he says, 'Oh, yes, yes.'

'And if I pay you 40,000 pounds, will you write a receipt out 'n' write on it "Completely paid" 'n' we'll hear no more of it?'

And the taxation feller says, 'Yes, I will.'

So the old man went over to his safe and he counted out 40,000 pounds in cash. 'Here yer go,' he said and he handed it over to the taxation accountant. And that happened just a month or so after the bank was robbed. As I said, that's common knowledge around The Curry because I once ran into a Cloncurry feller up on the Atherton Tablelands, many years later, and we got talking and he told me the exact same story I just told you – the cake of soap, the keys made and the 40,000 pound. You know, like, without me saying anything about it, he'd say, 'Yeah, 40,000 pound.' So that was a story I heard that I'm now telling you, and that's true because even though it was never proved, it was the local knowledge.

But, anyway, when I was out there at this place yard building with old Arthur Reid, them very same owners was making a big dam – massive, it was – and from the stockyard where old Arthur and me was working and camped, we had to go about thirty mile across this great big black soil plain to get to the riverbanks, where we got the posts from. And, see, the owners was working on this dam around the clock, with heavy machinery and all that. Oh, where they camped, they had a fly – a tent – and a kerosene fridge, all sorts of things. So they were pretty well set up, aye, and of an evening old Arthur and me had to go on the road, past where these owner fellers camped, with our load of posts, going back to the stockyards.

But, see, Arthur was a shrewd old feller because some of the bloodwood posts we got from down along the river, they'd have a big pipe in the middle. Yeah, a hole right up through the centre – about that round, maybe more. Not all the posts, mind you. Just some. But, see, you don't put posts with a pipe in the ground because they rot quicker. They don't last as long. But old Arthur, he was shrewd, aye, because what he done was, he'd cut a small sapling and he'd put a sharp point on the sapling and he'd ram it up the pipe in the bloodwood post. Then we'd make sure we loaded them posts on the driver's side of the truck so that, when we was on our way home and we pulled up to have a yarn with the owner fellers, they wouldn't see any pipes, aye, because they're on the other side of the truck.

So yeah, I learned a lot off Arthur Reid. He had a grown-up family, just about. And he taught me how to fell a tree. Well, just by looking at the branches, if most of the weight's on one side, it'll be more inclined to fall that way. Then he also told me how to tell if a tree was hollow on the insides or not. Like, if the limbs up on top of a tree have really dead wood sticking out, you'd guarantee it's hollow every time. And he was right. See, some yard builders have a brace and bit and they bore through the trunk and when they come to nothing, they know it's hollow. But not old Arthur. He didn't need to do that. He could tell by just looking at the tree.

Then we done all the cutting by axe so it was hard work. But I was getting good money – three pound a day, seven days a week. And, mostly, they was good posts. You know, about eighteen inches across. Then all the rails, we also cut by axe, from gidgee. Real tough timber is gidgee. And it was a big yard we was building. Five rails for each panel, to stop the yard jumpers. So the top rail was a bit under five feet. Then, of course, there was the crush, and that also had a lot of posts. To explain what a 'crush' is – well, basically, first you draft the cattle in the big drafting yard. Then after you get them in the yard, they head into what's known as a 'crush', which is only about three feet across, and that forces them to go through in single file into the dip, or plunger, which is about the same width as the crush and about as long as this room, about fifty feet. And they'd be dipped for ticks. But you'd have it all covered over because you don't want rain getting in the dip because it'd weaken the chemicals. So then they'd have to swim the length of the dip because they can't turn around in it and they'd come up out into what's called a draining pen. So that's the type of yard we was building.

And also, when I was out there, I saw me first min min light, aye. Well, we're coming back one night with a load of logs and I says to old Arthur, 'Look, there's a vehicle coming our way.' But it seemed a bit odd because it had only one light instead of two and the road we're on wasn't a main road or nothing. It was basically just a track that went from one mustering camp to where we was camped, and that's where it stopped. So we see this light coming and, out that way, there's lots of what's called gilgais, in among the gidgee. Gilgais are like saucer-shaped holes in the ground. Sometimes they're up to six foot deep and about the size of this kitchen. No, I don't know how they're formed but they fill up with water in the wet season. It's bad country to go chasing wild cattle. Yeah, a lot of blokes have broken their necks and killed their horses galloping through that gilgai country.

Anyrate, so this light appears and then it disappears again, and we just thought, Well, it's gone down one'a them gilgai. But then it appeared again and it's coming up closer and closer. And, you wouldn't believe it, then it starts to dance in the air. Yeah, dance in the air. Then it shot off into the sky. So that's the first min min light I saw, and it had a blue tinge to it, aye, like a ball. And that's true. Fair dinkum. Anyway, I'd been out there six weeks or something and we only had a couple of weeks to go till the fencing was all done, so old Arthur says, 'Sorry, Goldie,' he says, 'I can do it without yer now, mate.'

So then, that finished it. But oh, I had a good cheque, aye.

12

So I says 'Cheerio' to old Arthur and I goes back into The Curry. It's around the middle of 1953 by now – winter – and I'm cashed up, aye. Mustering season's not long over and so I runs into one of the ringers I'd met out on Canobie Station. Canobie's that place I was doing some building with the feller that Sam Thurleigh told me was going about of a night wanting to have sex with the other fellers in the railway's camp. Anyhow, this ringer's name's was Gordon Thompson and he says to me, 'Goldie, what're yer doin'?'

I says, 'Oh, nothin' much.'

He says, 'Look, I live up at Atherton 'n' I haven't been home in three years. I'm cashed up so how's about yer come up ter Atherton with me?'

Atherton's inland of Cairns. It's country I hadn't seen before so I says, 'Well, I'm cashed up meself, so yeah, okay. Beaut. I'll come along with yer.'

Now there was a steam train called the Forty-Two Up that used to leave The Curry on the Saturday night and it heads for Townsville, over on the coast. I don't actually know why it was called the Forty-Two Up, no. It might've been just a code name or something. It had two passenger carriages and it had a mixed goods van as well. Now, this train had a reputation in as much as it'd never been known to arrive on time. Yeah, it wasn't unusual for it to arrive up to eight hours late. That's fair dinkum. And the main reason was that this Forty-Two Up stopped at every little fettlers' camp along the way and the driver and the fireman and the guard, they'd all get out and wander over to have a yarn with the fettlers' wives and have a cup of tea with them and so forth and so on. Then, when all that was done, they'd wander back to the train and get on their way again till they reached the next fettlers' camp.

Anyrate, Gordon and me, we gets on this train, heading to Townsville. By morning we're going through all those little one-horse pub towns like Nelia and Nonda, where there's not much to occupy your time. All you see out the train window is big mobs of mimosa. Mimosa's a short bush. You wouldn't get one much over ten feet, but it has savage thorns on it. And, like, we're going so slow I can just about count the thorns on these mimosa bushes, aye. Then, I couldn't believe me eyes but, blow me down, the train starts to pick up a bit of pace. 'This's odd,' I says to Gordon.' But it didn't just stop there because the old Forty-Two Up kept picking up speed till we was really rattling along. So then I says to Gordon, 'Good, it's makin' up fer lost time.'

Then, just as we began to really rattle along, suddenly, the train comes to a screeching stop. 'Goldie,' Gordon says, 'maybe they just fergot where the brakes was fer a while.'

Anyhow, I took a look out the window to see what's going on and there's the fireman and the driver walking back along the track and one of them had a rifle in his hands.

'Geez,' I says to Gordon, 'take a look at this.' So we sticks our heads out the window and we sees them walk over to a dead dingo and they gets out a knife and they start to scalp the thing. So that explained why the train had been going so fast, aye. They was chasing this dingo, and they had their rifles up the front, in the cabin there, and they just shot the thing. Well, see, back in them days, there was a bounty on a dingo of about a pound, and sometimes the cocky – the property owner – would give them five pounds. But, blow me down, there I was thinking they was making up for lost time.

Anyway, we eventually ends up in Townsville. Then there's a train that goes to Cairns, so we gets on that and we're enjoying ourselves so much that the guard come along and he takes our bottle of rum and says, 'I'll give it back to yers when we get ter Cairns.' See, you weren't allowed to drink on trains in them days.

Okay, we gets to Cairns and the guard feller gives us back our rum and we're having a great time because, not boasting or nothing, see, I had good features when I was young, so the women was a bit attracted to me, aye. Then from Cairns, we catches this little train that goes up the Kuranda Range and when we gets to Mareeba we camped at the railway station. Oh, how I never poisoned meself I don't know because, see, we'd bought these oysters. You know, those oysters you buy in a jar that's already out of their shells. And, like, we're drinking and going on and I'm eating these oysters straight out of the jar. Then, when I wakes up the next morning, there's this terrible smell all about the place. Just horrible, it was. Anyrate, when I rolled over, there's still a few oysters left in the jar and, I tell you, they were absolutely rotten, aye. So how I didn't poison meself, I'll never know. Just by the smell of them, I should've died.

By then I've still got a few bob left, aye, so Gordon and me, we goes over and we books ourselves in at Memino's Cafe and Boarding House. Anne Memino ran it – Italian she was – and we're having a feed there, in the cafe, and this Gordon Thompson, he had a terrible habit of drinking the Holbrook sauce that the cafes had on their tables. True, every last drop. Anyrate, he downed the bottle of Holbrook sauce that was on our table, then he went over to the other table and he swapped the empty one for the full one and he starts into that too, aye. And this Ann Memino, when she saw what he was doing, oh, didn't she really blow up at him for drinking all the Holbrook sauce.

So that was at Mareeba. Then we goes to Atherton. Now, Gordon's old man was a woodcutter. He supplied wood for all the fuel stoves and that in town. Okay, so we gets there pretty late at night and Gordon goes in the house and wakes his father up and, before you know it, there's this big row going on. A huge row. What it's exactly about, I don't know, but, apparently, his mother had died years and years earlier and Gordon was always the black sheep in the family, so he and his father just never got on. That's why he'd cleared out from home in the first place. Anyhow, when things settled down a bit, the father says to Gordon, 'Look, I could do with you 'n' that mate'a yours ter help me cut some wood.'

By now all me money's gone so I had no choice. But, oh, it was hard yakka, aye. It'd still be dark and Gordon's old man, he'd be up and cook breakfast and make a few sandwiches for our lunch. He had this old truck. I think it was a Dennis or something. It didn't have pump-up tyres. It had solid tyres. It was one of them you had to crank up. So we'd crank this old thing up and away we'd go. It was still early so we'd have the lights on and we'd go down behind the Atherton rifle range, then away up in the rainforest, to cut this timber.

By the time we got out there it'd be just light enough to start. She-oak we cut. Most of the timber we cut by axe, other than the father had a one-man cross-cut saw. Well, with a one-man cross-cut saw you set it up so you had the inner-tube of a truck or a car tied to the tree then, when you pulled the saw towards you, the rubber would pull it back. Yeah, like a shanghai, sort of. But I was mostly on the axe. Then around mid-morning Gordon's old man boiled the billy and we had bit of lunch, and we'd be back into it again. Then, just on dark, we'd stop cutting and load up the truck and come home with the lights on. Then, when we got back to the house, we'd unload the truck and stack the wood in the pitch black. That's how long the hours was we worked. I tell you, it was tough, so hard in fact I'd be too tired to eat. Fair dinkum. Gordon's dad would cook a feed and I'd just lay down on me swag out on the verandah, and I wouldn't even bother eating. I'd just fall asleep. But, see, the feelings around the place wasn't good. You know, Gordon and his father was always arguing and going on. So then after a couple of weeks, Gordon says to his dad, 'I've had enough'a this. I'm clearin' out.'

And the father says, 'I don't need yers anymore, anyway.' Then he says to me, 'Here's five quid. That's all I can afford. There's not much money in wood cuttin'.'

Anyhow, when we gets into town I says to Gordon, I says, 'Look, Gordon, you gave me a spin because yer old man only gave me five quid fer all that hard work.'

And Gordon says to me, 'Well, Goldie, yer lucky because I got nothin'.'

So we're back in Mareeba, having a good time, mucking up and all that, and something I'll never forget. Have you ever heard of Bronco Johnson? Well, Bronco Johnson was in the fight game in the mid-fifties. A pub brawler he was, really, because he'd bring these haymakers up from the floor. But he was starting to build himself a bit of a rep – reputation – by knocking a few big-time fighters out. Anyhow, Bronco had a brother called Frank and Frank lived in Mareeba. A very quiet sort of feller was Frank. A nice bloke. And one night, Gordon and me, we're in the pub, drinking with this Frank, and I looked down beside me and there's this other feller laying on the floor, see, frothing at the mouth and kicking like he's having a stroke or a fit or something. So I says to Frank, I says, 'What's wrong with him?'

And Frank says, 'Oh, don't take no notice'a him. It happens all the time. He's been drinking that stuff over there.' And Frank points at these bottles behind the bar that are about two foot long, very thin, with a little bit of a bell at the bottom and there's a plant growing inside. So blowed if I know what kind of drink it was or what sort of plant was in it, but Frank says, 'Oh, he'll be okay, he's just been drinkin' that stuff.'

Anyrate, I says, 'Oh mate, by the way he's frothin' and kickin', ter me he looks like a dingo that's just taken a bait.'

13

Now, what happened to Gordon after that I'm not exactly sure, though I think – and I stand to be corrected here – but I think he got a job at a big timber mill up on the Atherton Tablelands, working on a machine that shaved the wood off huge logs to make three-ply. I ended up back at Memino's Cafe and Boarding House. That's the place Ann Memino ran – the one who got stuck into Gordon for drinking the Holbrook sauce.

Anyway, with Ann Memino being Italian, I pretty soon got a job tobacco picking on a place just three mile out of Mareeba, working for a bloke called Johnny Piagno. With all the bending down and that, tobacco picking's pretty hard on your back. But that was okay. I didn't mind hard work. I was young and fit. Well, how you go about it is – when the tobacco plant's about five foot high, it starts to die from the bottom up. Yeah, these big Virginia leaves about eighteen inches long and about ten inches or something wide, they narrow to the point of the leaf. Generally there's about three or four ripe, yellow leaves at the bottom of each plant and you just snap them off with your hand. They come off real easy. Then you plonk them in the cradle of your arm and you go to the next bush and do the same there. Then, when you can't carry any more, you put the leaves down on a hessian bag, like a stretcher. And when that's all loaded, you take it up to the barn where the leaves are threaded out on sticks, like tomato stakes, ready to be dried.

So you'd work your way through the crop and by the time you got to the end, more leaves are starting to die off, back at the beginning, so then you do a second pick, a third pick, and a fourth pick. Then after you've picked all the leaves and they're hanging up on the stakes in the barn, they burn wood and the heat cooks the tobacco leaves, nice and dry. No, no special wood. They just used what they could get because, see, there was a lot of tobacco farms around that area, all drying leaves. I mean, sometimes you'd have to go for miles to get wood from out of the forest.

Now what smokers don't realise – and I didn't at the time because I was still smoking – is that there's at least twenty-seven different poisons in tobacco. Twenty-seven! Because even before you start drying the leaves, the plants have already been sprayed with DDT and other poisons to stop the grubs getting into them. That's when they're only about a foot high. Then you spray again when the plant's about four foot high and you spray it again when it's about six foot high, and all those insecticides get cooked into the leaf. So not only does the tar from the tobacco kill people, but the insecticides are killing them, too.

But we never wore a mask or anything. No, we'd just go out barefoot and in a pair of shorts. That's all we wore. And after a while, there's all this sticky stuff in the tobacco leaf that gets on your arm and you have to use kerosene to get it off. Actually, a lot of the tobacco pickers used to shave the hairs off their arms so the stuff didn't stick to their hairs. So that's how you go about tobacco picking and, around the area, it was mostly Italian-owned tobacco farms. A big Italian population. I remember Johnny Piagno telling me how he'd once had a shortage of labour so he sent away to the Immigration Department to get people to come and work for him and they sent him all these southern Italians. But, see, the northern Italian doesn't like the southern Italian, aye, and Johnny, being northern Italian, he used to say, 'Oh, these-a Italians from-a Sicily, I don't-a like 'em. They's primitives.' That's what Johnny was telling me, anyway.

Then after all the tobacco leaves have been dried off in the barn the farmers put them in these big bags, like wool bales, and they truck them into this huge auction room in Mareeba where they're set up in rows and they're all given numbers, ready for the auction. Back then, there was two main tobacco companies up that way: Dimbulah Tobacco Company and North Queensland Tobacco, and they had buyers who'd come along and they'd open the top of a bag – say it was lot 107 – and they'd look at the leaf and they'd smell it and they'd get down inside the bag and pull it around, trying to grade it, like. Then after he's done that, the buyer thinks, Okay, I'll offer so much a pound for that. Then all the buyers bid for each of the bags. And that's what they done every year.

Then after they buy the tobacco, they process it and really cut it up. Like, there's all different grades and cuts, like ready-rubbed tobacco and fine-cut tobacco and all that. And Dimbulah Tobacco Company, when they processed their tobacco, they used to put traces of molasses in it to give it a bit of a taste. Dimbulah was about twenty mile out of Mareeba. Dimbulah Tobacco was in a blue packet. And the North Queensland Tobacco Company, they was right in Mareeba and, when they processed, they'd put traces of rum in theirs and, oh, you could smell it all over town. So I'd reckon North Queensland Tobacco was the more popular to smoke. But that was probably the rum, aye, and it did have a nice flavour to it.

So anyway, I was working for Johnny Piagno and he looked after me real well. Like, I had nice quarters to stay in and that. But it was pretty boring so, of a night, I'd walk the three mile into Mareeba to have a few ales. There was the Railway Hotel and then there was the Ted Marsterson Hotel, I think it was called. They're just two I can remember. But I was never a very heavy drinker. I'd go into town just to have a bit of night life – you know, to meet fellers at the pub. Most of them worked over the railways so when Johnny Piagno run out of work I just went over to the Railway Workshops in Mareeba and I says to the feller there, 'Can yer give me a job, mate?'

'Okay,' he says, so he gave me a short-time job, shovelling coal up on the coal stage, along with a local feller called Bill Seacombe.

Now, a coal stage is made out of very tall timber poles and up top there's a big holding bin thing. So they'd put a steam engine on the trailing end of some rail trucks that's loaded with coal, and they'd push them up a ramp, to the top of this coal stage, and we'd shovel the coal out of the rail trucks, into the holding bin. Then, when the locos came in, you'd lower a chute down into the coal tender of the train and you'd pull a lever and the coal would gravitate down into the tender. So that's what we was doing.

Anyhow, I'm back at Memino's Cafe and Boarding House, aye. A lot of railway workers stayed at Memino's. Now, I don't think Ann Memino had a husband but she had a sister – or it might've been her daughter – working there with her who'd make all the beds and that. That's right, Kitty her name was. It come to me just then, would you believe it? But, oh, they'd just about do everything for you. They'd even cut your lunch. And, oh, we had three good meals a day, and I had no trouble paying me board and I kept me room tidy. And one feller, one of the engine drivers, was always at me to learn to be an engine driver. And with all this stuff I was always going on about, about wanting to go out into the cattle country and go ringing, he kept saying, 'Listen, Goldie, that's no life fer you. Being a train driver's the way ter go. Once yer in, yer set up fer life.'

But it was me lifelong dream to get out into the cattle camps, aye. So anyway, like I said, shovelling coal was only a short-time job and me and this Bill Seacombe, we're only there for about a month and then the big boss from Cairns rings up and he says to our boss in Mareeba, 'Put those two fellers off. We've got no more work for them.'

Anyrate, our boss – I forget his name just now – he said to the big boss in Cairns, 'But these two coal shovellers, they're the best workers I've ever had the pleasure to have.' He says, 'I wanta keep them on permanent.'

But the Cairns feller said, 'No, sorry, yer can't keep 'em. Put 'em off.'

Yeah, so we was paid off. Then, lo and behold, about two or three days later, Cairns rings our boss feller back again and says, 'Oh, yer can put them two fellers back on again. We've got a fair bit of work lined up.' And I only heard about that later because, apparently, our old boss went round, from pub to pub, trying to find us. That's how much he wanted us back. But by then I'd gone picking tobacco out at Dimbulah. Now, I forget how I got that job but even though the tobacco season was winding down it was still very easy to get work around the area in them days, seeing it was the heart of the tobacco industry in Australia.

This was the second time tobacco picking, yeah, but another tobacco farm, different from Johnny Piagno. Now, these people, the second lot, they're real southern Italians – the ones Johnny Piagno reckoned was like primitives. And in many ways he was right because they couldn't speak much English. There was about three families out there, permanent, all in separate homes, but they're living very basic, like they would've done in Sicily or somewhere down the south of Italy. I mean, yes, the kitchen had a wooden floor and the little room I was in had a wooden floor but the rest of the house was all dirt floors. And the little Italian lady, she didn't buy a normal straw broom, no, she made one out of tea-tree, like what you'd call a witch's broom and she'd sweep everything with that.

Then there was a little girl there – I still remember her – and, while we're picking tobacco, she'd always be going round with a water bag, like Gunga Din. You know that film, *Gunga Din*, where he'd go about the soldiers in the front-line, giving them water. Well this little girl, she'd come and give us water. And because she was going to school she could speak English so, if you wanted to get a message through, you told her and she'd tell the farmer. Yeah, she was part of the family. Nice little kid she was, about twelve. But, anyway, before I went out there I was talking to the big main boss of the place, in town – he owned several tobacco farms around the area – and I said to this big boss feller, 'How long's the work gonna last for?'

'Oh-a,' he says, 'a month-a or six-a weeks then-a after dat you're goin' peanut-a pickin'. I've gotta acres 'n' acres 'n' acres of-a da peanuts.'

See, they was picking peanuts by hand back then and, of course, me back was good so I said, 'Yeah, I'll stick it out 'n' save up 'n' buy meself a ute.'

Yeah, that's what I told him. And I meant it, too. But then I start thinking, Oh, bendin' down, pickin' tobacco leaves again, then goin' out, bendin' down, pickin' up peanuts all day long. I don't know so much about that. So I was only out at this place for a week or so and the big main boss comes out one day from Mareeba and he stayed the night, then in the morning I says, 'You goin' back ter town, today?'

'Yeah.'

I says, 'I'm comin' with yer.'

'What? You got-a some busy-ness in-a town?'

'Yeah, permanent business,' I said, 'I'm pullin' the pin.'

And, oh, he went berserk, aye. 'Oh, I'm-a gonna miss you. The men out-a here say youse a very good-a worker.' So they must've told him I was a good slave, aye. And I was too. I always pulled me weight in whatever job I done. Anyrate, we goes into town and we get there at night and we goes to his house, right in the centre of town. A big flash place up on stilts. Huge, it was. But he's not in a good mood. He's going on about how disappointed he is that I'm leaving. Anyhow, I wasn't going to change me mind, aye, so we goes inside and he calls out to his wife: 'Get-a my pen! Get-a my pen!' See, he had to get a pen to write me cheque out. But, oh, he was real arrogant to her. She was Australian but because he was so cranky she must've misunderstood what he'd said because she comes back out with a pair of pants. 'Not-a pants!' he shouts at her. 'A pen! I want pen!'

Anyway, he give me two pound a day. Something like sixteen or twenty quid I got, which didn't last too long, I can tell you.

14

Anyhow, the mustering season was about to start, out the back country. But even though I still wanted to get out into the cattle camps and that, it was the same old story, aye; I still didn't have the experience. Anyrate, I says, 'Blow this, I'll head back out ter The Curry 'n' see what turns up.' So I went to Cairns and I finished up in Townsville, then I jumps this rattler, a mixed goods, heading out west. Like, quite often trains went out to Mount Isa to bring back copper and zinc and stuff like that. So them trains are going out to Mount Isa all the time and you can jump on one of them and nobody asks questions or anything. Yeah, well I'd had some money to start with, aye, but that'd all gone after a few nights, hadn't it? I mean, I also had to eat and things like that.

Okay, so I'm heading out to The Curry and the train pulls up at Nelia. There was a race week going on, so I goes for a walk around town and by now I haven't even got the price of a feed and there's this big two-up game going on in the street and, oh, there's five quid and ten quid notes flashing everywhere. And it just about broke me heart to see all that money going to waste when I was starving hungry. Yeah, I remember that real well, I do. So anyway, I gets back in the train and I ends up in The Curry. It's early '54 and I'm skint so I goes round to Phyllis Hawes' pub again, the Central Hotel. Yeah, Phyllis was still alive then and, as usual, she says she'll stick by me till I gets a job. See, the idea was to go out ringing. That's all I thought of, aye, but then I runs into this taxi driver feller by the name of Reid. Actually, he was a shearer but he was driving taxis about town during the slack season. No, he had nothing to do with old Arthur Reid, the feller I was yard building with, that time I saw me first min min light. No, it wasn't him. Anyhow, this feller says, 'Are yer lookin' fer a job?'

I says, 'Well, yes. I'm thinkin' 'bout goin' out ringin'.'

He says, 'Well, there's a real good payin' job goin' as a yardman, up at the hospital.' He says, 'I'll drop yer off up there. Just tell them I sent yer.'

By now I was owing Phyllis a fair tab so I says, 'Oh, yeah. Okay, then.'

So he drops me off at the hospital and they gave me the job straightaway. So now I'm a yardman at the Cloncurry Hospital and, oh, I'm getting three feeds a day, aye, and I'm getting ringer's wages and so I pays Phyllis back and they had good quarters up there, too. I even had me own little room. I suppose, it was about a forty-bed hospital, which was pretty big for a town the size of The Curry. But that's mainly because all the time the Flying Doctors was bringing in fellers who'd been smashed up out on the stations by bulls and horses and that.

Anyhow, I'd be up at the crack of dawn to light the fuel stoves. Then I'd be chopping wood to make sure the wood boxes was full. The cooks up there had this massive old stove where they done all the cooking. It was one of them stoves with an oven each side of the fire box. But, no, even though I was a yardman, I never mowed lawns or nothing. I mean, there was no lawn in Cloncurry anyway. I don't even remember a garden. But I had to go up the top of the hill and turn the water on from the town's main water supply tank, to gravity feed down to the hospital. Then I just did general duties around the place, like going down to the nurses' quarters and emptying their trash bins and I'd go round to the operating theatre with an Aboriginal orderly fella and we'd clean up all these buckets. And, oh, some of them had people's gizzards in them and all that. Oh, one time there, all this stuff fell out of a bag and oh, mate, I tell you what, it was like in a butcher's shop, aye. Just about put me off me tucker for a couple of days, it did.

Now I forget this Aboriginal orderly fella's first name but his second name was Thorpe. Nice bloke, he was. Actually, I once took his place in a fight. Like, I enjoyed a bit of a stoush. I don't know why but I just liked it, ever since I represented me platoon, back when I was doing 'nasho'. But I never looked for fights. Never, ever. Only once I picked a bloke in a hotel and I learned then that you can't fight when you're drunk. A tough lesson that one was, I can tell you. But anyway, with this Thorpe fella – see, we're down at the Queen's Hotel and it's raining and there's a fella there called Ernie Douglas. Ernie was a half-caste or something. Actually, he was a bit of a no-hoper about town but he had a bit of a rep as a fighter. Mind you, I don't know where he got it from. Anyhow, Ernie's picking this Thorpe fella, the orderly from the hospital. But this Thorpe, he's about twice the age of Ernie Douglas, so I sings out, 'Hey, Ernie, what're yer doin' pickin' 'n old man?'

Anyrate, one thing led to another and I said, 'Well, come on mate,' I says, 'let's go outside 'n' sort it out, then.'

'Okay,' Ernie Douglas says.

So we goes down the main street, opposite the Prince of Wales Hotel. It's pouring rain and we're into it, bare-fist, and I done me thumb on him. It still aches even today. It come out of the socket. But that's alright because I'm getting the better of him, aye, even with me thumb out of its socket. Anyhow, there's a fella drinking in the bar of the Prince of Wales by the name of Alfie Clay. Now Alfie was a big-time Aboriginal fighter down in Sydney. He come from The Curry and he happened to be up there in between fights. I'm led to believe he belted the living daylights out of Johnny Famechon's father. You've heard of Johnny Famechon, haven't you? He was the world featherweight champion. Anyrate, Alfie belted the daylights out of his dad. So when this fight between Ernie and me starts getting serious, Alfie rushes out from the bar shouting, 'I'll referee this. I'll referee this.' Then he says, 'Look, it's no good fightin' out 'ere in the pourin' rain. How's about yers come back tomorra 'n' sort it out?'

'Okay,' we says, and when I come back the next day for the fight there's about thirty or forty blokes gathering about to see it. But then this Ernie Douglas says, 'Look, Goldie, I don't wanta fight yer.'

And, by then, I didn't want to fight either. I mean, the blue was over. But that's where I done me thumb, on Ernie Douglas. And that's when I went to see the doctor feller who told me how the gin out on Taylors Plains had done a real good set on me broken wrist, aye. But with this Alfie Clay, I don't know what weight he fought under, but he wasn't very big. Like, he'd be under a welterweight. But he fought some good men and he could've even went further if he had've looked after himself. Now, here's a story – see, Alfie used to live three stations out of Central, at Newtown, and one time he had a big fight lined up at the Sydney Stadium. So the fight's supposed to start at, say, eight o'clock and at four o'clock they find him in a bar, almost paralytic drunk. So they drags him out and they puts him under a shower and cleans him up a bit and he went into the ring half-drunk and he still flailed through this other feller. And that's a historical fact.

Anyhow, I'd been working up at the hospital for about four months or so and I wasn't saving any money. Then I ran into the taxi driver again – the Reid feller – and I was telling him about it and he said, 'Look, would yer like ter go out inta the shearin' sheds?'

And I says, 'Oh, yeah, mate. Anythin' ter get outa town 'n' save money.'

So I gets a job with the shearing team that him and his other brother was with. This's around March '54. Now, I forget the name of the big boss of the shearing team, just now, but he come from Melbourne. His wife had a hairdressing shop down there and he'd hired a shed out at McKinlay, where he kept the truck to go out with his big shearing plant and that on it. But I never done any shearing. I just went picking up – you know, roustabouting. The first place we shore at was McKinlay Station, about fifty mile south of Julia Creek, just outside the town of McKinlay. The shearing shed there used to be fifty stands, twenty-five each side with the picking-up pen running down the centre. But with this big boss shearer feller, there was only eleven shearers and two picker-ups, me and another feller from The Curry. So that was McKinlay; then we went out to a big station called Eulolo. Then we went to another massive big station, north of McKinlay. I forget its name just now but it was so big it'd be on a map. Then we went to a place called Nithsdale, then to Toolebuc Station. Toolebuc was both sheep and cattle. About five hundred square mile, it was.

But this shearing business, it wasn't for me, aye. Well, you're looking at a clock all day and one thing and another. Anyhow, by now the shearing's winding down and some of the shearers had already left the team. Then, when we got to Toolebuc, I heard the station manager, a feller by the name of George Davis, was looking for a cowboy. Now a cowboy on a station isn't a ringer. He's just the feller who milks the cows and poddles around the yard and does the gardening and chops the wood and all that. That's what they call a cowboy. So I went and saw George Davis and I asked him about this cowboying job and he said, 'Can yer ride a horse?'

I says, 'Yeah.' Mind you I was no expert, but I didn't tell him that.

'Can yer milk a cow?'

'Yeah.'

'Alright then,' he says, 'yer've got the job.'

So I goes back down to the shearing shed and I says to the big boss of the team, I says, 'Look, I know I'm not leavin' yer short-handed but I wanta get out.' So he paid me off and I went back up the homestead and I started me job cowboying.

15

I'd only been cowboying on Toolebuc a month or so and one morning I'm carrying these two buckets of milk up to the cook's quarters and I starts feeling all stiff. And it got worse. In fact, I wasn't too good at all so the manager's wife, Mrs Davies, she rang Julia Creek Hospital and they said, 'It could be anything. What's the symptoms?' Anyrate, she took me temperature and it was below average and they said, 'Look, the Flying Doctor's on a mercy trip just now but we'll send an ambulance straight out.'

Now, well, Toolebuc's eighty mile from McKinlay. McKinlay's eighty mile from some other little joint, aye, and that little joint's fourteen mile from Julia Creek. So it was a fair way he had to come out and so the ambulance arrives at night and the feller comes over and all the ringers and that are there and he says, 'Squeeze me hand.' But I couldn't squeeze his hand very tight at all. He says, 'This bloke's got paralysis.'

So then they takes me into Julia Creek Hospital and I was there for about three weeks, not feeling too good, and they took some fluid out of me spine and they sent it to Brisbane. Well, it turns out I had meningitis, which was pretty serious because it can leave lifetime things on you; like, you might lose some vision out of one eye or you might lose some of your hearing or you might lose all of your hair. Those sorts of things. So I was in Julia Creek for about three weeks and that's where I met a nurse, Janet Wilson, from New Zealand and, mate, I tell you, I done them over her, aye. Oh, she was a flashing good sort, she was. Anyway, I could see she was a bit my way as well, like –

you know, that she was attracted to me. So when I come out of hospital I took her out to the pictures and that and I said, 'Look, how's about we write ter each other?'

She said, 'Oh, I'd like that.' Then she says, 'But I'm going back to New Zealand soon, is that okay? Perhaps you'd like to come over later on?'

So she was serious too, aye. But, oh, I was as keen as mustard so, when I gets back out on Toolebuc, we're writing to each other all the time. Yeah, even when she went back to New Zealand. I can still remember her address, aye – it was 45 Marsden Avenue, Mount Eden. That's what sort of effect she had on me but, oh, she was a good-looking sort.

Okay, but while I was back on Toolebuc I got a relapse of the meningitis so the boss, this George Davies, he sends me into Cloncurry to see the local doctor, Harvey Sutton. I've already told you about Harvey Sutton, aye. He's the feller who lanced me running sore that time. Actually, now I remember it, the locals named the road out to the Cloncurry cemetery the Harvey Sutton Highway. No joke. That's what they called it – the Harvey Sutton Highway. Anyway, Harvey says to me, 'There's no need for me to ring Julia Creek about your case history; you'll be right, just go back out to work.'

So I went back out to Toolebuc again. And other than cowboy-ing I'd also work in the yards when they brung the cattle into the main station. And I really enjoyed that. But being a cowboy who only done a little bit of cattle work wasn't good enough for me. Like, I was close to being a ringer but I wasn't one, aye, if you catch my drift, and that got to me. Anyhow, I was still writing to Vincent and Benny Smith – they're the ones I'd catch up with on the weekends, when I was fettling out at Oorindi – and by the flavour of their letters they seemed to reckon they could get me some ringing work up in the Gulf. And that started me thinking because, see, I'm still writing to this

Janet Wilson piece, in New Zealand, and now I'm wondering, like, if I should give up me lifelong dream of going ringing and go off to New Zealand chasing a bit of skirt. So I got pretty mixed up about it all, aye, and it all come to a head over the opening of a gate, believe it or not.

Well, what happened was, this George Davies, the manager feller, he's driving me back from somewhere and he says, 'I want yer ter shut that gate when we go through it.'

I says, 'But it's never been shut in the whole seven months I've been here.'

Then he gets angry and says, 'I told yer, I want yer ter shut that gate!' Like, in that tone of voice.

'Right,' I says, 'I'll shut the gate alright 'n' I'll shut a few more gates behind me round here, too.'

So when we gets back to the homestead there's a cattle buyer there and I says to him, 'Are yer goin' ter town today?'

He says, 'No.'

I says, 'Well, I would've went with yer. I'm pullin' the pin, here.'

Then I goes over to the quarters and I does all me washing and I hang the wet clothes over a bit of strung-out no. 8 fencing wire outside. You know, just tossed it over, and Davies sees me doing this so he knows what I'm up to. Anyhow, he had a carpenter feller camped there, not quite half a mile down from the homestead who was doing the shearers' quarters up and apparently Davies is telling this carpenter, 'Oh, my cowboy's leavin' me. I'm really fond of that boy.' He says, 'I thought he woulda been here forever 'n' a day.'

And I might've been too, aye, if he'd gone and put me out in a stock camp – you know, instead of just using me up as a cowboy. Anyway, he didn't, so I went over to the house and I says, 'I'm leavin'.'

Davies says, 'I saw yer washin' on the line so I reckoned yer was goin'.'

Anyway, I was pretty steamed up so I says, 'If I can't get a lift with nobody, I'm gonna walk inta McKinlay.' Mind you McKinlay's eighty mile from Toolebuc, so I wasn't thinking too right, aye.

'Well,' he says, 'if yer determined ter go, the nearest place where there's water is Cannington Station 'n' that's over twenty mile.'

'I don't care,' I says. 'I'm goin'. I'm walkin'. I'm off ter McKinlay.'

Actually, here's a story – see, the publican at McKinlay was an alcoholic, a very bad alcoholic. Like, he'd mess himself and that sort of thing. Anyhow, one time, the owner at Cannington said to the publican at McKinlay, 'I'll give yer a hundred quid if you can go without a drink fer twelve months. But if yer do break out 'n' have a drink, then you'll owe me a hundred quid.' So it was a hundred-pound bet. And, well, not only did the publican give the drink up for twelve months and get his hundred pound but he never, ever drank again. So that's just a little story and something good come out of it, aye.

Anyhow, this Davies, he scratches me cheque out and I goes over to the cook and she makes me up a tucker bag with some salted meat. Like, salted meat's the worst thing to eat when you're in the heat, even if you've got a water bag. So I rolled me swag and I'm off, on foot. But I was very inexperienced as far as the outback went in them days. Yeah, as green as next year's corn, aye. I went down to what they call the Hamilton Channels – they're like tributaries that eventually run into the Diamantina River – and I camped down there the night and I got stuck into this salted meat. Then, next morning, I'm walking along, carrying me swag and it's hot, and I starts thinking, Geez, I'm thirsty. But I said, 'No, I'll save me water.'

So I'm traipsing along, thirsty as, aye, and I'm carrying this water bag and the water's sloshing about inside and the top part of it's wet. But, see, what I didn't realise was that all this time the water in the water bag's evaporating. So I learned the hard way, aye. Actually, later on, I read where someone perished doing the same thing. Anyway, eventually, I noticed the water bag was getting a bit light and when I took a look there's hardly any water left, aye. So I drank that water. But now I haven't any water left, and it's still hot and I'm baking and I'm still walking.

Then along the way I traipses passed Nithsdale Station. The homestead's a fair way in from the road so I knew I couldn't make it into there. But what I did see on Nithsdale was this windmill shimmering up in the air a bit – you know, with the heat haze. By now I'm parched. Like me tongue's starting to swell and all that. So I'm tossing up whether to go in there to get a drink or not. Anyhow, I didn't. I just kept going. Kept walking. Traipsing along. Anyrate, I finally gets to Cannington Station. Apparently they saw me coming up the horse paddock because they came down to get me. But I wasn't too good, aye. Like, they had to virtually drag me along, and at one stage I wanted to jump in the horse trough, in with the water. Anyway, they finally got me up to the house and they put me under a shower. But, oh, I tell you what, I wasn't in too good a shape. I was almost gone, aye.

But on Cannington, the manager was a real gentleman. Very honest. I forget his name just now but he wouldn't eat anybody else's sheep if his life depended on it. So I'm recovering there for a couple of days and then the manager of Nithsdale, Doc Collins, comes in to see these Cannington people and they say to Doc, 'Goldie's just walked off Toolebuc.'

Well, in the seven months I was on Toolebuc, I was the third person to walk off. Yeah, the third. So the place was getting a bit of a reputation. Like, people are saying, 'Gee, Toolebuc can't hold their men. There's fellers walkin' off the place left, right and centre.'

Anyway, Doc Collins says to me, he says, 'I need a boundary rider.'

Then he asks about me experience and, in the meantime, though I still couldn't ride real well, I'd learned to shoe a horse on Toolebuc and all that. Anyhow, I knew I could do the job so I says to Doc, 'Alright then. Good.'

So I just rolled me swag and I went with Doc Collins. Nithsdale was a sheep station. Just a small tin-pot place, around 140,000 acres. And a funny thing, when Doc Collins was driving me back to Nithsdale in his ute, we're going back along the same road I'd traipsed along and I'm looking out to where I was nearly perishing and that windmill I saw – you know the one I nearly went in to drink from – well, Doc told me the water was bore water, as salty as salt. So, lucky I didn't go in there to have a drink because I'd have been a goner, aye. And that particular windmill on Nithsdale was one of the ones I was to check when I went out boundary riding, so I got to know it well.

But on Nithsdale, at last I was in the saddle nearly every day, aye, so I learnt how to handle a horse. Well, with boundary riding you go out to the windmills and make sure there's no dead sheep in the troughs. And I'd clean out the salt that'd built up round the edge of the trough, from the bore water. Yeah, they're all concrete troughs. You couldn't have iron ones because they'd rust. Then I'd go up on top of the windmill where the blades are to check how things are going up there and make sure it's pumping the water into an overhead tank and make sure it's being gravity fed down into the trough okay and sometimes I'd strip off and climb into the overhead tank and I'd swim in the salty water. It's good for you. Cleans all your nose out and all that, and you get a good view, as well, aye.

Then, other than checking on the windmills, you'd always carry a bit of wire and a forked stick and a pair of pliers so if there was a break in the fence or whatever, you could fix it.

Well, with the forked stick, you twist the wire round it and use it as a strainer. Oh, the fences was always in need of work because the neighbours, Chatsworth, see, they had a lot of feral camels and they was always trying to smash through the old dingo-proof fence. Then we'd make up these strychnine baits for the dingoes. Like, we'd shoot a kangaroo and we'd drag it along behind a four-wheel drive all around the boundary and throw out the strychnine baits every now and then. The idea there was that a dingo would pick up the scent of the dead kangaroo and they'd follow the scent along and they'd find the baits and they'd eat that and die.

There was other things I done, too; like, we'd muster and we'd earmark the ewes on one ear and the wethers on the other ear because, when you're getting them ready to go off for sale, you can tell real quick what's a ewe and what's a wether. Also we'd mark the lambs – you know, castrate the males. When we done that we'd always keep their stones – their testicles, like – and we'd curry them up to eat of a night. Beautiful. And, that's right, while I was at Nithsdale I saw me first Bedourie dust storm. See, that's when the big south-westerlies blow in from the desert country around Bedourie. We was drafting sheep at the time and I could see this huge wall of dust coming our way and when it hit, the dust was so bad we couldn't even see the ear marks on the sheep. That's ridgy didge. True, the dust was so thick we had to leave the sheep till the dust storm had passed. Yeah, red dust. It was pretty high, round six hundred feet. And another thing I'll never forget was, I turned twenty-one on Nithsdale. I remember that day real well see, because we was mustering sheep and it was pouring with rain. Pelting down, aye, and I sings to meself, 'Happy Birthday, Goldie.'

Anyrate, I'm still writing to this Janet Wilson piece, over in New Zealand, and I'm still writing to me mates, the Smith boys, up in the Gulf, and they was about to go ringing on a station called Glenore, which was owned by a feller called Reg Quilty, and they said, 'Come up here. We'll find ringin' work fer yer.'

And so I says to meself, 'Right, this's what I've been wantin' ter do fer years' – you know, to get out there on a big cattle property.

So I wrote to the Smith boys and told them I was coming up. Then I says to Doc Collins, I says, 'Look, all the lamb markin's finished 'n' I've got the troughs 'n' fences lookin' okay. I'm not leavin' yer in the lurch but I wanta go up ter the Gulf country 'n' do some proper ringin'.'

'Righto, Goldie,' he says. 'I wish yer all the best.'

Yeah, so I left Nithsdale. But it was a good parting because me and Doc, we was good mates. So I left there with a few quid in me pocket and I'm thinking, At last, I'm gonna get up inta a stock camp.

16

Okay, it's early 1955. January. After leaving Doc, I goes back into Cloncurry. Yeah, I'm still writing to this Janet Wilson, over in New Zealand. Oh, I was crazy over that piece. I still had intentions, big intentions. But anyhow, I'm off to Normanton to go ringing. I'm a bit cashed up so I books a seat on the plane, an old twelve-seater. It was one of them old drover Flying Doctors' planes with a propeller in front of the cockpit and one on each wing. It did the Cloncurry to Normanton run and stopped off at station places all along the way, picking up and dropping off ringers and that.

Anyway, I gets to Normanton and Vincent and Benny and their younger brother, Ernie, come to meet me. I hadn't met young Ernie before. He would've only been about fifteen, I guess. But one of Ernie's great claims to fame was that he'd once been donated a silver egg cup from the Queensland Minister of Health for being the first baby born in the new maternity wing of the Normanton Hospital. So yeah, that was young Ernie and he loved telling stories, aye. Anyhow, we went around to the Smiths' place and I met their mother, Lena, and their youngest sister, Margaret. She would've been about twelve or thirteen. I forget now where Bob, their father, was. Everyone called the father 'Dogger' Smith and Dogger did a bit of cattle duffing and that around the place.

I stayed with the Smiths for a few days, and, oh, the mother, Lena, she accepted me right off as one of her sons, aye. Like, that's how well we got on. She was the daughter of an Italian feller called Thomasini who'd had thirteen daughters and no sons. Fair dinkum. And I remember once seeing somewhere about a feller who had eleven daughters and no sons and they said it was some sort of Australian record. But it wasn't, because Lena's father, this Thomasini, he had thirteen daughters and no sons and I'm led to believe that one of them's still alive in an old persons' home in Cloncurry.

So then we goes out to Glenore Station to get ready for the mustering season. Mustering generally starts in March, after the rivers and watercourses have stopped running. So we're out there working around the homestead and because it's only fifteen mile into Normanton, every now and then we'd ride into town for a bit of a blow. Vincent was head stockman and there was Benny, young Ernie and me and a few Murries and, basically, the Smith boys took me under their wings and taught me everything. Like, they showed me how to break in a horse and we repaired saddles and we made hobble straps and corded-girths for the saddles. Glenore was 1800 square mile of country. Reg Quilty had bought it off the banks, dirt cheap, back in 1911, so, yeah, the banks must've taken it over from the previous owners. To give you some idea, it was seventy mile from one boundary to the other. Anyhow, old Reg always spent the wet season in Sydney so he wasn't back yet, not that he ever went out on the muster. Like, being the boss, he only came out to see the drover off on his way down to Julia Creek with the cattle.

Then not long before the muster started I met the Casey brothers, Jimmy and Geoffrey. The Caseys was well-known cattle duffers who owned Shady Lagoons. Shady was only a seventy-two-square-mile place that joined Glenore and they rode over to get the lay of the land and, before they left, they said how they're going to duff a few of Reg's cleanskins on the way back home to Shady. Cleanskins are unbranded cattle. Anyway, Vincent had his own brand, see, a (diamond) J4, so he decides that, while Reg's still away, we may as well join in and help the Caseys out and we'd split the profits. But, anyrate, as it turned out it was still a bit too wet and we only got about fifteen mile up to a stockyard – bronco yard – called Anabranch so we didn't get too much to worry about. But that was my first little adventure into the duffing game.

Okay, so it's time now to start mustering and I'm ready to go, aye. When you go out mustering each man takes about five horses from the home paddock, plus the ones you've just broke in. The just-broke-in ones only do little days till they're good and ready. Then you've got about seven or eight packhorses that carry all your gear, like your camp ovens, your swags, your flies (that act like a tent), and you have a set of billy cans – quart-pot shaped – flat on one side and round on the other so they fit on a packhorse. Then there's all the salt, flour, the rice, the treacle, Holbrook sauce, curry powder and all those sorts of things you take along as well.

In our camp there was about five Murries, meself and the Smith boys, and one of the Murries done the horsetailing. Well, the horsetailer's the feller who goes out before the crack of dawn and unhobbles the horses. Some could be up to a mile away. They usually have bells on but, because, say, if there's three horses that's always together, well, they'll mate up so you only need to put a bell on one of them. Anyhow, he brings them back on camp then hobbles them again and, when you're ready, you go out and pick what horse you're going to ride for the day's mustering. That's generally the run of the thing.

Well, I took to it like a duck to water, aye. Oh, this was me lifelong dream, mate, from right back when I was a little kid up in Springwood reading all the cowboy comics and from when I wagged school in Sydney and went to see cowboy films. And, now I'm here, and I'm doing it. And everything I had to do, I learned real quick – you know, I learned to repair saddles and make hobble straps real quick. I learned to break in horses and throw a bullock real quick. I even learned how to butcher a beast. Like, first off the Smith boys showed me how to salt the meat. Next time I'd take the shoulder off, and before long I could butcher a beast. And I just loved it, aye. It was like I was meant to be a ringer all me life. Yeah, you could say I'd got me calling in life, so to speak. Yeah, that's what you could say.

Now, our first camp was Anabranch. That's where we'd went with the Caseys. And it took about five days to muster round that area. There's bronco yards all the way up through them places. You know, some yards are only eight mile apart, some might be twelve mile. And after you get the cattle in the bronco yard, you spend a day branding the cleanskins and earmarking them and you castrate the males. With the branding, you've generally got two fellers: one catches the calf by throwing a greenhide rope over it from a bronco horse, then you drag it up to the bronco frame where the other feller brands it. Then after you done all that, you hold the bullocks and you bush the others, like the weaners and the female cows, yeah, so they'll go back out bush to mate up for next year's muster.

Now, because there wasn't many boundary fences, every station sends two men over to 'attend the muster' next to their property. Like, you'd work under the orders of their head stockman, just like ringers, then you'd take back any of your own cattle that's wandered onto their place. So the Casey boys mustered with us at the bronco yards on the Shady Lagoons side of Glenore, like Anabranch. Then from Anabranch we went another five or seven mile across to Bull Yard. We mustered there for five days and spent a day branding, earmarking and castrating. Bull Yard's on Claire Creek and it still had a bit of water in it from the wet season. Then from Bull Yard we went to Silverfish. Same again; we mustered around there for five or six days. From there we headed for Campbell's Yard to muster around there.

Then the Caseys left us after Campbell's to head back home to Shady Lagoons with what was theirs. Of course, we knew if they came across any of old Reg's cleanskins along the way they'd take them home as well. You know, duff them. I mean, that wasn't such a big deal because just about everyone done that. But, see, the thing was, the Caseys also took two of old Reg's favourite horses, Baldy and Robin, along with a creamy cleanskin colt. Now, both Baldy and Robin was handy horses. Like, they'd carry a man all day. They had a bit of clumper, or draughthorse, in them so you could also load them with packs and use them for bronco and pulling out calves. Baldy, in particular, was a good old faithful stock horse who'd never run away. Old Reg usually kept him in the home paddock so if he caught wind that there was duffers about, he'd be straight after them. Anyhow, as I said, when the Caseys went back to Shady, they took Robin and Baldy with them plus a cleanskin creamy colt. Like, I didn't really care what they took but, see, we had a quarter-caste Murri with us, Dinky-di Zana, and I knew he'd spill his guts to old Reg. Well, Murries are like that. They just can't keep a secret. But, anyhow, I didn't say nothing.

Actually, there's an interesting little story about how this Murri got to be called Dinky-di Zana. See, the local butcher, a German feller named Zana, tried to keep it a secret how he'd knocked over a gin and a son was the result. The only trouble was, the son turned out to look exactly like Zana, the German butcher, and that's why they called the Murri, Dinky-di Zana. And that's true. Fair dinkum.

Anyhow, each time we had about two hundred head of bullocks from mustering about the place, we'd send them across to a paddock called Scrubby. Scrubby's sort of smack-bang in the centre of Glenore and we held them there while we went and mustered around other places like The Lakes. Then it was about another eight or so mile to Broadwater, which was only a couple of hundred yards off the Norman River. Actually, during the war they used to land seaplanes at Broadwater. It's full of crocs. You'd put a torch out of a night and you'd see all these red eyes looking at you, aye, which made for a light sleep, I can tell you.

But Scrubby was quite small in the scheme of things and, of course, if you ended up with too many bullocks in there they'd eat it out pretty quick. So when we'd got a good few held at Scrubby, a couple of fellers would take those bullocks off to a hundred-mile-square paddock called Surveyors. Surveyors was on the boundary of Iffley Station, about fifty-two mile from Glenore homestead. It's the best part of the country and so that's where they'd be fattened and inoculated for pleurisy before the drover took them away. But anyway, while we was still camped at Scrubby, young Ernie was on a black mare called Jam Pot, and he's galloping after a beast and the horse tripped or something and he went down in a screaming heap, into an ant bed, and he couldn't move. Nothing broken, but he was sore and hurt internally and he needed to get to hospital real urgent.

So we gets young Ernie to what's called the Forty Mile Crossing, which is along the road from Normanton to Julia Creek. It's not a main road, just a road that goes from one station to another. But the river's up, see, and it's flowing pretty fast. Anyhow, on the other side of the river's a feller called Henry Butler. Henry had been a drover when he was younger but now he had a fencing contract out at Iffley Station. Anyrate, Henry's stuck on the other side of the river with a tractor and a trailer, with all his gear and his swag and his tucker and that, waiting for the water level to drop.

Oh, and that's right, Henry also had an old blackfella with him called Joker. Joker had walked barefoot all his life and his feet got so wide and thick he couldn't even get them in the stirrup iron. To give you some idea, Joker was down with Billy Campbell one time when Billy was blacksmithing. Anyhow, Billy thought he could smell something burning so he turns around and there's Joker standing on the red-hot coals. And Joker didn't even realise it. Fair dinkum. Bluey Ellis told me that, so it must be true. Anyway, poor old Joker's camped over there with this Henry Butler and he'd forgot to bring out a mosquito net with him so when we arrived, there's Joker burning this stack of cow manure and he's sitting in the middle of all its smoke, trying to get rid of the mosquitoes. Anyrate, we calls out, 'Any chance'a gettin' this young feller inta town?'

And Butler says, 'Well, if yer can get him across here, yer can put him on the trailer 'n' take him in on the tractor, if yer like.'

But, see, it was getting young Ernie across the river that was the worry because it's not only up high and flowing pretty rapid but there was also a big saltwater crocodile living in a waterhole about a hundred yards away. And he was a big boy, aye. He ate cattle and wallabies, the lot. Like, you'd see brumbies come

Glenore homestead

down to his waterhole and they'd drink like this – very wary – because they know the croc's there. Now, there was something wrong with him; I forget now whether he had a stumpy tail or a stumpy foot but, whatever it was, he couldn't run up the bank properly so he'd just lay up there sunbaking himself, and he'd have his big mouth wide open and there'd be all these white cranes in there picking all the bits of meat out of his teeth, keeping them clean. And, oh, you could see he was enjoying it, aye.

Anyhow, I'd guess it'd be about fifty yards across the crossing so, yeah, I says, 'Oh well, blow it, I'll carry young Ernie across.'

So I got him to put his arms around me neck and I picked him up and I started off. Okay, the water's above me waist and it's flowing so strong that, if I took me foot off the riverbed, I would've been swept away. So I had to slide me feet along the bottom as I went. But all I was worried about was that great big saltwater croc, aye. Anyhow, I just kept shuffling me feet, slowly and slowly, and eventually I got Ernie across to the other side, then I goes into town on the tractor and I gets him into the hospital and Matron Pit says, 'Now, what happened to you, young Ernest?'

And, see, young Ernie loves telling a story, so he says, 'Well, it was like this Matron. I was on old Jam Pot 'n' I was gallopin' after this beast ...' and on and on he went, giving a moment-by-moment description of what happened.

Now, because of the tucker we ate, we lacked vitamin C. Like, you'd burn yourself on a branding iron or you'd be galloping along and a branch cuts you and you'd come out in all these sores that don't heal. I think it's what's called 'Barcoo rot'. Anyrate, after Matron Pit has a look at young Ernie she says, 'I'm gonna have a yarn to that Reg Quilty. He's not feedin' you fellers properly. You should be eatin' lots 'n' lots'a green vegetables.'

And that's where I first met old Reg. He'd just come back from Sydney and arrives up at the hospital to check on young Ernie. And I even remember the first words I ever said to him. I said, 'Oh, we had a bit'a bad luck in the camp, Reg.'

17

Anyhow, Reg took me back out to Glenore, and we hit it off straightaway. Yeah, we got on real well, aye. Then before I goes out mustering again I'm working on this bad horse, in the round yard at the homestead, see, and I notice there's a white woman moving in there with old Reg. It turned out to be Mrs McQueen. Now, Mrs McQueen had been shacked up with the manager of Iffley Station, a feller by the name of Bill Young. So Bill Young was sweating her, aye. That's the term they use for people who lived with a women but didn't marry them – 'sweaters'. Now, what must've happened was that old Reg had somehow taken this Mrs McQueen off Bill Young because, all of a sudden, Bill Young turns up at Reg's place in his Land Rover. And, I tell you, he's meaning business, aye. He's got a six-gun stuck down his belt and all. Anyrate, he goes inside and he practically drags this Mrs McQueen out and throws her in the front of his Land Rover. He goes back inside again and, next thing I see, a three-foot stuffed crocodile comes flying through the air and lands in the back of his vehicle. Then out storms Bill and he takes off back to Iffley with Mrs McQueen and the stuffed crocodile. Anyhow, I thought to meself, Goldie, don't get involved. Don't say nothin' ter nobody. Keep well out of it.

Yeah, so as soon as I sorted out the bad horse, I went back out to the mustering camp and I said nothing about it. By then the horses we'd first taken out had done three months hard riding and fresh horses was always kept on Surveyors bullock paddock. So we took a mob of bullocks and all our horses back to Surveyors, with the aim of swapping them for fresh ones. And that's what we was doing, mustering fresh horses, when Vincent came down with a whitlow on his thumb. Whitlow? You get it on your hands. An old saying was it's caused by your hand jarring all the time. But that's not right because I think it's some sort of infection. Maybe even from a lack of vitamin C, but I'd have to look it up in a medical book. All I know is, it's terribly painful. Vincent's whole thumb swole up and it was hurting so bad that we had to hide the tomahawk from him because he was going to chop his thumb off. Fair dinkum. That's how bad it got.

So we had to get him off to hospital, aye. Anyway, there was a grader driver and his wife camped on the other side of this big waterhole at Surveyors. So I swims Vincent across this waterhole, on me horse, and I says to the feller, 'Look,' I says, 'me mate's crook, would yer mind takin' him ter town?'

And the grader driver says, 'What? I'm not takin' nobody inta town!' and he goes on and on, with one thing and another.

Well I was pretty shocked, aye, so I says, 'But mate,' I says, 'that's what we do around here. Everyone looks after one another.'

'Yeah,' he says, 'you might, but blowed if I do.'

And I just thought to meself, What a right mongrel you are. I'm gonna get you one day.

Then there was some Hungarians doing a bit of fencing for old Reg and they had a big five-ton truck. So I went and asked them and they never hesitated. They took Vincent to town, no problem, and they was Hungarian and the grader feller was Australian. You can't credit it, can you?

Anyhow, after they took off with Vincent, I went back to Surveyors. Then not long after that we started sorting out the first mob of bullocks, ready for the drover. I forget, just now, if it was a feller named Jones or maybe it was Arthur White. But by then we had about 1200 bullocks on Surveyors and so we started inoculating them for pleurisy. Now, the needle we used for that was what's called a wallaby claw. Like, you've got to keep this serum nice and cool, then you pour it into a little pannikin you have around your belt. And you have little bits of cut-up wool, like knitting wool, and you soak the wool in the serum. Then, while you've got the beast held in the crush, you put a piece of the wool in the wallaby claw and you whack it in, right at the end of the tail, and, when you pull the wallaby claw out, the soaked bit of wool stays in. So that's what goes on there. But you've got to be careful because, if you hit the bone, sometimes it'll start to rot and then you've got to cut the tail off three or four joints up.

Okay, by now it's smack-bang in the middle of the season and Reg turns up with Vincent, who's feeling a bit better. Reg's also come out to make sure things go okay with the drover. Well, Reg done that because, after the drover left, he'd have to go back home and arrange with Queensland Railways to pick the bullocks up when they was delivered by the drover at Julia Creek. So the drover turns up and all of a sudden Steve McQueen from Iffley Station, he's also in the camp. Now Steve McQueen's the son of Mrs McQueen, the one I saw Bill Young come and drag out from Glenore homestead. So it's all seeming pretty suspicious to me. Anyhow, after old Reg has been with us for a few days, one morning we're out on the flat having breakfast when he up and sacks the Smith boys. Yeah, sacks the whole three of them. Anyrate, I says to Reg, I says, 'Reg, why are yer sackin' the boys?'

And Reg says how their father, Dogger Smith, had been seen poking around Glenore somewhere, duffing cleanskins for that German butcher, Zana – the one I told you about who'd fathered Dinky-di. And old Reg reckons he couldn't have the Smith boys working for him because they'd cover for Dogger.

'Goldie,' he says, 'you know 'n' I know, how blood's thicker than water.'

But, see, that didn't ring true for me because, for just one butcher, Dogger wouldn't have taken too many at all; certainly not enough to make such a big fuss about. So then I says, 'Well, who's gonna run the camp now, Reg?'

'Oh, Steve. Steve McQueen,' he says.

And that's when the penny dropped, see, because my reckoning of it is that old Reg had somehow gotten the idea that, if he gets rid of the Smith boys and he puts Steve McQueen in as head stockman then, more than likely, Mrs McQueen would leave Bill Young and come over to Glenore to be with her son. Meaning she'd also be with old Reg, aye. Anyhow, so then I thinks, Geez, I'm right in it here. On the one hand, after years 'n' years, I'm finally ringin' 'n' I love it, but on the other hand I'd better stick up fer me mates. So I says to Reg, 'Well then Reg,' I says, 'I'm gonna pull out too. I'm not gonna work fer no jackeroo.'

Reg says, 'Sorry Goldie,' he says, 'but that's the way it is.' And that's when we left. We goes back to Glenore and Reg pays us off.

So I left there with a big cheque and I goes back into town and I'm stopping at the Smiths' place. I was sort of part of the family now. Anyhow, I'm still writing to this Janet Wilson piece. Oh, and that's right, she's even lined me up a job and everything over in New Zealand. So she's real keen, aye. And so now I'm wondering if I'll get a mate to go over to New Zealand with me, as well.

Anyway, a few days later, Reg drives up to the Smiths' house in his Land Rover. Us fellers are sitting on the verandah and he calls out, 'Vincent, you tell those Casey brothers ter bring back Robin 'n' Baldy 'n' that cleanskin creamy colt 'n' if they don't I'll get the police onta them.'

Well, the Smiths always said that one thing Reg never, ever does is go to the police. He's always said, 'If I can't work out a problem meself, well, I'll just cop it sweet.'

So he was only bluffing, aye. But, still and all, I thought I'd better go out to Shady Lagoons 'n' warn the Caseys that Reg was on to them.

18

The Caseys only lived six mile out of Normanton so I borrowed a horse to go out there. I'd never been out to Shady Lagoons before. It was on the other side of the Norman River so if you ever wanted to see them you either had to go across on the punt and ride out or you'd go up the river, to opposite where they lived, and sing out. Anyhow, I decides to go over on the punt. A bloke called Backhouse had a little hut there and he worked the punt, getting traffic and that across, twenty hours a day.

It turned out that Jimmy Casey lived in one house with a missus and a whole heap of kids and Geoffrey Casey lived in another house with his missus and a whole heap of kids. Jimmy was the eldest and Geoff was the youngest one. Their wives was part-Aboriginal, though not too much. In fact, if you took them to a strange town out of the Gulf, no one would hardly know. But they had whole heaps of kids, aye. So I pulls up at one of the houses and I says to one of the women, 'Are you Missus Casey?'

'Yes.'

I says, 'Where's Jimmy 'n' Geoff? I've got a message fer them.'

She points and says, 'They're down the paddock, killin' a beast, just over that little hill, there.'

So I rides down and there they are killing a bullock that belonged to a feller by the name of 'Womp' Burns. Womp's proper name was George, but he was always known as Womp. I don't know why they called him that but he was a real big feller, about eighteen stone. They used to torment him round the bars and that and sing a song about him – 'Hey there

Womp, over the swamp, there's a big mud turtle, that's a big fat lump.' Something like that. Womp's family owned a 400-square-mile station called Mutton Hole, which joined Shady Lagoons.

Now, here's a story. See, Womp's mother was a very good cook. Oh, she'd make these beautiful sponge cakes, aye, with an inch of cream on top and an inch of cream in the middle. Anyhow, out on Mutton Hole they'd get fellers to do a week's work branding or whatever and, when that happened, Womp always went up to the house to get everyone's smoko. So first he'd come down with a big bucket of tea, then he'd go back up and get the cake. As I said, this cake would be a big, round sponge cake on a plate, six inches high, at least. Beautiful. So he'd start walking down with the sponge on the plate but somewhere between the yard and the house there's a blind spot where nobody could see him. So when Womp got to the blind spot, he'd stick his finger up his bum and then go down to the boys and say, 'Oh fellers, isn't this cake beautiful? Just smell it.' And he'd hold up the plate for them to smell it and all they could smell was his finger. 'Yuck. That's shockin',' they'd go, and, of course, that was Womp's way of getting the lot, aye. So no wonder he was a big feller, and greedy too.

But anyhow, the Caseys, they was down there butchering one of Womp's bullocks. Yeah, they'd duffed it off him. I mean, the Caseys always used to kill Womp's bullocks and Womp always killed the Caseys' bullocks, so they ended up equal, I guess. I mean, the last thing anyone would do in the Gulf was to kill one of their own, to eat themselves. You always killed someone else's to eat. Anyhow, so I says to the Casey boys, 'Reg come in yesterday. He says he wants his three horses back.' I says, 'Yer know yerself you don't go takin' horses or nothin' in front of a blackfella because he'll spill his guts.' See, because I just knew how Dinky-di Zana would go and tell old Reg, right off, about the Caseys taking Robin and Baldy and the creamy cleanskin colt.

Anyway, they said I could have Robin and Baldy but they weren't sure where the creamy cleanskin colt had got to. Like, it was unbroken so it might've even got away with the brumbies or something. But that was okay because Robin and Baldy was old Reg's favourite horses. So then we got talking about one thing and another and they says, 'Goldie, how's about comin' in, duffing, with us? We'll go third shares in everythin'.'

I says, 'No. I'm cashed up. I'm goin' ter New Zealand. I've got a good-lookin' sort over there, waitin' fer me. She's even got me a job 'n' that.'

Then Jimmy says, 'Tell yer what, Goldie.' He says, 'You stay with us fer a couple'a years 'n' yer'll be able ter buy New Zealand.'

I says, 'What, are yer fair dinkum? So you reckon I'd be able ter buy New Zealand, aye?'

'Yeah,' they said. 'Just about.'

And that got me thinking, aye. Well, because duffing was something different; you know, something exciting, and it sounded like there was real good money to be made out of it, so I says, 'Yeah, okay then, count me in.'

So I left Robin and Baldy there and I went back into town and I told the Smiths how the Caseys had asked me to go in with them. No, they didn't seem to mind. I mean, duffing wasn't such a big thing for them and, also, I guess they was still a bit shirty about old Reg giving them the sack. So I started spending more time over at Shady Lagoons then. Like, I'd just throw me swag down on the verandah and that, then after a while I moved into a little hut, out on a permanent waterhole called Catfish. Catfish was the Caseys' main camp, halfway between the Glenore and the Shady boundary. It was just a bit of an iron thing, with a couple of bunks and a galvanised iron roof, with a bit of a wall around it.

Now, what happened to the Smith boys? Actually, I think that, not long after, they went down Cloncurry way, ringing on stations. I'm not sure just whereabouts but I do know they finished up on a place belonging to their uncle, Allan Richards. That was on Wernadinga Station, which was halfway between Normanton and Burketown.

So then, with the money I'd saved to get over to New Zealand, I bought five horses, aye, and I still had enough left over to support meself and buy tucker and everything till I got cashed up from duffing. And I guess it would've been about a month later, I thought I'd better take Baldy and Robin back to old Reg. Anyrate, I gets there and I put them over in the yard and I rides over to the homestead. Reg's on the verandah and, see, news travels fast in the Gulf, so I knew he'd know what'd been going on. 'Oh, how yer goin', Reg?' I says. 'I guess yer've heard I'm in with the Casey brothers, now.'

He says, 'Yes I have.' Mind you, he didn't sound none too keen about it.

'Oh,' I says, "n' I brought yer horses back – Robin 'n' Baldy.'

First duffing trip – the yard at Catfish

'Yeah, I see,' he says, 'but there was three of them. What about the cleanskin creamy one?'

I says, 'I don't know nothin' about a creamy one, Reg.' And, you know, because I liked Reg, I hated lying to him but I looked him straight in the eye and I said, 'No Reg, sorry, but there was no creamy one. The Caseys only took Robin 'n' Baldy.'

But old Reg knew I was lying, aye. Anyhow, he left it at that and he said, 'So I guess yer want a feed.'

'Too right,' I says.

So he got the Aboriginal cook there to sort me out some tucker and while I was eating it I says to her, 'So, where're the boys musterin'?'

'Oh,' she says, 'them's musterin' way up Surveyors.'

Now, Surveyors bullock paddock was just about the opposite end of Glenore from Shady Lagoons – well, enough distance apart, you'd be pretty much guaranteed that none of Reg's boys would be hanging around there. So when I gets back to Shady I says to Jimmy and Geoff, 'Well fellers,' I say, 'she's open slather on Glenore.'

Only me and Jimmy went on that first duffing trip and, oh, Jimmy, he was a true professional cattle duffer. He was good. He never done stupid things. Like, he taught me, 'You never interfere with a brand. It's like tryin' ter change a person's signature on a cheque. It's strictly a no-no.'

So Jimmy and me, we starts off from my little place at Catfish. We had two horses each, and, oh, I tell you what, I was frightened, aye. You know, I'm riding along and I'm looking around like this. Every which-ways. And, like, so that you always know where your horse is, you've got a strap around the horse's neck that's got a bell on it. But when you're duffing you put a slit in the tongue of the hobble straps you're also carrying and you the tie the donger part of the bell into that so the bell won't ring and give you away.

Anyhow, I'm frightened, aye. Then there's a chain of swamps on Glenore country. So we're in Glenore now and we musters from yard to yard. See, with duffing, you pick some cleanskins up here, then go to the next yard and pick some more up. Yeah, you just hold them in the yard. You don't earmark or anything. You do all that when you get them back home. For about ten days we mustered around the Glenore bronco yards. We went to Bull Yard. We went to Silverfish. Them places. But we never crossed the Croydon–Normanton Road. We kept away from there because Jimmy knew that Reg used to drive up and down there in his Land Rover, looking for any cattle tracks. So it was too risky, aye. Then we goes across to a place called Gum Hole. Reg rarely sends his men over there, and, in all, we got about thirty cleanskins. Then we brung them back to Catfish and we branded them and cut them and earmarked them in the bronco yard there. And I remember when we was branding them, I said to Jimmy, I says, 'Oh, what about my third, Jimmy?'

He says, 'Well, you'd better go inta town 'n' register a brand.' So I went to the stock inspector in town and I got me own registered earmark and brand – J (diamond) 8, it was. And here's another thing Jimmy taught me about the earmark – see, in the cattle duffing game, say you've got a beast that's already been cut and earmarked but it's got away before it's been branded. Well, what you do is, you grab the ear that's got the station earmark on it and you screw it around and you cut that ear half off. Then, when it unravels, it looks like a dingo's bitten it. Because, as you might know, when dogs pull cattle and that down, they always go for the ear. So that's what you do and then you put your own earmark on the other ear and no one knows the difference.

Then once we done all that, we sold them to different fellers. One feller was Hungry Dawson and another was Tom Wheelan, the manager on Wondoola Station. Tom was the main feller. He used to go around and buy crook cattle from all us little fellers – you know, a hundred here, two hundred there, so he'd end up with a whole big mob. Then he'd walk them down to his own property just outside Julia Creek, a place called Glenmore, and he'd leave them there for a couple of years to fatten them up, then he'd sell them at a good profit.

So that was my first cattle duffing trip. Mind you, we didn't get enough to buy New Zealand, not by a long shot. And I'm not real sure I got me three-ways cut of the profits neither.

19

So then after that first duffing trip we goes into town, aye. I'm in the top pub. See, in Normanton, there's the top pub, which was the National, then there's the middle pub, which was the Central, and the bottom pub was the Albion. But you always said, 'I'll see yer in the middle pub,' or 'the bottom pub', or 'the top pub', yeah. So that's how it went. Anyhow, I'm having a beer and, lo and behold, who should walk into the bar but none other than that mongrel grader driver who refused to take Vincent Smith into town when he had the whitlow, out at Surveyors.

So I sings out to him across the bar, 'Remember me, mate?'

'No.'

I says, 'Well, I'm the bloke who asked yer ter drive me mate inta town when he was crook, 'n' you wouldn't.'

'Yeah, so?'

I says, '"Yeah, so", alright.'

So I went round and I picked him and he says, 'Well, we'd better go outside 'n' settle this.'

I says, 'You bet yer life we will!'

Of course, half the bar goes out with us to see the stoush. But he's an old hand, aye. See, I had one of them coat shirts on and when we gets out the back of the pub, he grabs me shirt, and he goes like that, so me arms are pinned. Then, while he had me arms pinned, I tell you what, didn't he get some nice ones in? Anyrate, I finally tore me shirt off and I'm into him, aye. Oh, I was angry, and in the end they had to drag me off him. That's how stirred up I was. But he was down and out by then because they had to carry him from the back of the pub around to his ute. So I messed him up good and proper, aye. Anyway, then I felt bad about it all so I went into the bar and I took him out a beer. But he was that messed up, he could hardly drink it. Then his missus appears and she screams, 'What happened ter you?'

And then she got stuck into me verbally, which got me even more upset about the whole thing, like. So then, a couple of days later, I found out where he was staying and I went up to see him and I says, 'Look, I'm real sorry, mate.'

'Oh, that's okay,' he said, but he wasn't looking too okay at all, aye.

Anyhow, a few years later I run into him again and he said to me, 'Goldie,' he said, 'I've learned a lot about the back country now 'n' if anybody asks fer help, I give it to them.' That's what he said. So he humbled himself, aye.

Now, in the meanwhile, Larry Del Hunty came to town with his travelling boxing show, something he done every race week. And, as what happens with these things, when they arrive in a town, the boxers from the troupe go out and find who the local pugs are. So I'm in the pub and these boxers come in and start asking, 'Who around here can fight?'

And the fellers in the bar, they point to me. Well, I never had a rep or nothing, not back then, you know. But they're saying, 'Oh, him. Him. Goldie can fight. He's just cleaned up a feller good 'n' proper.'

So one of Del Hunty's men – Danny somebody or other – he gets me on the side and he says, 'So you're Goldie, aye? I hear yer can handle yerself.'

I says, 'Oh, no mate. I'm just an ordinary run-of-the-mill bloke.'

He says, 'That's not what I hear.' He says, 'Look, what I want yer ter do,' he says, 'tomorra night when we get on the board 'n' bash the drum 'n' call fer challengers, I want yer ter come up 'n' fight me.'

Well, see, this's me chance to have a bit of a lash. Oh, I loved it, aye. I didn't care if I got a hiding or not. I just loved it. So I says to this Danny feller, 'What's in it fer me?'

He says, 'Dello's payin' five quid', Dello being Larry Del Hunty.

So I thinks, Well, it sounds like everybody round town's talkin' about me so I'd better not let 'em down so I said, 'Okay, then. See yer tomorra tonight.'

Okay, so the next night I goes into town and I goes over and there they are, they're on the board outside the boxing tent, banging the drum and all that, and Dello's up there calling for fellers to come up and fight his boxers. So when he asks if anyone wants to take on this Danny feller, I shouts out, 'I'll have a go at him.'

So I climbs up on the board and stands alongside this Danny feller. There's another couple of pugs up there also and Dello gets some fellers to come up and fight them, too. Anyhow, comes our bout and everyone's there and, anyrate, Dello ended up stopping the fight in the middle of the second round because I'm chopping him up a bit, see. Actually, someone told me how they saw him later on, out behind the tent, spewing his guts up, aye. Yeah, Danny something, his name was. A few years later, someone shot him in the back while he was standing in a hotel bar drinking somewhere out in the back country. Yeah, shot him and killed him.

Now, one of the top boxers Dello had with him that race week was a feller by the name of Bill Sutton. Bill called himself 'Kid Dynamite'. He was an ex-eight-rounder from Brisbane and he had a bit of a rep. Actual fact, these days, he's got a butcher's shop in Rockhampton. Anyhow, after what I'd done to that Danny feller, word got about that I could fight a bit so, by the next night, of course, everybody's expecting me to challenge this Kid Dynamite. I was at eleven stone two. I was always eleven stone two. And Dello takes me aside and says, 'Look, Goldie, just put on a good show 'n' I'll get this bloke ter nurse yer 'n' I'll call it a draw, 'n' yer can take yer money.'

So it's set up to be a stew, aye. Well, a stew's when the other feller doesn't go all out to beat you or cut you up. Like, he looks after you. Well, that's what I thought was going to happen anyway, and so did Dello. But, see, unbeknown to both Dello and me, behind our backs, the manager of Miranda Station – a feller named Phil Shaffat – he'd heard I was duffing with the Caseys and he wanted to send us a warning not to go into Miranda. So he gets this Kid Dynamite on his own and he says, 'Look, I want yer to teach Goldie a real lesson so he won't come duffin' on Miranda.'

'But it's all set,' says this Kid Dynamite.

'How much?' asks this Shaffat.

'Five quid,' says Kid Dynamite.

And Shaffat says, 'Well here's ten quid. I want yer to knock him out.'

So anyway, when they get up on the board, bashing the drum and all that, Dello's calling out, 'Who's gonna fight? Roll up. Roll up.'

And when he starts spruiking about this Kid Dynamite being the main event of the night, I calls out 'Yeah, I'll have a go at him', and all the locals give me a cheer. But, see, I thought it was going to be a stew. Of course, nobody else was supposed to know that, except Dello, me and this Kid Dynamite. Anyhow, first up a couple of Murries have a fight with some of Dello's boys. Then the main event comes up. First round and this Kid Dynamite, he comes out and we're sparring around and he's bringing them in hard and I'm thinking, Gee, if this's what's called nursin' a bloke then I'd hate ter fight him when he's really havin' a go. Anyhow, Dello's not taking much notice. He's whipping everyone up: 'Come on crowd. Cheer fer yer local boy!'

So I gets through the first round and in the second round, boy, this bloke's back into me and he's really throwing them, aye. And, like, I'm finding it hard to get a punch in now because I'm too busy blocking his, see. But I'm still thinking, Why's he comin' in like this? Then I thought, Well, perhaps bein' an old eight-rounder from Brisbane, he's gettin' all stirred up 'n' he can't pull his punches.

Anyhow, I finally saw the three rounds through. But, boy, was I glad when it was over, aye. And afterwards Dello quizzed this Kid Dynamite about why he went in so hard and that's when Kid Dynamite told him how Shaffat had offered him ten quid to try and knock me out, as a warning to stop us duffing on Miranda Station. Like, not that it worried us anyway, because we took Miranda cattle without even having to go into Miranda Station. Yeah. Well, see, there was a 230-square-mile block called Timora that bordered Miranda. Nobody owned it and so, what we'd do was, during the dry season, we'd set fire to it. You know, burn it out. Then, when the first storms come, in about October, all this nice feed would shoot up and the Miranda cattle would wander across for a nice fresh feed. So, instead of us risking getting caught by going over into Miranda, the Miranda cattle, well, they'd more or else come to us. Yeah, so that's how we worked that one, aye.

20

Yeah, so then our next duffing adventure was when I went over to attend the muster on Glenore. I've already explained what that means, aye – you know, how each station sent a couple of men over to the neighbouring station to attend the muster there and they'd work in the camp while they collected the cattle belonging to their station. Anyhow, I goes over from Shady to attend the muster at Glenore. Yeah, Steve McQueen's still head stockman. Then, after about a month, we gets to the bronco yard at Scrubby. Scrubby's about forty mile from the Shady Lagoons boundary, an easy four days' ride. By now our cattle are thinning out so the Casey boys, they come over to help me take our cattle back home. Jimmy and me was on horses – we had about ten in all – and Geoffrey drove over in the ute to carry all our swags and stuff. But see, old Reg never trusted the Caseys so he turns up at Scrubby just to doublecheck we're only taking what had our brand on it. Then just before we left he says, 'So boys, what yard are yer gonna camp at ternight?'

'Down Broadwater,' we said, Broadwater being a yard about ten mile away.

But, see, we knew old Reg wanted to know where we was going to camp so that he could come down there and check we hadn't duffed some of his cleanskins along the way which, of course, was exactly what we had in mind. So we started out with around thirty head of our cattle, from attending the muster, and along the way we picks up a good few of Reg's cleanskins. Now, knowing how Reg was aiming to come down to Broadwater to check on us, we moved them on a bit and we went straight past Broadwater and camped at a yard called The Lakes. Of course, when Reg turns up at Broadwater and we weren't there, he smells a rat, aye.

Then, by the time we got to the next yard, Anabranch, we'd picked up a few more of Reg's cleanskins, plus some Vanrook Station bullocks that the drover had left behind because they'd gone lame. Well, with them having the Vanrook brand, we couldn't resell them, aye, so we just took them as killers, for us to eat. By now we had around ninety head, in all. The thirty of ours, plus old Reg's cleanskins, then these few Vanrook bullocks.

Okay, between Anabranch and the boundary to Shady Lagoons was the Croydon–Normanton Road and alongside the road ran the railway line. So we had to cross both the road and the railway line to get to Shady. The only trouble is, with Reg knowing we're up to no good, he's now driving up and down the road, trying to find us. Now, it's just lucky for us how each side of the road is so thick with timber that Reg can't get his Land Rover into there, to check on what we've got. So we kept the cattle moving through the timber. While all this's going on, Geoffrey Casey's driving up and down the road in the ute, aye, keeping his eye on old Reg. So when Geoffrey sees Reg take off back up to Scrubby to get reinforcements, that's when we said, 'This's it. It's now or never ter get these cattle across the road 'n' railway line 'n' home ter Shady.'

But there's another problem. See, a lot of these cattle are from deep into Glenore country so they'd never seen a railway line before. And, like, normally, in a situation like that you'd get them to the rail line and let them take a look at it, sniff at it, and then they'd decide whether or not to walk across it. But, of course, with Reg hot on our tail, we haven't got the time for that, aye. So we decided to risk it. We packed them in real tight and we got our whips behind them and – crack! – we galloped them across the road. Then, by the time the leaders baulked at the railway line, we had them going so fast that the others pushed them over. Momentum, yeah, that's right.

Okay, so we gets them across and we takes them into the thick tea-tree, well out of sight. Like, we can still see the road but Reg can't see us from the road. We're now only five mile from Shady's bullock paddock. We let them stand, let them settle. Geoffrey drives past, down the road. Then Reg comes racing along in his Land Rover. Steve McQueen and a Murri's with him. He stops when he sees the tracks across the road. Checks them. Now he knows we've got well over the thirty head of our own we'd started off with. Jimmy gets edgy. He says, 'We'd betta let Reg's cleanskins go. There's no way we'll get 'em home without him findin' us.'

I says, 'No way. They was too hard ter get in the first place.'

So we decides to hold them in the scrub till dark. But the Norman River's less than half a mile away and they can smell the river. See, they'd had a long day without a drink and so now they want to go to the water. So we had to double-watch them – you know, two fellers ringing them. Then, when night came we only kept the horses we was riding and we let the rest go. They'd head straight for home, see. Then in the dead of dark we starts them off again. Nice and slow, nice and easy. As little noise as possible. And when we got to Shady bullock paddock we didn't go through the gate because we knew that Reg'd check the tracks the next day, so we undid the strainer wires and put them through there. Then, next morning, real early, we took them to the house yard and branded them and earmarked them.

Then I'd say it was about three weeks later I saw old Reg at the bottom pub so I says, 'G'day, Reg.'

And he didn't say a word about it. All he said was, 'Goldie, two things: one, I'll buy them thirty head of yers fer ten quid each.'

That was a good price so I says, 'Yeah, okay, 'n' what's the other thing?'

He says, 'Yer good with horses, good with stock 'n' I like yer so, if ever yer want a job, just let me know.' Then he gives me a bit of a look and he says, "N' also, if yer workin' fer me I'll be able ter keep a close eye on yer.'

I says, 'Okay, Reg, I'll keep it in mind.'

Anyrate, I ran into Steve McQueen a while later. From what I gathered, Steve's mother didn't want to come across from Iffley Station so Reg'd sacked him as soon as the mustering season was over. But Steve was telling me how, when they couldn't find us with that ninety head, Reg had said to him, 'How can them fellers disappear into thin air with all my cattle?'

And Steve had said to him, 'Well, at least thirty of them weren't yours, Reg.'

Then Reg gave him a real dirty look, aye, and he said, "N' where do yer think they originally got that thirty head from? Duffed 'em off me, that's where!'

And he was pretty much right about that, too because, see, Terry McMahon, the copper, told me afterwards that Reg had said to him, 'One'a these days I'm gonna come down on those Caseys like a ton of bricks. 'N' even though I like Goldie, if he's gonna get involved with 'em, he'll have ter cop it, too.'

So Reg knew what we was up to, aye. But, from then on, even when I was with the Caseys, old Reg got me over to Glenore during the wet season to break in his horses. So for a couple of months at least, he knew exactly where I was.

21

Anyway, we duffed on and off all through '56, not only on Glenore but also places like Iffley and them. Oh yeah, we had some real close shaves, aye. One time I was in town at the Burns Philp store getting three or four pounds of tobacco and old Reg's in there buying bags of flour and rice – you know, all the sorts of stuff you'd take out on a big muster. So I says, 'G'day Reg.'

'Goldie,' he says, and so we have a bit of a yarn about this and that. But, see, mostly when Reg and me had a yarn I'd be feeling him out. Like, I'd be trying to find out where he was mustering; then, if it was far enough from Shady, me and the Caseys, we'd be into Glenore real quick. Reg, of course, tried not to give too much away because he knew what I was up to. It was sort of like a banter we always had. Anyrate, as usual, Reg didn't let much slip so, when I went outside, there's this Murri sitting in the back of old Reg's truck, aye. So I says, 'Where you bin' go muster now, bungee?', 'bungee' being Aboriginal for 'friend' or 'mate'.

'Oh, we bin' goin' muster Saxby River tomorra, Goldie.'

Now, Saxby's sixty mile from Glenore homestead, right at the other end of the Glenore boundary, and I knew that the Saxby muster generally takes around two weeks. So when I gets back to Shady, I says to Jimmy Casey, I says, 'We're on again, Jimmy.'

So we gave it a day or two, then we slipped into Glenore with a couple of packhorses and a few saddle horses and we mustered three yards. That took seven to ten days. If I remember correctly, all told, we ended up with around sixty head, which included some nice fat, branded cattle to eat ourselves, plus some cleanskins and weanable calves and wait-a-whiles. Wait-a-whiles are calves too small to wean off their mothers so you'd put them both in your paddock and wait till they was old enough to wean before you branded them.

Anyhow, we couldn't make it back to Shady in one day so we camped at a yard called the Twenty-Five Mile. Well, it was called the Twenty-Five Mile because it was near the twenty-five mile rail sign on the Normanton–Croydon line. So then, the next day, early, we got them back to Shady. Yeah, sixty head, thereabouts. So that seemed like an easy one, aye. But later on that copper mate of mine I told you about, Terry McMahon, well, he'd been talking to Reg and Reg had reckoned he'd nearly caught us red-handed. Well, because, see, unbeknown to us, Reg had somehow got wind that we was on Glenore. Just how I'll never know. So he decides to spring us, see. But on the Wednesday afternoon, just as he's about to set off after us, he gets this phone call, see, from some business associate who'd just flown into Normanton and this feller wanted to meet with Reg that very same night, the same night we camped at the Twenty-Five Mile.

Now, lucky for us, the meeting went late and so Reg had to stay in town that night. Then, next morning, after he saw his business mate off on the plane, he raced back out to see if we'd crossed the road, which we had. So he went down to the Twenty-Five Mile yard and saw that we'd camped there the previous night. Then he raced through the scrub, hoping to catch us up, but all he found was some cows we'd weaned off their calves. And when I got to working it out, my reckoning was that Reg had only missed us by a couple of hours. So that was a close one, aye.

But, of course, we wasn't the only ones duffing. As I might've said, it wasn't really considered thieving, as such, because there was lots of other fellers duffing, too, all over the place. And some of them was good, like Jimmy Casey – oh, he was real good – then there's other fellers who wasn't so good. Well, for instance, take the Priestley brothers: Dazzler, Seventy-Seven and Plaster. They had a little property out of Croydon. I forget the name of it just now. Yeah, all in their forties. And, now, this's going to sound hard to believe, but it's gospel truth – see, the Priestleys was notorious for getting lost. Notorious. Yeah, cattle duffers who always get lost. You wouldn't credit it, would you? But, because they was forever getting lost, what they did was, see, whenever they went duffing they'd take their cattle dog with them. Then, when they wanted to go home, they'd throw stones at the dog and it'd head for home, with its tail between its legs, and they'd follow the dog. Yeah, that's a fact. That's how they found their way home. Fair dinkum.

And one of them – Dazzler, or was it Plaster? – he used to forever dribble from the side of his chin. Well, he had some sort of indent or something at the side of his lips, where his chin started. Anyhow, he'd be talking away and, like, he's always reckoning how he's going to shoot somebody. 'I'm gonna shoot that mongrel. I'm gonna shoot that other mongrel', and there's dribble running down there and a bit here. Then just as it's about to break away, he'd suck it all back up like one of them yo-yos. Yeah, 'I'm gonna shoot that mongrel' – suck! – and up it'd come. Yeah, I think it was Dazzler.

Anyway, the Priestleys used to come down every now and then to give old Reg a bit of a rip. Actually, for a long time, Reg thought it was us. But it wasn't always us. Anyrate, this time, someone in Croydon rings old Reg up. 'Oh, Reg,' they say, 'the Priestley boys are headin' your way with packs 'n' saddle horses.'

'Oh, yes,' says Reg, ''n' when did they leave?'

'Yesterday arvo.'

'Oh, yesterday afternoon. Right, good, thank you.' So then Reg sits there with his map and he says, 'Okay, they'll take so long to get here 'n' then they'll muster there, at that yard, for about a week. Then they'll muster there, at that place. Then they'll head fer home via Cross Water yard.'

Cross Water's where the Glenore boundary went across the middle of a waterhole. It's a good fifty mile from Glenore homestead. So after he'd worked it all out, Reg gives them whatever days it was, then he sticks a mosquito net down his shirt, he gets Baldy, his half-clumper night horse – the one the Caseys took that time – then he sticks a bit of damper and corned beef in his saddle bag and he rides all night, out to Cross Water. Oh, yeah, he'd ride all night, would old Reg. Okay, he gets there. All's quiet. Sneaks up to the camp. Counts how many mosquito nets are pegged out. 'Yes, yes.' Then he goes and checks one of the horses that's hobbled out, to see what brand's on it. 'Yes, that's the Priestleys alright.' Then he goes up to the yard where his cattle are, he lays his swag out, and he camps in front of the gate.

Next morning, the Priestleys come to get the cattle out of the yard and there's old Reg, sitting up on the slip rails waiting for them. 'Nice muster, boys. Nice muster. Yes, there's a bullock there. He got away from me last year. "N' that big roan feller, he's mine. 'N' there's some others there that look like mine. In actual fact boys, I reckon yer've got a swagful of cleanskins that're all mine.'

So he sprung them, aye. But here's the interesting bit – see, instead of getting the coppers, what Reg does is, he gets the Priestleys to take his cattle back to Glenore homestead. Yeah, Reg rode with them. Then, when they get there, Reg gets them to brand the cattle with the Glenore brand, a V5T. And I reckon they'd wince every time they done a beast with the V5T instead of their own brand, aye. Then after they'd done all that, old Reg takes them over to the office, gives them a big nip of rum each, then he writes out a cheque for a week's wages and he says, 'See yer later boys. Thanks fer all yer help.'

Then he sends them on their way. Yeah, the Priestleys. But that's the sort of man Reg Quilty was. Like I said before, one thing old Reg never, ever done was to go to the police. He's always said, 'If I can't work out a problem myself, well, I'll cop it sweet.' And I've always admired old Reg for that. Yeah, he was a real good feller, was old Reg.

22

But the biggest hit we ever done was in the wet season of 1957. Actually, the story started before then when someone saw me riding the back way home to Shady Lagoons, along the Normanton–Croydon railway line, with split-bags across me saddle. Well, a split-bag's like a big chaff bag. See, if you can imagine, you sit on it and the sides are hanging down and you just cut the top, like that, and put your stores and things down there. Like, if you're going cattle duffing by yourself you'd usually take a split-bag because it saves taking a packhorse; instead of carrying your swag, you just carry a little blanket at the back. Anyhow, the local police sergeant, Sam Henry, he got wind of this so he thinks, Gee, this's pretty suspicious because, if I know Goldie, the only reason he'd be goin' along the rail line is so he doesn't leave any tracks.

But the thing was, I hadn't been up to anything. You know, I'd just been in town getting supplies for this big, sort of, droving trip we was about to go on and the only reason I was riding along the rail line was that it was too wet and boggy off the tracks, so I got on the ballast, where it's more solid under hoof. But, like, Sam didn't know all that. He just naturally thought I'd been up to no good. And then, when Jimmy Casey turns up at the police station and fills out a waybill saying '300 head. Destination, Julia Creek. Travelling for sale', that really got old Sam suspicious.

Now, in actual fact, we only had about a hundred and twenty head ready to travel. Well, we'd got them from previous duffing trips, aye. Oh yeah, we'd already branded them and all that so they was legally ours ... well, not legally but, you know what I mean, because, with our brand on them, no one else could put a claim on them, aye. But why Jimmy wrote down '300 head – Travelling for sale' was because, with the wet season coming on, mustering had finished and the stations had paid off all their men. So with hardly any men left on the stations, our chances of being seen was pretty slim, aye, which meant it was, pretty much, open slather to pick up any cleanskins we came across, along the way. And, of course, just as long as they all had our brand, it wouldn't have mattered if the coppers saw we had less than three hundred head because all we'd say was that they'd rushed one night and we'd lost some.

Anyhow, okay; we'd already organised to sell whatever amount of cattle we ended up with to a buyer feller named 'Hungry' Dawson for ten pound ten a head. Hungry had a station on the downs, the other side of Iffley. Beautiful fattening country it was, too. Well, he'd been named Hungry because of him being so mean and tight. One story goes that he once went into the Gilliat Hotel and the feller behind the bar shortchanged him. So they had a big blue over it. Then, after the blue, Hungry went and offered to buy the pub off the publican, on the spot, on the guarantee he'd sell it back to the publican for the same amount of money, the very next day.

'Why's that?' asks the publican.

'Because if I own the place, I can sack that mongrel so-and-so!'

Yeah, that's true. And, oh, that's right, another story about Hungry was – see, he used to have arthritis in his back, real bad, and someone told him to get a twelve-volt battery and, every morning, wire it up to his back and give himself a hit with it and it'd cure his arthritis. And he did that for years and years and he swore by it and even when the battery went flat he still reckoned it was doing him good. So yeah, that was Hungry.

Anyrate, the Caseys and me, we set off from Shady with this hundred and twenty head and we start picking up cleanskins along the way. And didn't we have a big hit, aye? They was everywhere on Glenore. Well, from around Anabranch, then we went to The Lakes, Broadwater, Scrubby for a few days. Then there's an old cattle duffing yard that'd been on Glenore for years and years. It was built with stakes in the ground and wire. Then, from Glenore, we went deep into Iffley country, to Vena Park, an outstation of Iffley. And, oh, mate, we finished up with three hundred head or thereabouts.

But anyway, while all this's going on, Sam Henry, the copper, thinks, Okay, it's about time I went out 'n' nabbed these fellers, cold.

Like, we didn't know any of this, of course. So Sam's all organised to go out the next day but then the Norman River came up that night and so he had to delay things. Of course, being the wet – and what a shocker of a wet it was – old Reg's away in Sydney, see. So Sam gets on to the new head stockman on Glenore, a feller named Arthur White, saying how we're in the area and up to no good and so they decide to jump in an aeroplane and go looking for us. Arthur was known around Normanton as 'Whale Bone'. No, I don't know why that was but I once sold him a mare. But, with having just taken on the head stockman job, Arthur wasn't too clued up on where all the Glenore yards was so they fly to Iffley Station to get the station manager there, that Bill Young I told you about, with Mrs McQueen. Bill knew the area like the back of his hand, aye. Then, when they gets to Iffley, they says to Bill Young, 'Have yer seen the Caseys 'n' Goldie yet?'

'No.'

So they jumped in a four-wheel drive and heads out to some high country where they come across the fresh tracks of around two hundred head. But that wasn't us. No. It turned out to be the Priestleys – you know, them cattle duffers from Croydon I told you about. They'd slipped into Iffley to give the place a bit of a tickle and they was lost out there somewhere. So then Sam and Arthur, they jumped back into the plane and they started out on a wide circle from the Iffley homestead, checking all the yards, but the heavy rain come in again, so they had to give up.

Well, the first we knew about any of this was after we'd left a yard on Glenore called Jumble Hole, and we're headed over to Surveyors. Surveyors had a crush so that's where we was going to brand, cut and earmark what we'd picked up along the way. So, yeah, that's when we sees this aeroplane flying round. Well, we pretty much knew it might be someone looking for us, but we didn't know who. Not at that time. But anyway, it got Jimmy all worried so we kept the cattle hidden in the thick timber all that day, then we walked them all that night, till we got to Surveyors.

Anyhow, as I said, a feller called Hungry Dawson's going to buy them off us for ten pound ten a head. But from Surveyors to Hungry's place was another eight days south, probably more. So we walked them again all the next night, across to the Five Mile yard on Glenore, which is about five mile from the Wondoola Station boundary. Anyhow, when we got to the Five Mile, lo and behold, down she come again. More rain. A good four inches fell so now we're stuck because we can't get them across the eighteen mile of black soil plain to Hungry's place.

Now, Jimmy always done our deals so, being so close to Wondoola, he went and saw Tom Wheelan, the manager there. I might've told you how, other than being the manager of Wondoola, Tom also owned a small station outside Julia Creek, called Glenmore, and he'd buy cattle off all the duffers and that from around the Gulf and take them down to Glenmore to fatten them up, before selling them. But, see, Tom knew we was stuck so he had us by the short and curlies, aye, and he only offered us eight quid a head on delivery.

'Okay then,' says Jimmy.

So we starts walking them over to Wondoola. Next thing, Tom comes out to say how Sam Henry had rang him, asking if he'd seen us coming through. Of course, Tom's the bloke who's just agreed to buy them off us so he says, 'No, Sam. Haven't seen hide nor hair of them.'

Sam says, 'Well, they're out there somewhere 'n', knowin' them, it's a dead-cert they'll be duffin' along the way.'

'Yeah, that'd be right,' says Tom.

'Tom,' Sam says, 'just let me know when they come through 'n' I'll fly straight out 'n' nab 'em.'

'Yes, Sam, all right. If I see 'em, yer'll be the first ter know.'

So Tom arrives and he says to us, 'Look, Sam Henry's onta yer so go wide around the station 'n' take 'em up to the Twelve Mile yard because I don't want the blacks here seeing yer with all these cattle.' That's because they're too honest, aye. They'll spill their guts every time, just like Dinky-di Zana done when the Caseys took Baldy and Robin from off old Reg.

'Okay, Tom,' we says, and so we heads out wide around to the Twelve Mile yard. That trip takes us a couple more days and, when we get there Tom takes them over then for eight quid a head.

So, yeah, I'm not sure exactly how many we ended up with but, after we divvied up the spoils, the Caseys give me 160 quid. And that's the biggest lot of money I got, on 'n'off, over me three years of cattle duffing. But, I mean, really, if you worked it out, I didn't even make wages. So I never made nowhere near enough to buy New Zealand, aye. And anyhow, by then, that Janet Wilson piece had given up on me good and proper. Like, all I got out of duffing was the excitement, aye. That's all. So then I thinks to meself, Goldie, it's time ter do somethin' else.

23

Anyhow, I'd been keeping in touch with old Arthur Reid from Cloncurry. Remember he was the feller I was building the yard with the time I saw me first min min lights? I told you about that, aye. Okay, so I goes down to The Curry because old Arthur wants someone to help him out for a week or so and we finished up fencing out at Devoncourt Station. Actually, I think Devoncourt belonged then to Australian Estates. Beautiful country. A big place about forty mile out of Cloncurry, just outside a little one-pub town called Malbon.

So we're out there, camped out on the flat, with swags and a fly, taking turns at cooking. There's not much bar and shovel work this time, which made it easier, because by this stage old Arthur's got himself a tractor, with a post-hole digger at the back. We done about a mile a week. Yeah, all wooden posts. Local gidgee, actually. It grew all around the place. Very tough timber. White ants won't touch it. Lasts a good fifty or sixty years. Very popular with fencing fellers, is gidgee. See, there's hardly any sap in the timber itself. No sapwood. Old Arthur also had a chainsaw by then so we'd cut all the posts ourselves. Then after we finished out there I come back into The Curry. I had a bit of money so I thought I'd buy a train ticket over to Charters Towers to have a look at what's going on around there. Like, work wasn't hard to find in them days. So I gets to the Towers and I'm walking down the road with me riding boots, carrying me swag, and a feller sees me. His name turned out to be Dan Gallagher. Dan was a mailman who went out to the different stations. So he says, 'Yer lookin' fer work, mate?'

'Well, actually I am.'

He says, 'Where do yer come from?'

I says, 'The Gulf.'

Well, Gulf ringers have got good names, see, because they're known as good horsemen and they're used to handling wild cattle and that sort of thing. So he says, 'Look, Mount Elsie's lookin' fer ringers. How's about I pick yer up tomorra 'n' I'll take yer out in the mail truck?'

I says, 'Yeah, okay.'

He says, 'What gear have yer got?' Well, I'd left me saddle and everything back in Normanton, see. So, straightaway, he went and bought a quart pot and he said, 'Here yer are. Here's a quart pot.' And, well, see, by giving me the quart pot, he's now got a bit of a claim on me, aye.

So he picks me up the next day and he takes me out to Mount Elsie Station. Mount Elsie's about eighty miles out from the Towers. Three sisters had owned it from since away back in the 1880s. One of the sisters, she'd married a feller, Frank Webb, a World War I digger. Frank was managing the place. Then another sister, Mrs Morrison, she lived in town. I ended up getting on real well with her. Then the third sister, I don't know what happened to her.

Anyhow, I worked in the mustering camps and all that – ringing, like – and because I come from the Gulf I got on real well out there. All brigalow and lancewood it was and cattle in that sort of country learn to get cunning and rogue. Like, they've only got to hear a whip crack and they'll hide in the timber. Then you've got to gallop after them and you've got to throw them. So, yeah, I got on well. But I missed the Gulf, aye, and I starts thinking how I might go back to Shady Lagoons and have another lash at duffing with the Caseys. So after about five months, I just pulled the pin, aye.

Now, I still had a bit of money left over from the big hit plus there was some more coming from Mount Elsie and, see, I always wanted to buy a vehicle. I'd never owned one before, aye. Mount Elsie always used a mechanic feller from town called Frank Stangar. Frank done all the work on their vehicles and everything. Now, I don't quite know how it all come about, whether I asked Frank about a vehicle, or if someone told me how Frank had a D4 International 15 cwt for sale. I even forget exactly how much it cost – 180 pound or something. But, the thing is, I just didn't quite have enough to buy it outright so I put a good holding deposit on it and the deal was for me to leave it with Frank and come back and pick it up in a few months' time, after I'd fully paid it off. So that was all okay. So then I went down to the air booking office – the TAA office. I had me riding boots on, me hat, a pair of jeans. I says to the feller there, 'Mate, when's the next plane goin' up ter Normanton?'

He says, 'There's one going tomorrow to Georgetown. You can stop overnight there and you can go on to Normanton the following day.'

I says, 'Oh beaut, book me down then.'

'Okay,' he says, 'and what's your name?'

I says, 'Jack Goldsmith. Call me Goldie if yer like.'

He says, 'And where are you staying, Mister Goldsmith?'

I says, 'The Southern Cross.' Well, in Charters Towers, the Southern Cross was known as the Blood 'n' Guts. Oh, it was a real rough place, aye. You know, you could get a fight there. You could get a woman there. You could get anything there.

So he looks down his nose at me, then he says, 'Oh, is that so? The Southern Cross? Well, okay then, that'll be so-many pounds.'

'Oh,' I says, 'she's right mate. Just put it on the slate.'

He says, 'Put it on the slate?' He says, 'Do you think just anybody can wander in here, off the street, and book themselves on a plane and expect us to put it on the slate when we don't know them from a bar of soap? Where do you work up there?'

I says, 'A place called Shady Lagoons.'

'Shady Lagoons?' he says. 'Never heard of it. Which company owns it?'

I says, 'It's not owned by a company. It's owned privately.'

He says, 'Privately. And you expect me to book you up because you work on this place called Shady Lagoons.' He says, 'So who owns this Shady Lagoons?'

I says, 'I do.'

Then he really changes his tune, aye. He says, 'Oh, do you? Well, that's different Mister ... err... Goldsmith. Very different. Just sign here Mister Goldsmith and we'll even come around at eight o'clock tomorrow morning to pick you up and take you out to the airport, Mister Goldsmith, err, Goldie.' And, you know what, I never, ever got a bill for that, aye.

So I gets picked up the next morning and they take me out to the plane and we flies to Georgetown where we stayed overnight. I knew the publican there, a bloke called George Dickson. Real good feller. I'll tell you a story about him later. Anyrate, next day, we get on this little single-engined plane. Four seats. There's the pilot. A seat next to him. I was in the seat behind that. The other seat's full of mail bags. Then this German feller gets in next to the pilot and we're flying along and this German's yapping away, telling the pilot what a great flyer he'd been during the war, and the pilot says, 'So yer flew in the Luftwaffe, did yer?'

'Yah, yah, I vos flyin' in zee Luftwaffe, yah, yah.'

'So yer musta shot some planes down?'

'Yah, yah, I ha'ft a lot of't victories in zer Battle of Britain, yah, yah, yah.'

Anyway, he's going on and on and on about his victories in the Battle of Britain and it gets to me, see, so I taps him on the shoulder and I says, 'Listen here, yer goose-steppin' Hun. If yer start shootin' yer mouth off round Normanton about how yer was shootin' down our planes in the Battle'a Britain, I can guarantee yer'll end up as crocodile crap.'

Well, didn't that shut him up, aye? Okay, so now we're going along in silence. Time's getting on and we're heading towards the sunset. It's all pink. There's no sun. And I'm looking out the window and I see this swamp and the pilot gets his map out and he's got all these plastic things and compasses and all that and he's looking confused, so I says, 'Geez, it's a pity there wasn't more daylight, mate, because I'd get yer to fly round the Twenty-Five Mile yard ter see if any of me cattle are there.'

And he says, 'Do you know where we are?'

I says, 'Yeah, don't you?'

'No,' he says, 'I'm lost.'

So I says, 'Don't worry mate, just keep headin' towards the pink 'n' when we hit the Norman River, I'll tell yer which way ter go, either up or down.'

24

Okay, it's early '57. I'm back in Normanton staying at the Caseys. But they're not doing much. You know, we'd just go out and duff a killer for ourselves every now and then and maybe pick up a few wait-a-whiles. But not much. So I'm at a bit of a loose end. Anyhow, a Northern Territory feller, Alec Baker, he's running the camp now on Glenore and I bumps into him in town one day and he says, 'You're Goldie, aren't yer?'

I says, 'Yeah. Why?'

He says, 'Reg told me about you. Can yer come out ter Glenore, there's a few colts need breakin' in.'

Well, wages are better than nothing, aye, especially seeing I had to pay off me truck. So I goes out breaking on Glenore and I wasn't there long when Alec Baker gets a call from old Reg saying he'd bought a hundred Hereford breeding bulls from a place called Taldora Station, just north of Julia Creek. Anyhow, because of the rain Reg can't get these Hereford bulls back to Glenore in a stock-freight truck, so he says to Alec Baker, 'Can yer send Goldie down ter Taldora 'n' bring 'em back up?'

At that time Taldora belonged to Duke Kerr. Duke was a massive round feller. His wife had to prop him up in bed with pillows, aye. Yeah, that's how big he was. Duke also owned Inkerman Station, up the York Peninsula, on the border of Rutland Plains Station. Now here's a story – see, when Duke was about fourteen, his mother was half-blind and she went somewhere for a holiday and when she come back, she came back on one of them old Cobb and Co. coaches. So Duke takes the sulky into town to pick his mother up and, along with him, he takes a Murri to help with the luggage. So they're waiting there and when the Cobb and Co. coach pulls up Duke sends the Murri over to pick up his mother's ports, to put them in the sulky. But, being half-blind, when Mrs Kerr sees this blackfella, she thinks it's Duke, so she starts kissing him and going on. And Duke's singing out from the sulky, 'Dat not me, mother. Dat not me. I'm over 'ere.'

Anyhow, that's just one I heard about Duke and he grew up to be a real big feller. So I goes down to Duke's place, Taldora, to walk this hundred head of Hereford bulls back to Glenore. Yeah, this's the first time I'd been in charge of anything, droving-wise. So we took the plant down – you know, the packhorses and the riding horses and all that. I went down with a little Murri called Tommy, a fella from Kowanyama Aboriginal Mission, up the Peninsula. Kowanyama was run by the Church of England Mission. They was good Murries from there. Reg had a lot of them.

But, see, bull droving's not real cattle droving, in the true sense of the word, where you have to go around of a night singing to them and all that. Bulls are real quiet. And, oh, I tell you, look, it was absolutely fantastic. I mean, yes, we watched them for the first couple of nights but after that they settled down beautiful. You'd just feed them up on camp and they'd all be around the fire, only ten feet away, and you'd be right there in the middle of them, aye. And I like my bullocks real close to the fire, see, because it's security for them and they get used of you walking around, singing or talking or whatever. They're calmer like that. Another funny thing's how the same fellers always camp in the same spot, every night. And once they're settled, every bullock walks in the same spot, in the mob. Like, you've got your tail-enders, who might be a little lame or not as long-legged. Then the long-legged fellers – the great big pikers; the big cock-horned fellers – they'd stride out the front. Then there's them that's been reared up together as calves and they stay mates for life. So you might get four or five in a little mob like that who'll always stick together.

Then as we got further on in the trip, I got to be real good mates with them. Like, I'd get off me horse and walk along with them. Talk to them, yeah. And there was one feller there and, oh, I had him broke in so tame I could ride him. True. He'd carry me along and, you know, I felt like I wanted to buy him for a pet. I just got on so terrific with him. You just can't help it. And in the morning they'll just hang around camp, waiting for you to crack the whip, to let them know it's time to walk off again. Then, when they see the dinner camp in the distance, they'd just drop their heads and they'd spread out.

And, well, there's this mate of mine from Murrurundi, Viv Walsh. He won't talk much, will Viv. He's very quiet and he's got a very dry sense of humour. Well, see, Viv had this contract to bring bullocks down from a place called Frogmore, to Singleton, in the Hunter Valley of New South Wales. He had that trip every year. It took him about four months. So one year he takes this eight hundred head over to Singleton but, when he gets there, the owner says, 'Look, there's no sale here, take 'em down ter Wangaratta.' Now Wangaratta's a long way away. It's near on five hundred mile as the crow flies over into Victoria and Viv wasn't flying by no means because now he's got to get this mob over the Great Dividing Range. So that's what he does. But when he finally gets to Wangaratta there's a telegram waiting for him, saying: 'Take them to Forbes.' So he turns around and he marches them back up to Forbes, in the centre of New South Wales. Anyhow, by the time Viv got to Forbes, the whole trip's taken him eighteen months and eleven days. So the next time I saw him, I says, 'I don't know about you, Viv, but sometimes yer get so close ter the bullocks that yer don't like lettin' 'em go, aye?'

And Viv said, 'Goldie, I know what yer mean but, ter tell yer the truth, after eighteen months 'n' eleven days, I was a little a bit keen on gettin' home.'

Anyhow, that's just a little story on the side. But, oh, I enjoyed it. Then, when me and Tommy got this lot back to Glenore I dropped ten off at Surveyors bullock paddock, then I went another day's walk and dropped another ten off at another yard, then another ten off at another yard and so forth, all the way back to Glenore homestead. Yeah, spread them out all through the property so they'd breed. And I tell you, when I got down near the homestead, I put what's left on a waterhole and a couple of days later they're still there, waiting for me to walk them off again. So that was me first droving trip. It was with bulls and, I tell you, it was just terrific, aye.

25

After we got back to Glenore, I went back horse breaking because I really wanted the horses to go right. Well, because, see, you can easy get a bad name if you break in a horse bad, you know. Like, I took a lot of pride in how I broke in horses so I always tried to make sure they was well mouthed and they could turn on a threepence and all that.

By now it's straight after the wet and they're ready to go out for the first muster of the season and, well, that Alec Baker feller, the head stockman I was telling you about, he says, 'Goldie, yer can come out in the camp now, if yer want.' And, see, I wanted to go into the camp because a breaker always likes to go out with the horses he's just broke in to see how they go, aye. And, also, I was keen to get a bit of a backstop – you know, some money to fall back on and help pay off me truck.

So I says, 'Okay, I'll go in the camp.'

So, next morning, we're packing the packhorses up, ready to go out to the camp. There was Fred Footscray, the cook. Old Dogger Smith, the Smith boys' father. There's me, Alec Baker, Pat Gallagher, Jack Chalkley. There was a big Murri, Tahmal Meenyarrawal. 'Adrian' was his Australian name. Well, 'Tahmal' means the 'ringtail possum' and the 'Meenyarrawal' was 'his tracks go back'. So there's him, then there's Lightning and another Murri. That might've been Tommy, the fella I'd brung the bulls back from Taldora with. So there's a fair few of us.

Now, this Jack Chalkley was a very surly sort of feller, a bad drinker. Very prickly. Hard to get to know. Like, he'd sit on his own and he'd eat on his own and sleep over by himself.

He'd done three months in Stuarts Creek jail, in Townsville, after some sort of trouble out on Iffley. Well, I don't know all the ins and outs of it but Bluey Ellis reckoned he got drunk and grabbed a .303 and started shooting the place up. But here's a funny thing – apparently old Fred Footscray, the bloke who was coming out cooking for us, well, he was also over on Iffley and when Chalkley started shooting the place up, old Fred's sound asleep in the truck, snoring away, with his feet hanging out the window, and there's bullets going left, right and centre. Yeah, that's what Bluey Ellis said, so it might be true, aye. But anyway, the night before we're going out on the run, Chalkley had gone to the kitchen and he'd gotten stuck into some sort of mix of lemon essence. I forget now what it was. See, sometimes they mix brake fluid with it. Of course, that's 60 per cent pure alcohol. So he might've done that. I don't know. But the thing is, he made a real mess of himself and he was still pretty much under the weather the next morning.

So we're packing up the packhorses and the last horse had a habit of bolting, or so they reckoned. Mind you, I'd never seen it bolt. But with Chalkley still being half-drunk the horse somehow knocks him over. Next thing, his hide cracks. He blows up and chucks in the towel and he resigns. 'I'm finished. I'm gettin' outa 'ere.'

Anyhow, Baker says, 'Okay. That's fine by me.' Then he says to us other fellers, 'Look, how's about we have a bit of a break 'n' go over fer smoko?'

So, okay, it was like this – see, the homestead was over there. The kitchen's just over here. Then the laundry's almost next to it, there. And over here's the meathouse or the butcher shop as they call them on the stations. Then the ringers' quarters are over there, about a cricket pitch away. So all us ringers and Baker, we head to the kitchen to have smoko and the Murries go and sit out there, cross-legged as they do, under a big ironwood tree.

Now, a Chinaman, Fred Ah Chee, did the market garden on Glenore. You know, like, he'd grow vegetables and one thing and another. Well, Fred had a big old chestnut gelding called Mango. A real beautiful thing. Pretty tall. That quiet a five-year-old could ride him. So while we're over having smoko, Chalkley goes and saddles up old Mango to take him the mile or so down to the railway siding to catch the rail motor back to Normanton. Now this's on a Thursday and the rail motor always comes down from Croydon on a Thursday. A diesel, with some flat-tops. See, they generally bring beer up from Cairns to Forsayth, then they truck it across to Croydon, then send it down to Normanton on the rail motor. Anyhow, we're all sitting there, having smoko, yarning about Chalkley and this stupid accident with the horse and Baker says to me, he says, 'Goldie, after yer drunk yer tea, take Chalk down ter the sidin' in the Land Rover.' Everyone called him 'Chalk'.

I says, 'Yeah, righto.' So I finished me tea and I drives the Land Rover over and I says, 'Don't be a blackfella, Chalk. I'll take yer down in the Land Rover.'

Okay, I'd say I was only about fifteen feet from the verandah of the ringers' quarters, not even that far. Chalkley's got old Mango outside the ringers' quarters and he's tying his port onto the saddle. His swag's down on the ground and his rifle's across the swag. A mongrel rifle it was, too. A .22. Real hair-trigger. You only had to look at it and it'd go off. Anyhow, so I picks up the rifle and puts it down in the back of the Land Rover, then I grabs his swag and throws it into the back of the Land Rover, as well. But Chalkley races round, grabs the rifle, and puts it up to me like this, like he's going to shoot me or something and he says, 'You put that swag back or I'll drill yer!'

Like, I only thought he was joking. But the bore hole of the rifle's staring straight at me. Then I sees the look in his eyes. And it wasn't a good look, aye. I thinks, Geez this feller's fair dinkum, aye. So I dived behind the horse, Mango. Just as I did there's this bang and Chalkley near blows the heel off me riding boot. Anyrate, he's got the rifle and he's going like this, under the horse, and I'm ducking and diving around this Mango, trying to get out of the way of the rifle and I'm calling out and going on, 'Don't be a silly so-and-so, Chalk! What's wrong with yer?'

Then – bang! – he lets go another shot. So there I am, I'm ducking and diving and I'm thinking, Oh, the fellers'll hear the rifle shot from up the kitchen 'n' they'll be down in a flash 'n' save me. But, see, they didn't – well, either didn't or they'd all went into hiding.

Now, the Murries, in the meantime, like I said, they're having their smoko over under the ironwood tree, just down from the kitchen. And there's one little Murri there, Lightning, and I can see him pointing all this out to this other Murri, Tahmal Meenyarrawal, the fella whose Australian name was Adrian. Anyhow, Chalkley's still after me, aye, so I dives around behind old Mango and I come up under his neck. But then he has another go at me – bang! – and the bullet goes through the ringers' quarters, just behind me.

And I'm real scared, aye, so now I'm starting to think about how I can get to me own gun, an old Winchester lever-action .32. It's propped just behind the door of the ringers' quarters, and I'm trying to muster me wits as to whether I can get to it before Chalkley shoots me. But I couldn't remember if there's a bullet up the breech or not because, if there was a bullet up the breech, all I had to do was to cock the rifle and I would've blown his head off.

Then I looks up, aye, and I sees this Murri, Adrian, creeping up on Chalkley. Pure-bred black, he was. Only about eighteen.

Tribal scars and all. A real big fella he was, sneaking up to Chalkley. Just putting one foot in front of the other. Step by step. Now, I dare not look at Adrian because that'd give him away and Chalkley would've turned around and shot him. But just then, from under the horse, I see the shadow of Chalkley and his rifle coming at me. So I jumps. And as I jumps, Adrian latches onto Chalkley with his big arms and, as he does, the gun goes off and the bullet misses me by a whisker. Yeah, I felt the wind of it going past, aye.

Of course, now it's safe, all the white fellers come running out of the kitchen. 'Hey, what's goin' on?' and all that. So everyone comes out now it's all over, aye. Anyrate, we tie up Chalkley, then Baker rings up Sam Henry, the copper in Normanton, and tells him what happened and Sam says, 'Put him on the rail motor 'n' I'll meet him when he gets ter town.'

So that's what we did and we didn't go out mustering that day. Then me and Adrian – this Tahmal Meenyarrawal – we had to go into Normanton the next day to make a statement. Like I might've said, Normanton's only fifteen mile from Glenore homestead. And I'll never forget, with this Adrian, he got so nervous along the way we had to stop just about every hundred yards or so for him to have a pee. That's how nervous he was about it all, aye. Anyhow, in the end we just told Sam Henry what had happened and then we went back out to Glenore. Then, the next day, when that drama's over, we all goes out mustering and I said to old Dogger Smith, I said, 'If I ever have a son, Dogger, I'm gonna name him after that Murri, Tahmal Meenyarrawal, because he saved me life.'

26

See, with only the Flinders River being the boundary of Glenore and Magowra, during the dry season, Glenore cattle would wander into Magowra and Magowra cattle used to wander into Glenore. So, after I'd been out on camp a while, Alec Baker says to me, he says, 'Goldie, go over 'n' attend the muster at Magowra 'n' take Lightnin' with yer.' Lightning's the fella who let Adrian know that Chalkley was trying to shoot me. A good little kid, about sixteen. Another Murri out from Kowanyama Aboriginal Mission or, as it was back then, the Mitchell River Mission.

So I goes over to Magowra with this Lightning and, see, when you attend the muster, you're under the orders of the head stockman from that station. A feller called Kevin Ross was running the Magowra camp. Actually, now I think of it, Kevin had a brother who died from tetanus out on Canobie Station. I forget his name just now but he was ringing out there and he started complaining about his jaw getting stiff. Now, a tetanus spore's a germ that can live for something like seventy years, because it's covered by a real hard coating. So in the manure in yards there's all these tetanus spores and he must've got staked or something and he got a tetanus spore in the cut and that's when he started complaining of lockjaw. Anyhow, the manager's wife got onto Cloncurry all about it and they kept saying, 'Oh, just give him whatever's in box 7 in the Flying Doctor's first aid kit.' But the thing was, see, all they was giving him was Aspros, which was doing nothing. So, yeah, in the end he ended up dying from the tetanus.

Anyhow, when we get to Magowra, this Kevin Ross gets me drafting horses. That's where ringers swing a gate to let a horse through into a different part of the yard. Well it depends on what they're going to do with the particular horse. Okay, so I'm blocking about thirty head of horses from coming in the yard. Then one horse come flying through. It knocks the top rail off. The rail whacks me forehead and it clean knocks me out. Of course, once the rail's down, all the other horses followed, aye. And, like, it was only a narrow gap, about as wide as this table. So I'm down on the ground but in me mind I think I'm floating up in the air. But I'm not, see, and all the horses gallop over me and not one hoof touched me, aye. Fair dinkum. Not one.

Okay, so I survives that, and after a few weeks on Magowra we get about 150 head of Glenore cattle. So I take them back over to Surveyors bullock paddock, with this Lightning. That's a good five days' walk. Then I puts them in Surveyors and we goes back to Magowra to get another lot. Now, one horse I had in our plant was a mare I'd bought some months earlier and broke her in. Miss Muffett I called her. Gee, she was the makings of a good mare. But by the time we got back to Magowra they'd shifted camp. Now, I didn't know that country too well so I had to try and find where they were. So me and Lightning, we camped down on a little gilgai – like a little waterhole. It's pretty muddy but we still made our tea from it. And I don't know how but, that night, Miss Muffett snapped her hobbles and she disappeared. The next day I has a bit of a look around and I can't find her anywhere. So we heads off and we eventually finds their camp and this time Kevin Ross gets me helping with the branding. Then after a couple of days, I says to Kevin, 'Look, mate, I've gotta go 'n' find me mare, Miss Muffett. I miss her.'

He says, 'Okay, but yer won't find her. The brumby stallions woulda got her by now.'

Anyrate, I went back to where me and Lightning had camped at the gilgai and I rode around and around. Then I see some tracks. Then I see some fresh manure. And, see, you can tell how old a horse is by their manure. True. So I think, That's her. She's still here somewhere. Now, I wasn't a religious or nothing but, see, the memory come flooding back from the day I was about eight years old and I couldn't find me socks. Oh, I'd looked everywhere. I'd looked in the cupboards, under the bed, everywhere, and they're not to be found and I just knew how the stepmother would give me a good thrashing if I couldn't find me socks. Like, to her it was just another excuse to belt me, aye. So I got down on me knees and I prays, 'Please God, will yer find me socks.' And you're not going to believe this but, when I opened my eyes, there they are, six inches away from me. And that's fair dinkum, as true as I stand here. To this day, I reckon God got an angel to put them there.

So now I says to meself, 'What I might do is that I love this mare, Miss Muffett, so much I'm gonna pray for her ter come back to me.' So I gets down and I says, 'Look, God, I know I'm not much chop. I know I do bad things 'n' I'm rotten to the soul but can yer please find Miss Muffett?' And after I prayed, nothing happened. Then I remembered the time I'd put the tuppence ha'penny in a little hole near the telegraph pole and offered it up to God so the stepmother'd stop belting me. But He didn't take it and she didn't stop belting me. And it was while I was sitting there thinking about all that, I heard the rattle of a hobble chain. And there she was. Miss Muffett. Right behind me. That's as true as I stand here. Funny, aye. Sometimes it works, sometimes it doesn't. Yeah, Miss Muffett. A beautiful little thing she was.

So I takes her back to the mustering camp and this time I'm over at Magowra for a few more weeks. By this stage we're getting further away from the Glenore boundary so they're thinning out. But, in amongst them all, Magowra had branded two Glenore cleanskin calves by mistake so they gave me a couple of theirs in exchange. I've got another two hundred head now, easy, so I heads back to Glenore and in the mob there's these two cleanskins Magowra had gave me and I'm thinking and I'm thinking, How can I put me own brand on them 'n' keep them fer meself?

Anyway, we come to the Milgarra–Magowra boundary and there's this new fence there and I see how the sawdust from the bit's only a couple of days old. So I leaves Lightning with the cattle and I follows it down and sure enough there's a fencer there, a part-Aboriginal by the name of Gilly Martin. I knew Gilly well. Actually, Gilly come about after his father, a copper, had a one-night stand with a gin. Not too many people know that. But he was good Murri, Gilly was, and a good worker. He's putting up this fence the old way – you know, with a crow bar, a shovel, brace and bit. So we got chatting and Gilly's telling me about all the trouble he's having with the brumbies. See, because they're not used to a fence being there, sometimes they'd race through of a night, getting rid of the mosquitoes, and they'd hit the fence wire with such a force, they'd yank the posts clean out of the ground. Some posts even ended up in the trees. Yeah, that's what Gilly reckoned, like. But here's me chance, see. So I went and got the two Magowra cleanskins and I come back down to Gilly and I fashioned my brand – J (diamond) 8 – out of some no. 8 fencing wire and Gilly gave me a hand to pull them down and we branded them and earmarked them on the spot.

So then we heads back to Glenore to get some fresh horses and go back to Magowra. Like, we wouldn't have got many but, see, Magowra was a bit of a bludge. When I say bludge, it was a good place to work, aye, and they had good tucker. But when we gets to Surveyors there's a message wrote on the side of the old hut, there, in charcoal. 'Goldie, don't go back to Magowra. I need you for the bullock muster. Meet me at Sawtell yard – signed, Tom Edwards.'

So now Tom Edwards was running the show on Glenore. No, I didn't know this. I thought Alec Baker still was. But he's not. Reg's got rid of Baker and Tom Edwards is now head stockman. Now, everyone knew of Tommy Edwards. He had a big rep as a fighter. Last I'd heard he'd been working on Dunbar Station, up the Peninsula. They called him 'The King of the Gulf'. Oh, yeah, you'd hear them going on in all the mustering camps about Tom Edwards. Oh, they reckoned he was a world-beater, aye. And also, see, I was starting to get a bit of a rep, meself, around the place and, of course, all the ringers, they'd be talking about some fight I'd had and they'd be talking about some fight Edwards had and then it'd get around to, 'Geez, I wonder how Goldie 'n' Tom Edwards would go?'

Anyrate, I gets fresh horses and me and Lightning, we heads off, two days ride, down to Sawtell yard where I gets to meet Edwards. And, yeah, we hit it off straightaway. So we musters up Browns Creek and all them yards up to Flat Hole, then finally we gets to Black Tar. Black Tar's all mongrel country, full of whipstick and minooka and wattle – not your normal wattle, this's long streaky stuff. But seeing how the cattle at Black Tar don't get handled much, they're real wild and you've got to use 'coaches'. See, coaches are quieter cattle that you run in with the wild ones to quieten them down a bit, aye. Like, there was a big, fat roan bullock that hung around there. It was his dunghill. But he was so handy, aye, because we'd get him in the mob and he'd lead them into the yard every time; that's till the next-doors feller knocked him over and ate him, aye. I forget his name just now but he was the sort of feller who had a very shallow character, you know. Not many fellers liked him.

We always kept good horses for Black Tar, ones that stand, because with the cattle being so wild, there was a lot of

Goldie on Iffley Station, ready to go out mustering

throwing. Okay, what I mean by throwing is, see, you carry three belts: one belt holds your strides up; one belt's got your pocketwatch and castrating knife – I generally carry two knives; then you've got a third belt which is your bull strap. So, say you're riding along and there's a mob of cattle with a big cleanskin micky. You take it easy. He might be a three-year-old bull who'd been missed in the musters before. So he's wild, aye. But he's real wary so, when he sees you coming, he'll look up. He'll watch you. He won't take off just yet because there's lots of wild brumbies out there, so he's used of seeing horses. But he thinks maybe there's something different with this one. Yeah, different. So he'll look at you and when he realises there's something different, the hair comes up along his wither. Often they'll come around the wind side to try and smell you. Then once he's got a whiff of you, he'll go. He'll cut. And for the first quarter of a mile he'll put everything he's got into it. So he's going flat out, aye, and you're after him on your horse. Right behind him.

And it's all to do with timing, see, because, after that first quarter mile, when he starts to half-flounder, that's when you jump off your horse and you half-hitch his tail. Yeah, grab a real good hold of him. And you run alongside him so he can see you. It's important he sees you because, when he does, he'll try and spin around to charge you. He'll dip his head, yeah, and when he does, he's off balance, and that's when you pull him down. Then, when he hits the ground, his hind leg's up in the air. But he's trying to get up. But before he does, you grab his hind leg and you stick your knee into his hamstring. Even then he's trying to get up, aye, but he can't get up because you've still got a good hold.

Then you get your bull strap. You tie his hind leg with the front leg and while he's tied down you go and get your horse and bring him over and you get the horn saw. I've got one here somewhere. It's like a pruning saw but it's in a sheath that's tied underneath the sweat flap on your horse. Okay, so you saw his horns off close to the butt. Real close. But he's not too happy, aye. He's really bellowing. But you've got him tied so he can't get up. All the while, your horse just stands there. If you had a horse that took off, you wouldn't have him in your plant. When I break in horses I make sure they learn to stand. That's what I mean by having a good horse. Then after you've dehorned him you castrate him and earmark him. Then you undo the bull strap. While he's struggling to get up, you jump back on your horse. But, when he's up, he's real angry. He's hooking, aye, like he still thinks he's got his boxing gloves on – his horns. Sometimes he'll charge you and, if he does, you turn the rump of your horse onto him so he can't toss you over. So, yeah, that's what throwing is and that's how you go about it. Now he's ready to be branded the next day, when he's back with the mob.

Okay, so we gets them cattle together and take them back to Surveyors. We inoculate them, muster the bullocks and put them in the holding yard. There's about a thousand head or so and the drover's about to turn up any day. So then old Reg turns up. Anyway, we're all sitting around the campfire there one night and I says to Reg, I says, 'By the way, Reg,' I says, 'there's two of my bullocks in that mob I brung over from Magowra.'

'Oh,' he says, 'is there?'

I says, 'Yeah, they've got my brand on them.'

He says, 'Well, I'll buy 'em off yer fer ten quid a head.'

I thought, Gee, that's alright. So I says, 'Alright. Good.'

Then Edwards says, 'I didn't know yer had any cattle, Goldie.' And, see, he says it like he's wanting to challenge me over it, aye. You know, like he wanted to pick a fight about it. And Reg notices all this and he thinks, What can I do here? I don't want these two fellers in the same camp. They both love a fight 'n' I want a peaceful camp. See, there's nothing worse than an unsettled camp and Reg's thinking how Edwards and me, we'll either end up having a big stoush or maybe we'll get together as mates and come up with a bit of skulduggery, like duff a few of his cleanskins. Anyhow, so old Reg's wondering how he can get rid of one of us before there's some sort of big blow-up or other.

Then Chalkley turns up. He'd been over at Iffley, attending the muster there. Yeah, the same feller who nearly shot me. Well, they only fined him twenty-five quid or something, then they let him go and Baker had got him back on Glenore, while I was over at Magowra. You wouldn't believe it, aye. Oh, it didn't worry me. In fact, he was overly friendly – like, it was 'Mate' this and 'Mate' that. Anyway, while Chalkley was over on Iffley he'd took the camp horse, Bowershed, over with him. Well, a camp horse is what you use for cutting out a beast from the mob. Some horses, like this Bowershed, are so good that, if you show him the beast, you can just about sit there and he'll cut it out for you. Anyway, so then Edwards turns around and says to Chalkley, 'Chalkley, when yer go back ter Iffley, ter attend the muster, don't take Bowershed. I want him here.'

Chalkley says, 'No, I'm takin' him back. I want him.'

So Edwards turns around to Reg and says, 'What's it gonna be, Reg? Am I havin' that horse or is Chalkley havin' it?'

And, see, this's Reg's chance, aye, so he says, 'Chalkley can have him.'

Then Edwards says, 'Well, Reg, I'm head stockman here so it's either me or Chalkley.'

Reg says, 'I said Chalkley can have Bowershed.'

Edwards says, 'Alright then.' He says, 'You can stick the job. I'm finished.'

Of course, this's exactly what Reg wants. Edwards has pulled the pin. Anyhow, there's a feller there in camp called Bud Lane.

In fact, it'd been him who'd made Bowershed a camp horse. Bud was part-Aboriginal, but he wasn't under the Act. He was a good man. A good stockman. So Reg says, 'Bud, will you run the camp now?'

Bud says, 'No, I don't wanna run the camp.'

Then he comes over to me and says, 'Goldie, will you run the camp?'

I says, 'On one condition, Reg. I'll only run the camp till yer find someone else.'

'Alright then,' Reg says, 'yer've got the job.'

So I took over the camp. By now the season's just about over. So then, after the drover leaves on his final trip, we did a quick ride around to different places and found another four to five hundred head and we put them in Surveyors, as a bit of a starter for the next year's muster. Then, after we done that, Reg sent a couple of us up into Iffley to bring down a dozen or so big fat Iffley bulls, to put in there so he could keep the calf quality up.

Then, most ringers, after the muster their hides are starting to crack and they just want to head for somewhere like Cairns to get into the women and the grog and all that. Like, have a real blow-out. So most stations pay their men off and they only keep two or three on during the wet to repair the pack saddles and do a bit of breaking in, and that's what old Reg wanted me to do – stay on. But, see, I'd been writing to the Smith boys and they'd asked me to go over to Wernadinga Station. Oh, to do a bit of ringing but, also, they wanted some droving done, which I was real keen on doing. So I told old Reg I wouldn't stay on with him. And, well, that was the wrong thing to do, aye. I mean, I should've stuck with old Reg because he would've given me a job for life, you know, on wages. And I liked Reg and, in a funny sort of way, he liked me too, aye.

27

After I pulled the pin at Glenore, I went back to town and stayed out at Shady Lagoons. Well, I'd just throw me swag down on the verandah and that. The Caseys still wasn't up to much; not that I'm too worried because now I'm looking forward to joining the Smith boys out at Wernadinga and doing some more droving, aye. That's what I really wanted to do, more droving, because, see, I sort of felt more confident with cattle than I would've as head stockman, with all the responsibility of fellers under me.

So I'm at Shady and I goes into Normanton for a drink and I runs into a feller – Norman Smith. No, Smithy was no relation to Vincent and Benny and them. This feller was a professional barramundi fisherman around the place. Anyhow, there's Smithy and he's been smacked around a bit. Like, he'd been roughed up, with a black eye and that. So I says, 'Geez, what happened ter you, mate?'

He says, 'Boy, am I glad ter see you.'

I says, 'Why?'

He says, 'Well, I had a bit of a row with a feller, Ronny Paul, 'n' he hit me about a bit, so I said to him, "I'm gonna get Goldie onta you".'

Well, I didn't know nothing about all this till now, aye, so I says, 'Oh, that's very nice. Thanks, yer've just gone 'n' fixed me up fer a scrap with a feller I got nothin' against.'

Actually, I was of the mind to tell Smithy how he'd better sort out his own problems but, apparently, word was already about how me and Ronny Paul was going to have this fight, bareknuckle, out at the Normanton Golf Club. Oh, it was only five holes or something – you know, out on this salt-clay pan. And, also, Sam Henry, the copper, well, he pipes up and says 'I'll referee.'

Then Smithy says, 'Well, whoever wins outa you two, I'll give 'em five quid.'

So now, it's all organised, so I says, 'Yeah, alright. Okay then, I'll have a go at him.' 'Him' being this Ronny Paul.

I guess Ronny would've been about thirty, a bit older than me. He was a retired eight-rounder from Brisbane who was working somewhere around town. I forget now what he was doing but he had a bit of a rep and I'd begun to get a bit of a rep, too. Anyhow, news spread pretty quick how this stoush was being held out at the golf club and Sam Henry's going to referee the thing and so the whole town turns out to see it. Well, there would've been about twenty or thirty people, I guess. I mean, it wasn't race week or nothing so the town was pretty sleepy. Anyhow, they're all there to see this fight. Then, when Ronny Paul turns up, he's got his hands all bandaged like you do when you're a pro who's going to have a fight. And, when he gets in the ring, there he is, he's prancing around, looking so pretty that one feller says to me, 'You wanta watch him Goldie, he's been at the game before.'

I says, 'He don't worry me', because, see, I can tell by the way someone walks as to how they can fight. Like, if you get someone who walks along like this – real loose – well, you can tell he's a hard hitter but he's slow. Then you get a feller who walks along like this – real tight – well, he's fast but he can't hit hard. And that's just how this Ronny Paul was. He was fast but he wasn't a hard hitter. Anyhow, Sam Henry ended up stopping the fight, aye. Well, I was chopping him to pieces, wasn't I? Now, I'm not trying to make out I can scrap or nothing. Don't think that, but I just couldn't understand where he got his rep from. I mean, he's supposed to be an eight-rounder from Brisbane.

But I couldn't see it. So, yeah, Sam Henry, the copper, says, 'Look, Goldie, I've gotta stop this.'

And I says, 'Geez, yes, please, Sam. The poor bloke's a mess.'

After the fight, the publican from the middle pub asked us all to go back there for a drink. Anyrate, Ronny Paul cleans himself up a bit and we had a few beers together, aye. Actually, I sort of liked the feller, so I ended up spending the five quid Smithy gave me on drinks for us both. But, see, there was three coppers in Normanton at that time and one of them, Terry McMahon, he'd seen the fight and he gets me aside and he's on to me about going to Brisbane to train to be a pro boxer. 'Look, Goldie,' he says, 'yer've got a real future in the fight game. I'll even write yer an introduction letter ter Snowy Hill.' Apparently, this Terry McMahon knew Snowy very well. Everyone knew Snowy Hill. Oh, Snowy was a big-gun boxing trainer. He trained a lot of title holders.

But, anyhow, I said, 'Look, Terry, thanks very much but we'll have ter put it on the back burner fer a bit. I promised me mates I'd go out ter Wernadinga. I wanta do some drovin' so perhaps I'll go down ter Brisbane after that.'

And Terry said, 'Any time, Goldie. Just let me know when 'n' I'll write ter Snowy.'

Anyhow, I goes back to Shady and I'm getting ready to go to Wernadinga. But, see, after Ronny Paul, me confidence is a bit high. But still people are saying to me, 'Goldie, yer'll meet yer match if yer tangle with Edwards', which was like hanging out a red rag to a bull, to me, aye. But Edwards was a good twelve and a half stone. Heavier than me. A good man with wild cattle. So now I'm thinking, Tommy Edwards. I've gotta get this Edwards. Like, not to build up me rep or nothing, but I just wanted to see how I'd go with him fair and square. Because – how do I say it? – like, if he was in a pub somewhere and some feller who didn't know him started to pick him, someone would step in and say, 'Hey, don't pick him. That's Tommy Edwards, the King of the Gulf. He's a world-beater.'

Then I went into town for something or other and I went down to the bottom pub to have a drink and, lo and behold, there's Edwards. Now, I don't know if he'd seen me fight Ronny Paul or not but, we're having a drink together and he says, 'Pity Dello isn't in town, aye, because then you and me, Goldie, we could have a bit of a spar in his tent.'

And I says, 'Well, I'll be comin' back in town in a couple'a days ter change me mail address, so how's about we have a bit of a spar then?'

'Okay,' he said. 'Good. See yer in a couple'a days.'

So everything's all set – me and Edwards, we're going to have this scrap behind the bottom pub. Now, I might've mentioned before how the township of Normanton was over the other side of the Norman River from where I was at Shady, and to get to town, a feller, Backhouse, worked a punt, getting traffic across twenty hours a day. He had a little hut over on the town side. So I'm heading off for this fight with Edwards and I comes in to where the punt lands and there's a yard there for the horse and a thing there to put the feed in and there's also a big brass bell. Now, when you ring this bell, this Backhouse's supposed to come over in the punt and pick you up. Anyhow, I rings the bell and Backhouse sticks his head out from his hut and sees me and he thinks to himself, Oh, it's only Goldie. Then he goes back and sits down or whatever. So I'm ringing the bell and he's not doing nothing. He's completely ignoring me.

'Well, stuff yer,' I says and I took me boots and me clothes off and I tied them to me head with me belt and I starts to swim across the river.

Now, the Norman River's pretty wide – very wide, in fact. What's more, it's known for its crocs. Like, you've only got to go

Norman River, where Goldie swam across it

out four foot and it's over your head, so a croc can sneak right up on you and you wouldn't even see him coming. That's true. At Shady, goats was taken all the time. Anyhow, so I'm swimming and I'm swimming and I'm thinking how this's probably about the most stupid thing I've ever done in me whole life, because I can feel how I'm starting to get washed down the river and it still doesn't seem like I'm getting nowhere and I'm thinking about the crocs. Then halfway across, me foot hits something, aye, and, oh, I just about shot out of that water. I tell you, I was more frightened and terrified right then than what I was when Chalkley was trying to shoot me.

So I'm swimming and I'm swimming and I'm getting knocked up and I'm struggling, and then I sees a bloke called Jack Smurdens. He'd come down to the punt to see Backhouse for some reason or other. Well, Jack sees me out in the river so he turns around and he takes off up town, singing out: 'Goldie's swimmin' the river. Goldie's swimmin' the river.' Yeah, that was

Jack Smurdens. No, I don't know what happened to Backhouse. I never saw hide nor hair of him.

Anyrate, I eventually got across. Don't ask me how, but I did. Then, with the scrap with Edwards – well, see, after he'd left Glenore, Edwards had been drinking a fair bit and he'd gone all puffy. He couldn't even pull his riding boots on. Anyhow, we goes round behind the bottom pub and everybody comes along to have a look. But he marked up easy, see, so I said to him, I said, 'Look, why chop each other to pieces just fer the enjoyment of the crowd watchin' us?'

'Righto. Fair enough,' he says, so we just had a bit of a spar, aye, and in the end they stopped it and called it a draw and then we all went and had a beer.

But I found out something about Edwards that day – see, he was slow. And in the fight game, I'm what's called a head-hunter. I generally hit me opponent around the head. But you couldn't do that with Edwards. With Edwards, if you wanted to put him down by hitting him around the head, the only way you could do it was to use a pick handle. But I found one weakness. See, he was open to the left with the ribs. He was easy to hit there and I reckoned, if I ever got a good one in, he'd fold up like a camp stretcher.

So, no, it didn't eventuate into much, really. But the point of the story is – you remember that feller, Womp Burns. I've already told you about him, aye – the fat feller who'd stick his finger up his bum when he offered some of his mum's cake to the other ringers and that. Anyhow, Womp done some droving as well and just three days later he was swimming some bullocks across the river, right where I swam across it, and a big croc took one of his bullocks. Fair dinkum. Right where I swam.

And what's more, up till the time I done it, only two other people had swum the Norman River and got across safe. One was that feller Norman Smith who'd fixed me up for the scrap with Ronny Paul. Smithy swam it for a bet. Then the other one that swam it was a feller called Harry Readford and, if you know your history, you'll know that Harry Readford was also known as Captain Starlight. Now, there's a well-known feller for you. A drover and a cattle duffer, too, I might add. Yeah, Captain Starlight. He was the other feller that swam the Norman River. So I'm in pretty good company, aye. And they still talk about that in Normanton and it's been written up in the newspapers and all. I'll even show you the piece out of the paper, if you like.

28

Okay, I'm out on Wernadinga now, with the Smith boys. Yeah, still in the Gulf. Wernadinga's a 1000-square-mile place over near Burketown that their uncle, a feller called Allan Richards, owned. I think he married the mother's sister or something. Actually, years before, he'd owned Mutton Hole, just out of Normanton, where he did a bit of cattle duffing and he also bought off other duffers. Then he sold Mutton Hole to Womp Burns's father, old Tom Burns, and he walked all his stock to Wernadinga.

Now, just one thing that might give you some idea how big the place was – see, we're out mustering, one time. But instead of a packhorse plant, we had an old Bedford truck to carry all our gear. So we went from camp to camp and when we had about four hundred head of bullocks this Allan Richards decided we'd take them back to the homestead. Anyhow, on our way back, we went through country on Wernadinga that this Allan Richards had never been through before. He said, 'Blowed if I know where we are, so let's just keep goin' till I get me bearings.'

So we kept walking these bullocks, then we come into country we couldn't even drive the truck through. So the truck had to go the long way around, and, of course, it took all our gear with it. So there we are, we're still walking this mob, and we're all tonguing for a drink, and we're hoping Allan Richards will soon find his bearings. Then we see some brumbies come up from out of a gully, where they'd been digging for water, so I says to the fellers, 'Geez, I'm tonguin' fer a drink. I think I'll go down where them brumbies come up from.'

'Okay,' they said, 'you go down 'n' we'll keep goin on fer a bit.'

So they went on with the cattle and I tied me horse up and I went down into this little gully with me quart pot. And, like, oh, the water's real soupy, aye. The brumbies had made a real mess of it. Manure and everything. Now, I'm used of drinking crook water, but this was foul. Terrible. Anyway, I gets a gutful and I rides back up to the mob. And, you won't believe it, there's all the fellers, up with the cattle, and they've found some old Aboriginal springs. Yeah, these lovely rockholes about three or four feet wide and you could look in and reach in and there's all this beautiful crystal-clear water. And Allan Richards didn't even know they was there.

'Oh, Goldie,' they said, 'have a taste'a this. It's beautiful.'

'Thanks very much fer callin' out 'n' lettin' me know,' I says.

Anyhow, we eventually got them back and, not long after, I went with a drover feller, Ray Findlay, taking bullocks from Wernadinga, along the Leichhardt River, down to the railhead at Kajabbi. Ray was a well-known jockey. Actually, now I think of it, he was only one of two hoops in the Commonwealth to have ridden every winner at a race meeting. True, the Queen even presented him with a saddle with a big brass thing on it. The other jockey got the same. Anyhow, that was Ray, and he was still jockeying, on and off. But I remember we had exactly 808 bullocks and there was six of us: Ray. Meself. A young white kid. Then we had two Murries and a cook. The cook was Ray's brother-in-law. He had a broken arm which made it a bit hard, cooking and packing and unpacking the packhorses.

But I just loved droving. Just loved it, aye. Like I said before, after you spend some time with them they get so broke in, they're almost tame. Like, the main thing is to keep both wings straight and when they're broke in and you're moving them along and they're strung out and you see the lead start to swing over, all you've got to do is ride up, halfway along, and call out,

'Move over boys', and they will. Or if that doesn't work, you might just have to crack the whip and the whole lot up front will swing right over.

But, like, droving's all different, aye. There'll be other times when you can sense trouble. I don't know. It's a feeling you get. Like when we had a couple of rushes at a station on the Leichhardt River called Augusta Downs. And when one bullock goes, the whole lot go. Yeah, they'll rush. We don't call it a 'stampede' like the Americans do, we call it a 'rush' or a 'jump'. And when there's a rush, the next morning after you've got them back together, you glance your eye over the mob and maybe there's one little feller that's always been with his mates, well, he'll be looking around going, 'Moo! Moo-oo!', singing out for his mates and if he doesn't get an answer, then you'll know there's some still missing out there somewhere.

And that's why you always camp near the fire and close to a tree because, see, if they rush, the fire'll split the mob and you might just have enough time to jump out of your swag and get behind the tree. Yeah, one of the rushes we had at Augusta Downs, I got behind a tree and when they'd gone past, the bark of the tree was all torn. That's fair dinkum. Ray told me that after one rush he had, a couple of bullocks ended up hanging up in the forks of a tree with their necks broke. Oh, he'd seen it all, had Ray – broken horns, broken legs, the lot. Terrible, aye. And, also, when it's raining or just lightning, you never lay in your swag. Even with two men on nightwatch you're still on tenterhooks, waiting for them to go. They don't always go, mind you, but you can't take the risk because, if they come your way, you could well be trampled to death. True – I've had them come through the camp and there's flour everywhere and they've smashed all the pack bags.

Then other times they'll rush for no real reason. Not one you can pinpoint, anyway. They're funny, aye. Something upsets them and away they'll go, just like that. It depends a lot on what sort of day they've had. That's why, when they're on a waterhole or a bore or whatever, Ray always gave them a great big gutful of water, of a night, before we spread them out to feed. Yeah, as a rule, the bigger the gutful they get, the more they'll feed and the better they'll settle. But the ones in the mob that you've really got to watch are the milkers' poddies. See, they're the poddies that've been reared up by hand, around the station. And sometimes they get homesick and try and sneak off of a night to head back home. Then, when the other bullocks see them walking away, they'll want to follow them. Oh, they're a nuisance, them milkers' poddies. Any drover'll tell you that.

And with the rushes at Augusta Downs, when we got them back together, the next day, we had the same as we'd left Wernadinga with – 808. That's why I remember the number 808 because we had to count them again. But, see, one funny thing, Ray always had a difficulty counting the bullocks. Now, how I go about it is, I always count them as if three is one. Like, when three bullocks go past, I count them as one. And when you get up to thirty-three, you just add one and that's the hundred and, when I got the hundred, I'd tie a knot in me whip. But Ray didn't count them that way. He'd count them the hard way. Like, three would go past and he'd say, 'That's three.' Then two more go past and he'd say, 'That's two, plus the three, so that's five.'

Anyhow, one time after we counted them, Ray was two out, so I says, 'How do yer count 'em, Ray?'

And when he told me I says, 'Ray, yer don't count 'em like that. Yer count 'em as three is one.'

He says, 'Yeah, really?'

So there we are, we're lying in dinner camp and a mob of galahs goes past, so I says, 'Okay, Ray, count them galahs your way, then count 'em my way, 'n' we'll see how yer go.' So he starts counting the galahs his way, then he counts them my way and he says, 'Geez, Goldie, yer right, that's the way ter go.' And from then on that's the way he did it.

Anyrate, so we're past Augusta Downs and, one day, we're going along and Ray comes up and says, 'Oh, they're settlin' down now, aren't they Goldie? They're settlin' down real well, aye?'

But, see, I wasn't quite too sure, especially so soon after Augusta Downs. But anyway, to save any sort of argument, I said something like, 'Yeah, they're settlin' down a bit, maybe.'

Then the next day he comes along and he says the exact same thing. 'Oh, they're settlin' down now, aren't they Goldie? They're settlin' down real well, aye?' And this went on for about a week. Each day he'd say, 'Oh, boy, they're settlin' down now, aren't they, Goldie, aye?'

But I'm still not too confident they are. Then, one day, out of the blue, this ute pulls up and a feller jumps out and calls out to Ray, 'Are yer ready, Ray?'

And Ray says, 'Yeah, mate, they've settled down beautiful.' Then he unsaddles his horse and says to me, 'Oh, look, Goldie, you take 'em along now. I've gotta go 'n' ride at a race meetin' in Townsville. See yer later.'

So he left me there – yeah, with this young white kid, the two Murries and his brother-in-law, the cook with a broken arm. By then we're about halfway down to the railhead at Kajabbi and, really, they was a good mob of bullocks. But still, I did feel a bit short of hands and, just after Ray left, that's where I run into a bush Murri and that's one thing I'll never forget because, see, back in the fifties there was still a few bush Murries roaming around. I say 'a few' because the missionaries used to send out other Murries to coax them in. But anyhow, I had this pocket watch, see, which had Roman figures on it, not numbers but Roman figures. So we're taking these bullocks along and one of my Murries, he comes around and he says, 'Goldie, big Murri up 'em tree like 'im goanna.'

I'm at the tail of the mob, like, so I goes over and there's this bush Murri. He must've seen the bullocks coming and he scarpered up the tree to wait till they'd passed. Now, I reckoned this fella didn't speak much English because I could see how he hadn't had much contact with whites. Well, like, he had no shirt on and just a bit of a pair of trousers. His tribal scars was across his chest and down his arms. Then he had a sugar bag, his spear, his woomera, and he also had his firestick for when he wanted to light a fire.

I says, 'Where you bin' go, bunjie?', 'bunjie' meaning 'friend'.

'Bin' go so-and-so,' he says. It was to a place not far from Julia Creek.

Anyrate, I thought I might be able to use him, so I says, 'You bin' tell 'em when other ringer Murri come along on yarraman – horse – you bin' tell 'im boss says you come along with us.'

'Yeah, righto, boss.'

So the other Murri gets him and gives him a shirt and we saddle one of the packhorses for him and, when we get him up to camp that night, the other Murri makes up a bit of a swag for him. Then I got him to wash his hands and things and we give him a feed. So I kept him for a couple of days, then I says, 'Now look here, bunjie.' What was his name, now? Yeah, that's right, it was Drumduff because I think he might've been born on Drumduff Station. I says, 'Drumduff, you bin' watchin' them other Murries ridin' round minya – cattle. Now you ride round night time, watch them minya.'

'Yeah, righto, boss.'

So I gets him to ride around with one of the Murries to get the hang of it. Then, when I thought he'd be okay, I decided to give him a go. Now, at midnight, bullocks always stand up and wander off to have a bit of a pick and a crap. You can just about put the clock to it. So just after midnight I made sure I had them all settled down again then I goes to this Drumduff.

'Righto Drumduff,' I says, 'now you bin' do 'em watch now like 'em migalo – white man.'

'Yeah, boss. Yeah, boss.'

So I took out me watch, the one with the Roman figures, and I tied it around his shirt with a bit of string. Like, he'd never seen a watch before so I explained. 'You bin' watchin' here,' I say, and he looked at the watch. 'See, there's a little man 'n' a big man – that's the hour and minute hands. Little man he bin' goin' across that first post – one o'clock – then he bin' goin' across to second post – two o'clock. Now, the big man, he bin' goin' right round 'n' round all same alonga boundary rider. So when him come up 'n' meet the little man at the second post, you bin' come 'n' wake me up.'

'Yeah, boss. Yeah, boss.'

Then I wound the watch around again and I made him repeat it a couple of times, just to make sure he's got the hang of it.

'Yeah, boss, 'im bin' right, boss.'

Anyhow, there's these two dingoes that trot into camp. But I don't worry about them, I just go and lay down and I listen to this Drumduff sing. And, oh, I tell you, there's nothing more wonderful than to hear a Murri sing in his own lingo as he goes around the bullocks. Oh, it's really something. Anyhow, I gets to sleep and I vaguely remember the horsetailer getting up. He's the first one up, see, because he's the one who looks after the horses. So that would've been well past two a.m., but I'm sort of having a good sleep. But, when I hear the cook stirring the fire, I wake up in a bit of a panic. I think, Oh, he's cleared out on me. So I look around and then I see him, he's on his horse, round the other side of the mob.

'Hey, Drumduff!' I call out.

'Yeah, boss.'

'You bin' come here.'

So he comes around. 'Where's bin' watch?' I ask.

He says, 'Here, boss' and he gets off the horse and I get the watch and I put it to me ear and it's still ticking away, beautiful.

'Why you no bin' come 'n' wake me up, Drumduff?'

'Well, boss,' he says. 'I bin' watchin' dat little man boss, watchin' 'im go past dat first post so I put 'im in me pocket 'n' I sing 'im songs round minya 'n' I bin' lookin' watch again boss 'n' he bin' comin' round 'n' dat big man 'im bin' goin' round alonga boundary so I put 'im back in me pocket 'n' I ride 'em round minya again, singin' 'em songs 'n' I bin' watchin' 'im again 'n' dat little fella he bin' comin' up real close ter dat second post 'n' dat big man he bin' comin' right up close, too, so I puts 'im back in me pocket 'n' I bin' ridin' round minya 'n' I bin' singin' 'em songs 'n', when I look again boss, dat little man 'im bin' gone right past dat post, chasin' dat big man. So I bin' tryin' ter catch 'im next time. But I keep missin' 'im, boss. I miss 'im past der post, every time.'

Oh, yeah, I'll always remember that one, aye. So then we continues on and when we gets about seven days out of Kajabbi, Ray turns up one night. Someone drove him out in a ute. 'Have yer had any trouble?' he says.

I says, 'No.'

Then the next night we butchered a bullock and we give half to the feller who drove Ray out. Yeah, apparently, Ray'd done well at the race meeting. I think it was the Townsville Cup or something. Oh, he was a good hoop, was Ray. Very much sought after. But, mind you, he was also pretty selective so he only rode the best of horses. I mean, if you could get Ray Findlay for a hoop then you was pretty sure of a winner.

But, see, Ray was always at me to go in with him. He had a small property, himself, just outside Kajabbi, and he wanted us to duff a few poddies. He had some very big neighbours and, of course, I had a bit of a rep for scrapping so I guess he reckoned if I was there, I'd also be a good backstop for him. But, really, I wanted to give the duffing away, aye. I mean, I was tempted, but then I thought, No, I'll get a job 'n' go back on wages. But, don't get me wrong, Ray was a fantastic feller. Very well respected. Very well liked. Nobody said a bad word about Ray Findlay, and he was a very knowledgeable drover. He taught me most of all I know about droving. In fact, just about everything I know about droving he'd already forgot.

29

So we gets to Kajabbi and Ray pays me off and I goes down to Cloncurry. There's a big trucking firm there called Hudson's Trucking Company. A family thing, I think it was. Anyway, the feller there, I forget his name just now, well, he had something like 150 drums of petrol to take up to Normanton so I says, 'Can I cadge a lift, mate?'

'Yeah, okay.' And I got a lift with him. But, oh, it just rained and it rained and it absolutely poured down and we got up to a place called Donors Hill Station, just south of Wondoola, and we gets bogged. We're stuck good and proper. So then we had to cut some wooden rails by axe and we rolled each one of them 44-gallon drums onto the rails, down off the truck, then we had to push every drum through all the mud and the slush, up on to hard ground. That took a couple of days, at least, then we had to push the truck up there also, so the wheels could get traction. Anyrate, we had to leave the drums behind then and, when we finally gets to Normanton, I says to the bloke, I says, 'Oh, mate, how much do I owe yer fer the trip?'

And he says, 'Geez, Goldie, it's more like how much do I owe you?'

Anyhow, while I was in town, I run into the new manager of Iffley Station, a feller named Alf Filo. Yeah, by then Bill Young had left Iffley and he'd gone over to Alexander Station, in the Northern Territory, and he'd taken Mrs McQueen with him. Oh yeah, he was still sweating on her. Actually, she wasn't a bad-looking bit of gear, if the truth be known. Now here's a story I was told – see, when Bill and Mrs McQueen went over to

Alexander Station, of course, the first thing he does is, he invites all the surrounding managers and that over for a big barbecue to get to know everyone. Anyhow, there he is and he's introducing this Mrs McQueen as his wife, aye. Like, 'G'day, nice ter meet yer, I'm Bill Young 'n' this's me wife, Mrs Young.'

So he's now introduced this Mrs McQueen as his wife so everyone knows them as Mr and Mrs Young. But in fact, what he'd done was, some time back, he'd chucked the real Mrs Young out to sweat on this Mrs McQueen. Like, there'd been no divorce or nothing. So they're starting to settle in and then on Saturday nights 4LG had a music session where everyone sends cheerios and requests out over the radio to all the station workers and that. So everyone's sitting around their homesteads on one of these nights and this request comes over the radio: 'Here's a song for Mr Bill Young, out on Alexander Station, and also to Mrs Young who, for everyone's information is, in fact, Mrs McQueen. A big cheerio, Bill, from the real Mrs Young.' So everyone now knows he's sweating on her, aye.

But, anyway, where was I? Yeah, that's right, I'm in Normanton, aye, and I runs into this Alf Filo from Iffley and Alf says, 'Goldie, are yer lookin' fer a job? I'm after a horse breaker.'

Well, I still had all me breaking in gear out on Shady Lagoons so I says, 'Too right, I am.' I says, 'I'd love ter go breakin' in.'

Okay, so I goes over to Iffley and I'm breaking in. Now, I've been out with other horse breakers and you never stop learning but, see, this's generally the way I go about it. For instance, let's say I'm breaking in a young colt. First of all you need a very quiet and calm breaking-in horse, a companion horse. Now, a round yard's generally about twenty-two or twenty-three feet across and I'm on the breaking-in horse and I get the colt between me and the rails of the round yard and I trot the colt around the yard.

Then I have the halter with the throat lash undone and I slip the halter over his head, then lean over and do the throat lash up. When that's done, I get off the breaking-in horse, take the saddle off, and I'll have it so it's standing alongside the colt, up against the rail. They're both standing there. Okay, then I get a pair of front hobbles and I get under the breaking-in horse so the colt can't see me and I'll slip the hobbles on his front feet. Then there's what's called a sideline – that's a chain with another hobble strap on it – and you get that between his front leg and his nearside hind leg, then you pull his leg a little bit forward till, eventually, you get the sideline on it.

After you've done that, you lead the breaking-in horse out of the yard. Of course, the colt wants to follow but he can't move, aye, because he's tied up with the hobble strap and the sideline. So then there's just you and him in the yard. Next, I get a saddlecloth and I put it on the end of a long stick and I rub him around the head with it, round his head, going down his ribs and shoulder. It's what's called 'bagging him down'. At first he'll flinch but then, after he gets used of that, I take the saddlecloth off the rod and I get the cloth in me hand and I start rubbing him around the head, and talking to him. Round the head. Round the shoulders. And talking to him. Keep bagging him down till he stops flinching away. And around the hind legs especially. Bag him. Bag him. Then you pull him around and you do the off-side. Bag him down. Bag him down. Bag him down till he stops flinching.

Okay, something important, if a young horse shows the whites of its eyes, it's a bad horse and I dodge them. Yeah, I dodge them. They're not worth the trouble because, see, on stations they've generally got two to three hundred horses, so you don't waste your time on any bad ones. Well, I've broke in bad horses, aye, and they come at you, the mongrel things, with their ears back.

So after I bag him down I get up close, see, and I start patting him. I pat him down there. I pat down there. Pat around. Pat around. Get his hind feet and pick them up. Pick them up. Get him quiet so he knows he's not going to get hurt. Get him to trust you. When he gets used of that then I just sort of jump up a little bit on him to let him feel me weight. Just a little bit. Then I come off. Then up again. Down. But still keep patting him, especially round the head. It's just a thing of mine, all the time I like to pat him around the head, and talk to him. Always talk to him. And I rub me hand under me armpits and I let him smell me. But always pat him. Always be talking to him.

Then after I've got him extra quiet I take the hobbles off him and I put what they call the tackling on him. The tackling's a leather strap that goes over near his wither. And then I put a bridle on him. Now he'll be chewing at the bit that's in his mouth because it's uncomfortable, aye. Then I get the reins and I'll cross the near one through a little pulley thing and I have a little cord and when I pull it, it pulls his head down a little bit. Not much, just a little at a time. It's called 'tying the head down'. Any horses you break in, you must tie their heads down so they've got a nice arch in the neck. Otherwise he'll always be looking around like this, up in the air. Stargazers, they call them. So then you tighten the cord a little bit more. Then after about an hour you tighten it a bit more and you eventually get the head tied right down.

But I make them walk around as much as I can. Make them walk. Make them walk. Then I lunge him. I pull his the reins around. Keep pulling his head around. Pull him around this way. Pull him around that way. Keep pulling him around. That way, when you've got your horse broke in, and you pull the reins to turn his head, he'll feel the pull on that side and he'll go around. Anyway, by then, I've still got quite a few more to break in so, while he's in the tackling with his head down, I'll get another colt or a filly and start going through the same thing with that one. Then, after I've got the second one in the tackling, you come back to the first feller and you teach him to lead. Now, most stations, they'll ask me, 'What do yer use ter lead them?' and I say, 'I use a whip,' and they'll say, 'Good, that's what we want. We want them led to the whip.'

See, that's when you get your colt and you tie him up to a post, reasonably short, and you flick him with a whip. Not to sting him but just to annoy him. And when you flick him with the whip, he'll pull back. He'll pull back. But you keep flicking him. Flick him around the legs and he's pulling back like this and sometimes they get right down and he'll try and pull away like that and he'll get up and he'll try and get away that way, then he'll pull around. But you keep flicking him till, in the end – not long, half an hour at the most – he'll lead like a baby. And all the while I keep rubbing him over the head and the face. Keep picking his legs up. Keep patting him under where the girth goes. Talk to him. Go on the other side. Do the same thing.

Ringers at Iffley Station, Goldie second from left

Next, I'll let him smell the saddle. Then I'll throw it on. Then I'll take it off. Throw it back on. On and off till he gets used to it and he just stands there. Then I put the saddle cloth on and I put the saddle on and I girth him up. He's pretty used to the girth now because I've had the tackling on. So I girth him up, then I lead him around. Lead him around. Now, because there's this strange thing on his back, that's when he might buck or do a crow hop or hump up. That's okay, then when he's settled, maybe I'll get a bit of hessian and tie it on the stirrup irons so he gets used to seeing feet there.

After that I put me foot in the stirrup iron and let him feel me weight. Get back down again. Get up again. Up, down. Up, down. And I always get on and off on the off-side too. Break them in both sides. Then slowly I put me leg over him. I'll get on and then I'll let him walk me around the yard. If he doesn't want to move, I might jog him on a bit. And, really, that's enough for one day. If you give them too much the first day they go sour. They just sort of stand there and you can't do anything with them. Generally, I break in about four a week so I'll work on breaking in another one for the rest of that day.

Next day I'll bring him back into the round yard, saddle him up, and lead him out into the big receiving yard. That's where I teach him to lead off another horse. See, I generally have a halter strap on my breaking-in horse, with the girth going through it so if he tries to pull away he can't because he's got to pull the weight of the other horse with him. So, yeah, then I give him a bit of a ride, not far, only a couple of hundred yards. Walk him around the homestead. Let him go past a car. Walk among the chooks. Keep patting him. Keep talking to him. And when I've got confidence, I'll get him out in the bush a bit and I'll walk him around there. Then, after he can walk a couple of mile, he goes out into the mustering camp. There was two mustering camps on Iffley. And, to start with, when he goes out in the camp, the fellers only use him for just little stuff, like to hold cattle. Next, they might trot out and bring a beast back in. Then after about a month he's fully seasoned and broke in to do cattle work. But you only give your horses three months out in the camp before you let them go for a spell. And when you bring them back, after a spell, and you ride them for the first time, they're likely to do anything. Oh, they'll climb and buck and all that, aye.

Anyway, so that's what I was doing out at Iffley. But, while I was breaking in I'm starting to feel sawing pains down in me groin and a little egg-shaped thing come out, like a bulb, and it got so bad that I had to lay down in the round yard and put me feet up on the bottom rail to make it go back in. Anyway, I finished up going over to Alf Filo's wife. See, she talked to the Flying Doctor every couple of days and she got on the radio and said, 'I've got a white stockman here. Looks like he's got a pretty bad hernia.'

The doctor says, 'Well, he'd better get it done straightaway or else he could end up with a strangulated hernia.' That's when your intestines get knotted up and, apparently, you get septic, like blood poisoning or something.

I says, 'Okay then,' so I left Iffley and I goes into Normanton to see the matron there. I says, 'Matron, I'd better go 'n' get this hernia done.'

'Well, don't go to Cloncurry,' she says. 'I don't like the surgeon there. He's made a few boo-boos. Go down to Charters Towers.'

I says, 'Oh, okay then', which was going to work out well because, see, by then I had a bit of money and I was thinking how I'd go to the Towers to pay off the rest of me D4 International 15 cwt, I'd left there with that mechanic feller, Frank Stangar. Yeah, so now I could pay that off and pick it up at the same time I got me hernia seen to.

So it's now November '57, aye, and I was only in Normanton for a couple of days and, see, there was an Aboriginal woman,

Gladys Grogan. Gladys was very, very attractive. Pretty light. I knew her well. She'd had kids before, two boys; one was by some station manager and the other one was from a saddler in Normanton. He had the mail run. I forget his name just now, but she'd also had a kid to him. Yeah, both white fellers. Anyhow, I'm staying at Smithy's place – the feller who dobbed me in to fight that Ronny Paul – and I'm lying down on the verandah one night and Gladys walks past so I says, 'G'day Gladys, where yer goin'?'

She says, 'Oh, g'day Goldie, I'm goin' up ter Miles' place.'

I said, 'Well, I'll come up with yer.'

'Okay,' she says.

Anyrate, we goes up there and the long and the short of it is that we fooled around at her mate's place, aye. I was twenty-two and she was twenty-five and, in them days, it was under the Act – Section 28A – that anybody who was found out to be having an intimate relationship with an Aboriginal woman, no matter how old she was, well, you'd get charged and they'd fine you for carnal knowledge. Yeah, Section 28A. I remember it. Anyhow, that was that, and then Alec Baker, that feller from the Territory who'd been the head stockman on Glenore for a while, well, he had a Land Rover and he wanted to go back home to Nebo for Christmas, so I asked if I could cadge a lift with him down to the Towers to get me hernia seen to and to pick up me truck.

30

So then me and Alex Baker, we heads off to Charters Towers in his Land Rover. I remember we got to a place called Forsayth, just south of Georgetown. Now, wherever I went, I used to pour curry powder all over me tucker. It wouldn't matter if it was salads or corned beef or damper or what, I'd plaster it with curry powder. Rumours even got around Normanton how I'd put curry powder on me pudding, which I never done. But that was the rumour. So anyway, me and Alex Baker, we're having a feed at this hotel at Forsayth, see. I forget what I was eating but there's a whole lot of us sitting around this one big table and I asked the little piece that served the tucker out, I says, 'Have yer got any curry powder?'

'What for?' she says.

I says, 'Ter put on me tucker.'

And the bloke next to me pipes up and he says, 'Curry powder's fer babies, mate. If yer wanta make it real hot, put some chilli in it 'n' see how yer go.'

Then Baker pipes up and he says to the feller, 'Watch what yer sayin' mate or Goldie'll take yer outside 'n' show yer just how hot things can really get.'

So yeah, I was a fanatic on curry powder, aye, plus me rep as a fighter was growing, especially with Alex Baker, aye. Anyhow, we finished up in the Towers and we booked ourselves in at the Southern Cross Hotel – the Blood 'n' Guts, aye. And did I tell you it was owned by a woman named Bennett? Everyone called her Mother Bennett. Yeah, anyway, so we're in the bar, me and this Alec Baker, and a big lump of a feller starts trying to pick me. Like, he'd say 'You're a this 'n' you're a that' in a real loud-mouth sort of way.

No, I didn't know him from a bar of soap, and no one else knew much about him, neither. So I says, 'Righto, mate, let's sort this out then.' Then I said to Mother Bennett, I says, 'Ring up a taxi. We're goin' outa town ter have this scrap.' See, because you don't much go fighting in towns or that because, next thing, the police are there and you're up for disturbing the peace or whatever. So I says, 'We'll go outa town.'

'Okay,' he says.

Next thing, Mother Bennett steps in and she says, 'Goldie, yer not goin' nowhere ter fight 'cause yer've got a hernia 'n' yer about ter book yerself into the hospital.'

And when this other feller hears this, oh, well, he's real apologetic. 'Sorry mate,' he says, 'I never knew yer had a hernia. Real sorry.' But, see, he must've heard about me somewhere, aye, and all he wanted to do was to build his own rep up by picking me. So I nearly had a bit of a stoush there, aye, and, of course, one of us would've got done like a dinner and it wasn't going to be me, if I could help it, hernia and all.

Anyhow, then Alex Baker leaves for Nebo soon after and I says to Mother Bennett, I says, 'I'm off up ter the hospital now ter see what they can do.'

So I'm walking up to the hospital and there's this older woman and a younger woman sitting in a Land Rover, up inside the hospital grounds, and I says to them, I says, 'Excuse me, where's the Outpatients?'

'Oh, just up there where that buildin' is.'

I says, 'Oh, good, thanks.'

Then as I walked away I heard the older woman say to the younger one, 'Boy, he's not a bad line, aye?'

Of course, I didn't think any more of it and I gets to the hospital and I sees the doctor and he took one look at me hernia and he says, 'Geez, I can tell from the bulge yer've had it fer a fair while, so we'd better get it fixed, 'n' soon. How about tomorra?'

Three weeks I was in there. Oh, they just cut it open, then they pushed it back in, where it was bulging. Then he had this big hunk of gauze and they put gauze in there. It strengthens it better. Then they sewed the insides part back up, where it was coming out. Then they sewed the outside part up. So I'm in hospital, recovering, and I gets talking to this nurse and she turns out to be the younger one of the two women I'd seen in the Land Rover, the day I first went up to see the doctor. Edith Combridge, her name was, and the older one turned out to be her mother, Elma. Anyhow, this Edith piece was doing her nurse's training and so I got to know her pretty well. When I say I got to know her pretty well, I mean that she was me favourite nurse, like. Yeah, so when I got out of hospital, just before Christmas, Edith's mother, Elma, she invited me to go around to their place to stay because she said she wanted to learn about the Gulf and things like that. Elma was a widow. Her husband had been in the 6th Division over in Egypt and he got discharged in 1942 from war wounds and he died as a result, some time in the late forties.

So I stayed with them and Elma's two young boys, Ben and Aubury, over the Christmas. Oh, and the younger sister, Pearl, she would've been there too. And during that time I also went around to Frank Stangar's place and paid the final payment on me truck, the D4 International 15 cwt. But, see, I found out that Frank had done the wrong thing by me because someone told me how, whenever Frank was servicing Dan Gallagher's mail truck, he'd let Dan take mine out on the mail run. So that's not right, is it?

Then, with the truck – see, the mother, Elma, she wanted some crates brung up from Townsville Railway Station, up to

Charters Towers, and my little truck was just the bee's knees
for that. 'Okay,' I says. So there's me, Edith and Elma and
Pearl, we all goes down to Townsville to get this gear and, while
we're there, we goes round to the beach part where there's a
picnic area and there's a little food place and I'm looking at the
sea and especially all the waves. I mean, in the Gulf there's lots
of water but there's no waves, aye. So I'm looking at the sea,
looking at it, and anyway the girl behind the little serving thing
says, 'What's wrong with 'im?'

Elma says, 'Oh, he's from the Gulf. He's lookin' at the waves.'

And the girl said, 'Oh, whereabouts in the Gulf?'

Elma says, 'Normanton.'

'Oh, I've got a brother up there.' She said, 'His name's
Norman Smith.'

And blow me down, it's the same Norman Smith – Smithy –
the fisherman who orchestrated me into that blue up there,
with Ronny Paul. Yeah, it's a small world, aye? So anyway we
had a bit of a chat for a while, then I went back to looking at
the sea and I remember it as clear as day – I was looking at the
sea and I said to meself, 'I really like this Edith. I'd like ter come
down this way 'n' see more of her.' Because, see, also, I'd
noticed how the ringers around the Towers got it real easy. Well,
like, at a lot of the stations they'd camp at the homestead every
night. They've got electric light, not the old carbide lamps. No
packhorses. They've got cars so they can go to town on
weekends. There's picture theatres. There's lots of white women
so they had girlfriends. Oh yeah, Charters Towers was noted for
having three girls to every one man. Yeah, noted for it. And so I
thought, Well, this's the only way ter go ringin', you know. And
that's when I decided to go back to the Gulf and tidy things up
there, then come back down to the Towers to start courting this
Edith Combridge piece. So all that was on me mind and so,
anyrate, one time I was talking to Edith and I said, 'What do yer

say if I come back down here 'n' live 'n' we can go out together 'n' all that?'

And she said, 'Yeah, I'd like that. I'd like that very much.'

So she was pretty much my way too, aye. And that was 1958, early. So then I was looking about for someone to go back to Normanton with me, in me truck, to help with the driving, like, and that's when I met up with Neville Huxley. Neville was a bit younger than me. He only had one ear. He lost the other one in a truck accident or something. Anyway, I says to Neville, I says, 'Do yer wanta come up ter Normanton with me? I need someone ter share the drivin' with.'

He said, 'Yeah, I'd love to but I can't drive.'

I says, 'Oh, don't worry about that. I'll teach yer as we go along.'

'Okay, then,' he says.

So that was all set. Then, just as we was about leaving, Del Hunty and his troupe arrive in town for race week, so I goes around to say g'day.

'Goldie,' he says, 'great ter see yer. Are yer up fer a fight?'

I says, 'No, Dello. Not this time.' I says. 'I'm goin' back ter the Gulf fer the last time 'cause I'm keen on comin' back to a nice little piece down here.'

He says, 'Good on yer.' He says, 'So, how're yer travellin' fer money?'

I says, 'If the truth be known, mate, I'm not doin' too good just at the moment.' So then he give me ten quid and I says, 'Oh, Dello, I won't be able ter pay this back.'

He says, 'Don't worry, Goldie.' He says, 'I made a fair bit'a money outa you.'

So he must've backed me somewhere in a fight, aye. Then, anyway, me and Neville – the one-eared feller – we headed off after that and he sort of learned to drive along the way. Yeah, that little International was the first vehicle he ever drove.

31

Yeah, so I'm pretty keen on this Edith, aye, and I'm on me way back to Normanton with this Neville Huxley to sort things out. Oh, yeah, he came in handy with the driving. Actually, he was pretty good and also, because it was the wet season, he also came in real handy helping push me truck out of bogs. Anyrate, we gets to Georgetown and I still had a little bit of Dello's money left, so I goes into the pub and, blow me down, there's Tommy Edwards. 'Goldie,' he says. 'Boy, am I glad to see you.'

'Yeah, same here,' I says. 'So what's doin'?'

He says, 'Mate, I'm lookin' fer a fight 'n' nobody'll fight me.'

I says, 'Well, yer can't blame 'em, can yer?'

He says, 'Well, what about you, then? Are yer up fer a scrap?'

But, see, I wasn't that long out of hospital after the hernia, so I explains it to him and he says, 'Oh, that's alright. I just won't hit yer down there.'

And that got me thinking, aye, because I'd never had a real good go at Edwards. But, see, I'd lost a lot of weight, being in hospital. I was only about ten stone by now and seeing Edwards hadn't worked for a while, he was every bit of thirteen stone. Anyway, like I might've said, when I'd sparred with him before, one thing I worked out was that Edwards was easy to mark. You know, you'd just scratch him and he'd mark up. So I says, 'Okay, then, I'm up fer a scrap.'

He says, 'Look; tell yer what we'll do. I feel like fightin' right now so how's about we have an argument, 'n' then we'll go outside 'n' have a good go.' He says, 'But I'll look after yer.'

So we made something up – I forget what it was – and we had

this argument. Okay, we goes outside, out the back of the pub. Someone sings out 'Fight! Fight!' and all the bar comes out. Then we're just about to hoe into it when a copper arrives, a feller called someone Aarons. A real good copper, he was. A good bloke, too. He says, 'Look, I don't want you fellers scrappin' here, like this. I've got some gloves up the police station so how's about, tomorra, yer have the fight up behind there, with gloves on.'

We said, 'Yeah, fair enough. Tomorra it is, then.'

So we goes up there the next day and, of course, half the town turns up and I'm barefooted and there's stones all over the ground. Yeah, sharp stones. But, see, the truth of it is that I wasn't ready for a real good go at Edwards. Not really, not then, especially so soon after me hernia, and they stopped the fight after about three rounds. Well, he was getting on top of me, aye. In the end I could hardly lift a glove up and, also, I'd cut me foot on one of these stones. Still, no excuses. On the day, Edwards was the better fighter and that's that.

But, see, I cut me foot pretty bad and when I got back to Normanton, I'm staying with Smithy and there's a ship called the *Wee-wack* that comes up the Norman River from Cairns about three times a year, with supplies for the town. A diesel thing it was. Not very big. I think it only had one hold. So the *Wee-wack* arrives with supplies and cement and drums of fuel. It was a long weekend. A Monday, public holiday. So the stevedore, a feller called Charlie Pointon, offers eight pound for the day's work and, of course, all the Murries turn up and I also join in. But eight pound – I mean, the usual wage was something like twelve pound ten a week and we got eight quid, just for the day, just because it was a public holiday. Anyhow, I'm working there barefooted and some cement got into the wound on me foot and I finished up in hospital with it and they pumped me up with penicillin and all that till they got it cleaned up. Then, when I gets out, it's now just after the wet in 1958 and I runs into this feller. I forget his name right now but I knew him from somewhere. He says, 'Goldie, are yer lookin' fer work, mate?'

'Too right I am.'

'Well,' he says, 'they want ringers out on Talawanta Station 'n' if yer go out there yer can help me kill two birds with the one stone.'

I says, 'Why's that?'

It turns out he delivered the mail out that way and he had a buyer for an American army jeep at Talawanta and he wanted me to drive it out for him. So that's what I done; I drove the jeep out to Talawanta. Talawanta's an outstation, about thirty mile from the main homestead of Lorraine Station. Oh, Lorraine's a big place on the Leichhardt River. Massive. Over three thousand square mile, maybe. To give you some idea, just on Lorraine itself, they branded something like fourteen thousand calves a year and that's not counting Talawanta. No, I don't know how big Talawanta was, but they done a lot of branding there, too. So I drives this American army jeep out and when I gets to Talawanta I gets me swag and me saddle and I takes it over to the ringers' quarters and, blow me down, there's all these crook fellers everywhere. Well, there was about six in the camp, I guess. All whites. There was no Murries there. But, oh, they was crook.

Now, from what I gathered, apparently the manager – a feller called Doug Campbell – he'd hired a plane and he'd took the ringers into Burketown for a big burn-up and they'd got on the grog. Then, when they come back, they brings four gallons of rum back out with them but, instead of just having little bits to nurse themselves back out of the DTs, they went and got stuck into the whole lot, straightaway. So after they'd knocked off that lot they went a bit crazy, aye, and they tried to break into the store to get the metho and in the end the manager's wife, she had to lock the store up. So then someone had the bright idea of draining the brake fluid from out of all the trucks and mixing it with cordial. But, oh, they was real, real crook, they was, so I just sat down for about a week waiting for everybody to sober up, aye. Anyhow, my room mate was a bloke called Jack Gill. His family owned a buck-jumping show. The Gill Family. A good ringer he was, too. And I had a bottle of rum and I felt a bit sorry for him, so every now and then I'd say, 'Here Jack, have a bit of a nip just ter help yer through.'

'Oh yeah, thanks, Goldie. Good on yer mate. Just a little nip'll do me fine. Just a nip.'

Then a few days later I'd say the same thing and he'd say. 'Oh yeah, good on yer Goldie. Just a little nip.'

Then after about a week or so I gets me rum bottle out from under me pillow and the colour of the rum wasn't red any more. It's gone brown. So I tastes it and you could drink it like soft drink, aye. Well, the mongrel had been bulling it, aye. You know, helping himself. And, oh, I was crooked on that, aye. I mean, to kick a man's dog and to bull a man's rum's about as low as you can go. But, no, I didn't do nothing. I mean, he was real crook, anyway.

So we finally gets out on the muster and there was one young feller – a bit of a lout – he'd leave possum tracks up and down the horse's shoulder. See, he'd dig his spurs into the horse's shoulders; that's the term, 'possum tracks'. They're the little marks the rolling of the spurs makes when you're cutting into him. Like, he had no reason to because the horses was pretty quiet, anyway. So, anyway, the manager feller, Doug Campbell, he's real crooked on this young ringer for leaving possum tracks. So we're drafting horses there, one time, and Doug Campbell thinks he'll really give this young feller something to think about so he says to the feller, 'Alright then,' he says, 'you can ride the Queen terday.' See, there was a mare there with a big rep for being a bad horse – the Skating Queen. A chestnut mare with four white feet, a white mane and tail.

Anyrate, we're all sitting on the top rail of the round yard watching this horse, the Skating Queen, and we're thinking, Oh, this'll be good. So the young feller saddles her up. Tightens the girth. But while the saddle's on her he lets her buck, see, to take some of the wind out of her. Yeah, this's even before he got on her. Then, when he gets on, see, the wind's already been taken out of her so, of course, she didn't do much. Oh, maybe just a bit but he hung onto the jug-handles to keep himself in the saddle. They're two brass things on the pommel of the saddle. But he handled her alright.

Okay then, we're out mustering now and this young feller's still on the Skating Queen. It was only a short day and we're coming back up to the house and I'm on the wing of the mob and this young feller's riding a couple of hundred yards in front of me. It's open country, but there's this timber called gutta-percha running right along the fence. Low mongrel stuff it is. Wherever you see this gutta-percha growing you know just how high the flood goes in the wet season. Anyhow, this Doug Campbell, he gallops up behind the young feller to go up and open the gate. Now, I'm not real sure if Campbell meant to do that on purpose or not because, one thing you never, ever do, is gallop up behind a bad horse, and he should've known that. Anyrate, this mare takes off. It bolts and it takes the young feller through all this gutta-percha and, oh, I tell you, it ripped him to pieces. Oh, he was a mess, aye.

So anyway, Campbell undoes the gate and we take the cattle through. By then this young feller's got the Skating Queen under control and we see him ride up and go into the station, past where we're going to cut the cattle out. Yeah, camp-draft them. It's only a couple of hundred yards from the house. So we're all there and, next thing, we hears this bang! And the manager, this Doug Campbell, he races over and there's this young feller, he'd shot the mare. Yeah, he shot it dead, aye. The Skating Queen.

'What did yer do that for?' shouts Campbell.

And the young feller says, 'Look, I know I'm gonna get the sack fer this but, one thing's fer sure, that horse'll never bolt 'n' smash anybody up again.'

Of course, Campbell gives him the push straightaway and so we had to go over and undo the bottom rail of the round yard and drag the mare out with the truck. Now, for the life of me I can't remember that young feller's name. But one thing I do know, he was a thieving mongrel. See, just before he left on the mail truck, he had to go over to the house and sign to get his cheque and one of the ringers unrolled his swag and there's his mate's nice gabardine jacket. So he thieved that. And he thieved my bull strap, too. So he didn't have a very good character, aye. And I never ever got that bull strap back. It was somewhere in his swag. I reckon that's where it went.

But I was only there for about five weeks or so and I left. Well, I pulled the pin, aye. Oh, well, pretty much the muster was over, really. No real reason other than that. But I was getting keen on going down to the Towers, you know, to get courting Edith.

32

Right, so I'm back in Normanton, staying out with the Caseys. Oh, and that's right, yes, that's right. I remember now. See, I wasn't long back from Talawanta and I'd come into town from Shady Lagoons and I was drinking with a feller by the name of Jack McNab. Jack was a saddler and he also had a mail run. So me and him, we're up in the top pub – the National – and we'd been drinking on and off in the afternoon. You know, not downing one after the other like, just steady drinking. Anyhow, by about ten o'clock that night, we're starting to get a bit argumentative with each other and this argument's getting pretty warmed up. I forget what it was about, just now.

Anyhow, Sam Henry, the local sergeant comes in. Sam's the feller who refereed that fight with me and Ronny Paul. Yeah, so Sam Henry comes in and he's sitting down the other end of the bar and he's thinking, Geez, it looks like a blue's on the cards here between Goldie and McNab. So Sam comes up and he goes through all the change we had on the counter and he hands it over to Ted Kershaw, the publican. 'Ted,' he says, 'give us a dozen beer.' In them days all the beer was in 26-ounce bottles. The big ones. There was no stubbies. So Ted gets the beer, see, then Sam says to me and Jack, 'Righto youse fellers, come with me,' and he puts the carton on his shoulder and he walks out of the pub. So me and Jack, we follow him out. We're just talking and going on because, by now, there's no arguing, just talking.

Then Sam gets in his vehicle. We get in the back and he drives us out to the edge of town to an old timber church. Now this old church was built round the turn of the century, early 1900s. It's weathered a lot of cyclones so it's leaning over at about a thirty-degree angle. It was one of them old weatherboard ones that's up on stumps, you know, with the white-ant caps on top. They didn't even hold services there because there wasn't much floorboards left. Like, anybody in town who wanted a bit of timber always went down to the old church to get it. Yeah, that's where they went for their timber.

So Sam drops me and Jack off out there with this dozen beer. Now, outside the front of the church, about thirty feet or something, there was still the original old bell and it had a length of rope hanging off it. Anyrate, Sam plonks us there and he says, 'Righto, fellers, go fer yer life. Do what yer like.' Then he jumps in his car and goes back to town. So me and Jack, we're left sitting there. We'd both long forgot what the argument was about so we're looking for something to do. And, see, around Normanton there's goats walking around all the time. So I says, 'Let's have some fun. We'll catch a goat 'n' tie his back leg ter the rope on the bell 'n' as he's trying ter get away he'll be ringin' the bell.' So then we tried to catch one of these goats, aye, but we're too drunk to catch a goat. They kept getting away from us. 'This's no good,' I says to Jack. 'How's about we ring the bell ourselves?'

'Good idea,' he says.

So I'm ringing this bell, aye. By now it's about two o'clock in the morning and we're ringing away and there's all these house lights going on around town, left, right and centre. Now, at that time, there was only one minister in Normanton. I forget his name just now but he belonged to what they called the AIM – Australian Inland Mission – and he lived away over on the other side of Normanton. So I must've been making a real racket, aye, because, next thing, he comes flying down in his car.

I says, 'Oh, how yer goin', Padre? Have a drink.'

But he's in no mood for that, aye, because he gives us this big lecture on the evils of drinking, then he says, 'You shouldn't be ringin' that bell.'

I says, 'Why's that?'

He says, 'Because when a church bell's rung, it's meant to be the call for all sinners to come to church.'

So I says, 'Well, this must be a pretty righteous town, aye, Padre?'

'Why's that?'

I says, 'Because, you're the only person who's turned up.'

After that he sort of gave up on us and he got back in his car and he drove back into town. But, see, that time back in Normanton, I'm at a bit of a loose end, aye. Really, I would've liked to have gone straight down to the Towers and got courting Edith. But, see, the thing that was holding me back was that I was still waiting for the money from Talawanta, so I was pretty skint, and the last thing I wanted to do was to turn up on Edith's doorstep as a down'n'out. You know, I wanted something behind me so I could take her out to the pictures and all that sort of thing.

But, anyhow, I'm back out there staying with the Caseys at Shady, just sleeping on the verandah and that. It was sort of like a second home. And the Caseys was trying to get me in on another big hit on Glenore like we'd done before. But, oh, I don't know, I wasn't keen on it, aye. Well, I was tempted because I needed the money. But, really, I wanted to make a clean start now I had this Edith piece. Anyrate, I thought to meself, I'm wasting me life up here. So, in the end, I knocked the Caseys back, aye. And, well, also, the duffing game brings out the worst in people. I mean, the Caseys was like brothers to me but I'd always had the slight feeling that instead of us going three ways in everything we duffed, it was more like they looked after themselves first and I come in third.

Well, I suppose I first started to notice things, right back, after the first duffing trip we did. See, we got about thirty cleanskins that time and so ten of them should've been mine, aye, and I remember we was branding them back at Shady and I said to Jimmy, I says, 'What about my third, Jimmy?'

He says, 'You can have yer third when yer get a registered brand in town.'

Which I went and did. But even after I registered me brand, I never got ten of them cleanskins. So there's little things like that. I mean, I was still good mates with them and all that. But there was just little traits of things I was a bit concerned about. Like the time we done the big hit, well, I should've got four or five hundred pound out of that. But I didn't. And other times I'd notice the ones the Caseys earmarked was the better ones, the ones they'd get more money for, and that was a bit deceitful, aye. So I noticed a slight part of their character that wasn't too good.

But the overall thing that was the final nail was, while I'd been working up on Talawanta, the Caseys loaned me brand and things to a cattle duffer by the name of Hewetson, for him to use. See, this feller, Hewetson, he'd took up a 200-square-mile block called Hereford, about fifty mile from Normanton, on the Croydon road. Actually, at one stage I was nearly going to take it up, aye, but there was no permanent water on it. Now, Hewetson's one aim on Hereford was to build up a herd from cattle duffing, so he got a notorious duffer by the name of Charlie Coleman to go in with him. Charlie was a yella fella, a great mate of mine. Then this Hewetson, he hadn't been there long when him and Charlie Coleman duffed something like thirty cleanskins off Glenore and the Caseys lent him my brand. So then Hewetson brands these cattle with my brand and, when he sells them to a buyer in Croydon, he says that he'd bought them off me. And that's when all the trouble started because, not long after, Sam Henry, the copper, was in the middle pub and he overhears someone ask a feller if he'd sold some cattle up Croydon.

And the feller says back, 'No.'

'Oh,' says the first feller, 'I seen a few head goin' ter Croydon. Thought they mighta been yours.'

So then Sam Henry starts thinking to himself, Well, I wonder what cattle they'd be? If it isn't this feller's cattle then whose cattle are they? They must be this feller Hewetson's, that's new in town. He musta taken 'em. So Sam decides to take a look. He goes down to Croydon and he goes out to this buyer feller and there they are with my brand on them. But, see, it's still peeling and, what's more, he can see that their ears have just been cut because they haven't healed up yet. Then Sam goes out to see this Hewetson and he says to him, 'Where'd yer get them cattle from?'

Hewetson says, 'I bought 'em off Goldsmith.'

'Oh, really,' Sam says. 'So when did yer buy 'em?'

'Just last week.'

Of course, Sam Henry knows I'd been out at Talawanta, see, so there's no way Hewetson could have bought them off me. So he charges Hewetson for stealing thirty head of cattle. Then he confiscates the cattle and he holds them in the police yard in Croydon, as evidence, and, just in case, he puts a black tracker up there, camped with them. Yeah, at the police paddock. But talk about honour among thieves, aye – see, all the duffers in the Gulf all used to look after each other. Now, do you know what a Bedourie dog is? A Bedourie dog's an empty old square kerosene tin and, of course, from the Croydon gold-rush days, they was everywhere, aye. But when an empty one hits the ground it makes a big echo of a noise. So anyway, one night, pretty soon after, some mob threw a Bedourie dog in with the stolen cattle – boom! – and, with it being only a wire yard, the whole thirty head took off in thirty different directions, see. They rushed, and it give the black tracker such a fright that he took off with them. So then it takes the coppers a few days to get the evidence back together again.

Anyway, things are getting pretty serious now, see, so Sam Henry gets the big chief inspector of the stock squad to come to town and they work out their battle plan, you know, to put this Hewetson away. And with this Hewetson having put my brand on them illegally, Sam Henry comes and informs me how I'll soon be getting a summons to appear in court because I'm now the main Crown witness for the prosecution. So, yeah, that's a bit of a turn-up, aye, what, with me being a cattle duffer meself. But anyhow, like I said, I'm pretty skint by now and I'm booking up me grog and everything while I'm waiting on me Talawanta cheque. Then, one Sunday, I'm down the bottom pub and a feller comes in and he says, 'Goldie, somebody wants to see yer outside.'

I says, 'Yeah. Who?'

So I goes outside and there's this Hewetson and he takes me round the back and he explains what a mess he's got himself into and he offers to pay me money if I'll backdate the sale receipt he's got. You know, to make it look like he'd bought the cattle off me before I went out to Talawanta.

I says, 'Geez, I don't know so much about that.'

He says, 'Well, how's about I also buy yer brand 'n' all yer horses 'n' gear as well.'

I says, 'Well, it's gonna cost yer.'

'Here,' he says and he hands me a 120 quid to backdate this receipt and for me brand and for me horses and everything. I mean, 120 quid. That's two months wages, cash in hand, and here I am stony broke, and I'm booking up me grog and everything. So I says, 'Okay, mate, where's the receipt yer want me ter backdate?'

So I did that and he gives me the money and he tells me not to worry about anything because he's just been to Cairns and he's got this big-gun solicitor. And, like, this solicitor feller must've been pretty good because Hewetson told me how he'd once got a feller off a rape charge after he'd pleaded guilty and there was five witnesses saying how they saw everything. So that's how good he was, aye. Anyhow, this big-gun solicitor from Cairns, apparently it was his suggestion to pay me to backdate the receipt, then he'd said, 'After yer get Goldsmith ter do that tell him that when the prosecution gets him in the witness box, he's ter say just three things: "'Yes", "No", 'n' "I don't know". Don't go sayin' stuff like "Oh yes, I remember that cow, I got her up Sandy Creek" or none of that because then they've got a little bit of meat to go on.'

'Okay,' I says, 'don't worry, mate, I don't know a thing.'

So that was that. I now had 120 quid in me pocket. So I pays off all me debts, then I thinks to meself, I reckon I'd better make meself a bit scarce about the place. I'd better get outa town fer a while. The only trouble is that I'm still a bit shy on going down to the Towers, just yet, because, with the court case and all coming on, Edith might want to know about everything – you know, all about my duffing and things – and she might've gone off me if she knew about all that side of me life.

33

Yeah, so then there was a feller called Tom Wheelan. I've told you about him, aye. He was managing Wondoola Station and he'd buy two hundred here, a hundred there and another three hundred off some cattle duffer at another place, then he'd take them down to his own station, a place called Glenmore, just outside of Julia Creek. Good fattening country. Anyhow, Tom had bought this mixed mob of around eight hundred cows, calves and store bullocks and he'd got a boss drover and four Murries to take them back to this Glenmore and he wanted someone to go along to share the cooking. 'Count me in,' I said.

Actually, I enjoyed cooking and it got me out of town for a while. So now I'm on the road with this mob. I'm ringing and sharing the cooking and we're camping about forty mile out of Normanton, at a place called Walkers Bend. So I've got me pack saddles laid out. The horsetailer's with me. The horses are all hobbled out. I've got a stew cooking and a damper and everything's alright, and I'm waiting for this summons, see. Sam Henry said it was floating in the air. It's all around town and everything. Actually, it was a bit of a joke about the place how me being well known for cattle duffing was now acting for the prosecution. Anyway, apparently, one of the local coppers, a feller called Don Condie, goes into the middle pub and he says to the publican, 'Oh, give me a beer, Fitzy.' Fitzgibbons was his name. Don says, 'I gotta go out 'n' find where these cattle are that Goldie's with.'

Then someone in the bar said, 'Is that fer the cattle duffin' bluey yer've got on him?'

QUEENSLAND.

—

" JUSTICES ACTS, 1886 TO 1949."
(No. 7B.)

Summons of a Witness—Copy to Serve.

(Fee—One Shilling.)

To JOHN GOLDSMITH of NORMANTON

To of

To of

To

WHEREAS a complaint was, on the Thirteenth

day of March , 19 58 , made before a Justice of the Peace for the

said State that on the 18th day of February 1958 at Hereford
Normanton in the Petty Sessions District of Norman in the
State of Queensland, one Geoffrey Lionel Banbury Hewetson
had in his possession seventeen bulls, fourteen heifers,
one cow and one calf suspected of being stolen

These are therefore to require you to appear at the Police Court of Petty Sessions
at NORMANTON
in the said State, on the NINETH day of APRIL , 19 58 ,
at 10 o'clock in the forenoon, before such Justices as may then be there, to testify
what you know concerning the matter of the said complaint. (and you are further required to
bring with you, and produce at the time and place abovenamed (a)

GIVEN under my hand at Normanton in the said State,

this Nineteenth day of April 1958

J.P.

(a) Here describe the documents to be produced.

G.P. Ref. No. 45   Govt. Printer, Brisbane.(%)

Goldie's summons for cattle duffing

He says, 'Yeah.'

And there was a tourist in the bar, see, like with his camera hanging down and his little touristy shirt on with palm trees and things on it. I tell you, out there in the back country these tourists, they stand out like a fly in a bucket of milk. So this tourist says to Don Condie, 'Are you going out to issue a summons?'

Don says, 'Yeah.'

'And this's for cattle rustling?'

Don says, 'Well if yer lived in America yer'd call it that.'

'Oh, can I come along?'

'Okay.'

So Don brings this tourist down. And so I'm cooking, like I said, and I see this vehicle coming down the way and I just knew it was the coppers, so I thought, Hello, here's me bluey. Anyhow, Don pulls up on the bit of a road there, going to Cloncurry, and he walks over to where we are. 'Well, Goldie,' he says, 'I guess yer know what this's for, don't yer?'

I says, 'Yeah mate. When's it on?'

So he tells me whatever the date the court case is on and we start having a bit of a chat. Now, while all this's going on the tourist bloke's taking photos – you know, taking photos of the horses, taking photos of me, taking photos of the camp. Then he says, 'What have you got cooking there?'

I says, 'I got a stew there 'n' I got a sod there.' A sod's a damper. See, a lot of them go soggy in the middle, so you call them sods.

And I can remember as plain as day, this Don Condie gives me the bluey and he's walking away and Don's pretty big and this little tourist feller, he's strutting alongside him yabbering away, 'What did he call that thing? What? A sod? What's a sod?' I tell you, I reckon it might've been the highlight of that feller's trip. I reckon his mates and his kids, even his grandkids, would've never heard the end of how he'd gone out with the police to hand a summons out to a feller who was involved in a 'cattle rustling' case. Yeah, so you can't beat them, can you, aye?

Anyhow, then, a few days later we're going past Wondoola homestead and a young Murri who was with us, well, his wife – a gin – was working there, on Wondoola. So, being so close to the homestead, he takes advantage to go in and see his wife. Then when he comes back he's got this letter, see, and he's looking pretty serious. He says, 'Goldie, yer'd betta 'ave a reada this.'

So he hands me the letter. It was from Gladys Grogan – remember that Aboriginal woman I'd fooled around with before I went down to the Towers for me hernia operation. Anyhow, it turns out that Gladys is friends with this Murri's wife. So I reads the letter. 'Oh, hello Sandra,' Gladys said. 'I got some news for you. I've got a bun in the oven and Goldie's the father and it's due in July.'

Well, it knocked me for six, aye. Here I am, I've met someone I really want to get on with and start courting and now this – a letter saying how I was going to be the father of a child to another woman. You know, I just couldn't believe it. Like, it was all too much to take in. But I'm thinking it all over. You know, what will I do here? Maybe she just wrote how I was the father because she wanted to impress this other gin? Was I the real father? You know, there was lots of questions I didn't have the right answers for.

Anyhow, we're walking these cattle and I'm mulling all this over and I'm starting to think it's some sort of mistake or something and then four or five days later, we get held up at a place called Cleanskin because the bullocks ahead of us had red-water fever. That's tick fever. So they're quarantined and held up and, of course, they stop any more cattle going through till they've worked out what to do. But there was a hut there at

Cleanskin and while we're camped there someone says, 'Goldie, there's some mail here fer you.'

'Oh yeah.'

So then I gets this letter. It's a letter from Gladys herself ... what's the word? ... yeah, 'confirming' how she's in the family way and how I was the father. She even wrote, 'Goldie, please marry me for the sake of your child. I won't keep you tied down. You can do what you like.' And, I tell you, mate, it's a funny feeling, you know, when you read how you're going to be a father. You sort of feel good but then, what do you do about it? You know, aye, because there's no one to advise you about what to do or nothing. So it was good but it was bad, if you catch my drift. Yeah, real bad, because, like, I'd come back to Normanton to tidy everything up so I could go and start a brand new life with this Edith, down at the Towers, and now everything was turned on its head, what with the duffing court case and now this. So I'm thinking to meself, Geez, Goldie, yer've got yerself inta a right mess here.

34

So we're camped at this Cleanskin, okay, waiting for the go-ahead to move on, and me mind's all on about this Gladys business. Anyhow, amongst it, we runs out of tobacco. So I'm tonguing fer a smoke, aye. We all was. And oh, we tried everything. We even tried horse manure. Actually, horse manure's the closest thing to satisfying you, even if it does burn your throat. But, see, because I'd worked on Canobie that time with that queer carpenter feller, I knew a few fellers from over there, so one day I says, 'Blow this, I'm off ter get some tobacco.'

So I gets on me horse and I swims the Flinders River. The crocs didn't quite come that far up. Well, very seldom one might turn up but it'd only be little feller, ten foot at the most. Then I goes a few mile further on and I comes to the Cloncurry River, and, oh, he was a good horse, this bloke. See, I'm riding him down into the river, we're getting deeper and deeper, and I could feel him going up on his toes. See, usually, as soon as they get in deep water they strike and lunge which makes it hard for you to stay on. But not this feller. He's right up on his toes, aye, and he swims me across without striking out or nothing.

Okay, so we gets up the other side and there's this fence – the Canobie boundary. I rides along the fence and I come to a wire gate. It hadn't been used in years. I goes through the gate, goes over a bit of a hill and there's a ploughed track – a firebreak. Now, because I knew I'd be coming back that night, while I'm on this fire track, I'm looking around to get a direction by the stars as to where the gate is. So I took me bearings and I say, 'Okay, Canobie's over that way.'

A mate of mine was a cowboy there, a bloke called Maurie Lee. When I gets to Canobie, Maurie says, 'Goldie, come in. What're yer doin'?'

I says, 'I ran outa tobacco 'n' I'm tonguin' fer a smoke.'

He says, 'Here, have some'a mine.'

So I rolled a smoke and, I tell you, I made it so fat that I could barely get the cigarette paper rolled around it, aye. Anyway, then I goes over to the cook, old Mrs Campbell, and I says, 'If it's okay with you Mrs Campbell, I'll stay fer tea.'

See, they all knew me because I was getting a bit of a rep around the Gulf now, for one thing and another, aye, so she says, 'Yeah, righto, Goldie.'

So then I goes up to the bookkeeper and I says, 'I'm after a pound'a tobacco, mate. Can yer book it down ter Tom Wheelan?'

'Okay,' he says and when I went to sign the book for the tobacco I says, 'What's the date?'

He says, 'The twelfth of April 1958.'

And it struck me. It was me brother's twenty-first birthday, aye. Yeah, David. No, I hadn't had anything to do with them at all. Not a thing. But, so, I spent my twenty-first birthday mustering sheep in pouring rain and I spent his twenty-first birthday swimming across rivers to get tobacco. And then, out of the blue, I started to imagine them having a big party at home, like, with the grog flowing and everything. But while that might've been a good memory, then came back all the bad ones. So party or no party, I was still pleased to be out of there, even if I did have me own problems to deal with.

Anyhow, after I signed for the tobacco, I goes back down and Maurie gives me a nip of rum. 'Here's ter me brother, David,' I says, and then I have a feed there and have a good yarn with whatever fellers was still around the station. Then after that I says goodbye and I takes the tobacco and I goes back to where

I'd come in, on the fire plough track. So it's real dark now and, as I said, I'd pretty much worked out where I'd hit the gate by using the stars. So I gets me direction and I says, 'The gate'll be there.'

Then I'm only a couple of mile along this track, heading for where I've worked out where the gate is, and I hits the fence and I rides along the fence and suddenly the horse stops. Yeah, suddenly he stops for no reason. Just like that. So I niggled him with me tacks – tacks are spurs – and he goes a couple of more feet and he stops again. 'Come on,' I says, 'what's wrong with yer?' But he won't move, see. He's stubborn. So I has a bit of a closer look around and, blow me down, there's the gate. He'd stopped right at the gate. Amazing, isn't it, aye? Oh, I tell you what, that horse deserved to go to heaven. So I goes back to the Cloncurry River and I tied the tobacco on top of me head with me belt to keep it dry and I did the same when I come to the Flinders River, just in case. Then a bit further on I heard the horse bells in the distance, you know, from where the horses are hobbled out. So I was coming back with the tobacco, aye, and, I tell you, weren't they all keen about that!

Anyhow, not long after, they sorted things out with the redwater fever. I forget just now what they did but they said it was okay for us to go on. So we heads on south, leaving the big runs – the big station properties. The big runs are wide, open spaces, thousands of square miles, and, with them being that large, the cattle don't come across too many fences. But as you work your way down the stock route towards Julia Creek, you start coming into the smaller cocky places where there's lots of fences.

Now, the drover's worst enemy is these little sheep cockies and, the law of the land is that, whenever the stock route passes through these places, you've got to give these fellers notice. And more often than not they'll come down to the boundary gate and see you through, just to make sure you stick to the stock route and you don't let your bullocks loose into their property, where the feed's better. Oh yeah, these little cocky blokes, they're a wake-up to all that. Then after they've seen you through their property they'll go back and they'll get on their little peddle wirelesses and make sure their cocky mate next door knows you're coming through. So then he'll also come down and meet you at his gate. Oh, they don't trust you, these fellers. Not one bit.

By this stage we'd been on the road for well over a month. It's near the end of the droving season so the stock route's been pretty much eaten out by now. So for three days this mob hadn't had a real good feed and we're trying to push them a bit to get an extra couple of miles a day out of them. And that's when the boss drover feller got word that his father had died, so he went back to Normanton and he left me in charge of the four Murries we had with us. Anyway, we come to the fence at one of these little places and the cocky wasn't there to keep an eye on things so, of course, I let the cattle wander into his place to get a decent bellyful of feed.

Then after they'd had a good feed I camped them in the corner for the night and we just watched them from the fire. Now, one thing – you should never camp cattle on a fence line or in a corner. As I said, they'd come from the big runs so they aren't used of fences so they're likely to get their horns hooked up in the wire, which causes them to panic and then the whole lot will go. They'll rush. Anyrate, they just wouldn't lay down like usual, which was a bad sign because it means they're worried about something. Then at about two in the morning there must've been some kangaroos fighting either side of the fence down'a'ways because the fence wire twanged and it frightened them. They panicked. They jumped. They rushed. And when they go like that the whole ground sounds like it's all thunder underneath. Yeah, just like thunder. So they rushed and, of course, they took a good part of the fencing with them: wires, posts, the lot. Now, lucky for us, out from the fenced area was pretty open country and, with a couple of night horses, we managed to wheel most of them around and block them up.

Next morning when we counted them, we was still a hundred short, so we sort of patched up what was left of the fence the best we could, which was pretty rough, then I sent a couple of the Murries out to get what's missing, while me and the others moved the rest on. Okay, so we're into this little cocky place and there's this bore drain, see, which is where the water comes out of the bore and it flows down a man-made creek sort of thing. Now, these bore drains, they're only about a foot wide and the cockies have this tractor that straddles the drain and for about two foot either side it keeps it very nice and neat and clean of grass. Yeah, because these sheep, if you ever see them, they come tippy-toeing down to the bore drain and they'll have a little sip and then they tippy-toe back to the gidgee.

Anyhow, it comes to dinner time and these Gulf cattle they're looking for a drink, aye. But, see, they've never tasted bore water before. They're used to monsoonal water and waterholes. So here's my lot trudging up through this bore drain, hock deep, making a real mess of it. Like, they'd have a bit of a drink and they wouldn't like the taste, so they'd walk up along the bore drain, hoping the water might be better further along, which it wasn't. But just in case the cocky who owned the place arrived and saw the mess we're making I sang out to one of me Murries, 'Hey, bring 'em back outa the bore drain 'n' put 'em back on camp again.'

Then, just as he was doing that, down come the owner feller and, oh, I tell you, he was your typical chief cocky, aye. He had braces. His bottle of Stockholm tar was in his saddlebag. He had a pair of hand shears to crutch any old maggoty sheep he comes across. He had a bit of wire around his saddle. A straining fork. Anyrate, he sees all this and he's giving me a real serve for messing up his bore drain. Just then, blow me down, who shouldn't appear but the other Murries, along with the missing hundred head. And I tell you, this mob, they're not only turning this cocky's bore drain into a complete mess but they're also dragging fence posts and they've got wire and bits and pieces strung out all around them.

'Hey, what happened 'ere?' the cocky says.

I says, 'Oh, we had a rush the other night out at the Millungera horse paddock and these fellas are just bringin' 'em back in.'

Now, the Millungera horse paddock was the only nearby place I could think of that had a fence around it, other than this cocky's place, of course. But I wasn't going to tell him that, aye. Anyhow it's enough to get him going again. He gets on his soap box and he's going crook about how the drovers from the Gulf are bullying all the little fellers like him and how rotten they are and about all the damage they cause and so forth and so on. And all this whingeing's got to me so I says, 'Look mate,' I says, 'how big's this farm'a yours?'

And I remember as if it was yesterday. He stuck his thumbs in his braces, puffed out his chest and he said, 'This place's sixty-six thousand acres.'

I says, 'Blimey, sixty-six thousand acres, aye?'

He said, 'Yes.'

'Well,' I says, 'that's almost as big as the smallest paddock back where I come from.' So that put him back in place, a bit. Then I said, 'Look mate, yer gettin' on me goat 'n' right now they're gettin' another mob'a bullocks ready fer me ter bring down this way 'n' if I hear that any of me drovin' mates have trouble with you then, the next time I come through, I'll let the red bull go.'

See, if any of those small cockies gave us a real bad time, that's what we'd do – we'd burn them out. Yeah, so they know they can't push us around. It's what we call letting the red bull go. Burning him out. Sometimes you can put the wind up these cockies just by asking if they've got a box of matches. Anyhow, boy, didn't that shut this little cocky up! After that he saw us to the boundary gate, as quiet as a lamb, and when most of the mob had gone through, he turns around and rides away. But I'll have to tell you this: see, this cocky also had a few head of cattle and just as he disappears, down trots this big fat bullock of his to have a stickybeak at our mob. And, boy, is he fat. Anyway, to cut a long story short, we run this cocky's bullock into our mob and we knocked him off the next day and we ate him. Beautiful he was, too, aye. Just beautiful.

So we moves on from there and we delivered them to Glenmore about eight days later. But, anyhow, like I said, all that time I'm tossing things around in me head about this business with Gladys and I got pretty mixed up about it all. But, the long and the short of it is that, I suppose, just on principle-like, I should've married Gladys, you know, to give the child a name, aye. Though I wouldn't have stayed with her. So in the end I decided not to do anything and go after Edith. Yeah, maybe that was weak of me. Maybe not. But that's the decision I made and it's the one I had to stick with all the rest of me life.

35

Anyhow, while I'd been on that trip Tom Wheelan had gone and bought another nine hundred or so head of bullocks off Mitchell River Aboriginal Mission – Kowanyama. It was run by the Church of England or someone. So Tom says, 'Look Goldie, go ter Georgetown 'n' help organise the plant up ter Kowanyama, then come back with the bullocks.' He says, 'I've got a boss drover bloke called William Butler. He wants a cook but, Goldie, whatever yer do, don't call him "Bill". He don't like it.'

'Okay,' I says, 'the money'll come in handy 'cause I'm headin' off ter the Towers soon. I've got a woman there.'

'Good on yer,' says Tom. 'About time yer settled down a bit.'

As it turned out, this William Butler was the nephew of Henry Butler – remember that feller who lent us his tractor and trailer at the Forty Mile Crossing the time young Ernie Smith got bashed up on Jam Pot and needed to go into town? So I goes down to Georgetown. I didn't know this Butler from a bar of soap but he knew of me. So we musters about ten packhorses, thirty or so riding horses, plus a couple of spares at a place out of town. There's six of us on the trip: Butler; his younger brother; there's Graham Seacombe, who was from Georgetown; me, of course; and two Murries. So we're in Georgetown, we've got the plant organised and we're packing up everything, ready to head off, and me and this Graham Seacombe, we'd had a few drinks and I said, 'Look, we'd better go up the Chinese store 'n' get some tins'a tucker.'

So we goes up there. The actual store was built in the copper-rush days, in the 1880s, and the floor was made out of logs, squared off by axe. Beautiful old floors. The store was owned by a Chinese feller by the name of Georgie Buk Chung. So we grabs a few tins of this and a few tins of that and some bully beef and we goes over to pay and Georgie says, 'Dat two pound. Dat two pound.'

I says, 'Okay, I'll write yer out a cheque.'

'Oh, no. No cheque.'

I says, 'Look I'm well known, so don't worry, it won't be a dud or nothin'.'

'No. No. No. I wan' cash.'

Anyway, I snapped, see, and there was a real wide counter and on the counter there's a pyramid of a pile of packets of them old blue-green peas. You know the ones you've got to soak for a month before you can eat them. Real hard things. Anyway, I snapped and I leans over the counter and I grabs Georgie and I give him a bit of a shaking, then I got stuck into these packets of peas and peas went everywhere, all over the floor. Then, when we gets outside this Graham Seacombe says, 'What the hell do yer think yer doin'?'

I says, 'Oh, he stirred me up when he wouldn't cash me cheque.' Then I thinks about it and I says, 'Yeah, yer right. It was stupid of me, aye? I'd better go 'n' apologise.'

So I goes back in to apologise and there's Georgie Buk Chung on the phone, see. It's one of them phones where you turn the handle to get put through to the exchange and they put you through to whoever you're calling. Georgie's ringing the coppers, aye. But as soon as he sees me, he thinks he's in for another shaking up, so he drops the phone and he takes off and he leaves the phone dangling, so I goes over and I picks it up and I says in the mouth part, 'Please cancel that call.' Then I had thoughts of Humphrey Bogart in that film where he yanks the phone cord out of a wall. So I does the Humphrey Bogart trick, I rips the cord out of the wall. Then I go and try and find

Georgie, to apologise, but Georgie's nowhere to be found. He's off hiding somewhere. Anyhow, then I goes back down to the packhorses, Butler turns up, and we're just about to head off when the local copper, Aaron Hillard, arrives. He sees me and he says, 'Oh, Goldie, I thought it'd be you.'

Of course Butler doesn't know what's happened, so we explain, then we all head up to the shop to work out the damage. But as soon as we walk in Georgie dives around behind the counter, to hide, see. Anyhow, Hillard asks, 'Oh, how much is the damage, Georgie? How much? Goldie wants ter apologise 'n' pay fer all the trouble.' The only trouble is that Georgie doesn't understand much English, see, and he thinks the copper wants to know how much the cans of tucker cost. So there's Georgie, calling out from down behind the counter, 'Dat two pound. Dat two pound.'

Anyrate, Butler pays him in cash and away we go. We left Georgetown with the plant and we headed west for a couple of days to the Gilbert River, then followed the Gilbert up till we got to a station. I forget the name of the place just now, but the people there made us very welcome and they give us a good feed. From there we went on to Strathmore Station. The Murries with us knew Strathmore pretty well because they'd done ringing there, one time or other. Then we camped maybe three nights or so on our way through Strathmore till we got to a yard with a crush, called Wilson. I remember that because 'Wilson' was painted on the covering of the cattle dip so aeroplanes could see it.

Okay, then after we left Strathmore there was no fences and we're in country none of us had been in before. But being just after wet season, there's plenty of water and plenty of feed. So we kept heading north, day after day, till we eventually hit the Kowanyama–Mungana Road at Dunbar homestead. Dunbar was sixty mile from Kowanyama and we camped down by the waterhole there and these Dunbar ringers came down to have a yarn and one of them was saying how he'd just been down in Georgetown and he'd seen Georgie Buk Chung walking around with his neck to one side so he said, 'What happened to yer neck, Georgie?'

And Georgie had said, 'Oh, some winger f'om Normanton, he shakie me neckie 'n' my neckie still sore.' So we all had a great laugh about that.

Anyhow, all told, from Georgetown to Kowanyama, it took us just under a month, then we spent three or four days mustering the bullocks for the trip back. But one thing – when we got on the stock route, blow me down, the flour's all full of weevils, aye. Oh, huge, big weevils. Some of them even in cocoons. And even if you took out as many as you could, like, there'd still be some left in the flour so, when I made the damper, the heat made the weevils explode ... pop! ... and so you got all these little dots everywhere in the damper from the pink of the weevils. Oh yeah, it still tasted okay. I mean, you could eat it.

Then, see, on droving trips, cooks and horsetailers, they always help each other. But the horsetailer I had, oh, he was a bludger, aye. A pure-blood Aboriginal he was and, I must say, Aboriginals are generally very good. But this fella was cunning. Like, what he'd do was – see, the horsetailer's first up of a morning to go and get the horses. On this particular trip we had about forty head of horses plus about ten packhorses and a spare. So he'd go out before first light and bring in most of the horses – most, but not all – and he'd bring them in, then he'd hobble them out around the camp. By now the ringers are having their breakfast. Then he'd say to me, 'Bin' another four horses somewhere. I gotta find 'em.'

So he'd go off while the ringers unhobbled the horses they wanted for the day and away they'd go with the bullocks, just on daylight. So I was left to get the packhorses and I'd have to load them up with all the pack bags, evenly weighted and with the ringers' swags on and everything. Then the last packhorse in the team is what you called the 'tuckerhorse'. That's where the damper is, the cooked corned beef, tea, sugar and milk and the plates and mugs and all that. So I'd have to leave that one unpacked till the horsetailer come back and had his breakfast. But, see, the bludger would work it so, as soon as I'd finished packing all bar the tuckerhorse, suddenly he'd turn up with the four missing horses, aye. Then, while he's having his breakfast, I'd have to pack up the tuckerhorse. So he was bludging see, when he was supposed to be helping me pack the packhorses.

And also I noticed how he'd mumble to himself, under his breath. Anyrate, all this's going on and I'm getting pretty steamed up about it all and we're only about four days off delivery. We're down the Walsh River. It's a pretty deep river and, see, the horsetailer and the cook, they generally catch up with the mob later on in the day, when they're on the dinner camp. So when we gets to camp Butler says, 'Goldie, go about two mile further on 'n' pick out a spot 'n' we'll stay there the night.' He says, 'Oh, 'n' don't go over the river where the drovers in front of us had went. Go a bit higher up. It's a bit shallower up there.' See, because the last thing you want is to get the flour and everything wet.

Okay, so this horsetailer and me, we starts taking the packhorses up further and I hear him mumbling and I catch what he's saying this time. 'Him don't know what him's doin'. He should be goin' across where other minya was goin'', 'minya' being Aboriginal for 'cattle'.

This's still in sight of the other fellers, see. Anyway, I snapped, aye. I'd had enough. So I drags him off his horse and I'm into him and when Butler sees all this, he sings out, 'Don't go beltin' him up, Goldie. Leave 'im.'

So I left him. But, like, I'm still steamed up about it all. Anyhow, later on we're in camp and this Murri's sitting on a log and, see, he had a fish hook in his hat. Most ringers carry a fishing line in their saddlebag just in case there's a waterhole and you might catch a fish. But I'm still fuming, aye, because I didn't get a decent whack at this fella for being such a bludger. So I snaps again and I up and into him and he starts fighting back. So I grabs his hat to pull it over his eyes so I could get a decent lunge at him but, like, the fish hook gets caught in me hand, so I calls out, 'Stop! Hang on. Sit still. Be quiet. Don't move. Yer fish hook's got stuck in me hand.'

And you won't believe it but this fella stops still while I get the hook out and, when I get the hook out, oh, I'm right back into him, aye. Anyhow, Butler comes along and says, 'Hold it Goldie. We'll get inta a lot'a trouble if we go roughin' Murries up.' So I stopped then. But, mind you, next day this fella's got all the horses up on camp and he's helping me pack up all the packhorses. So I should've given him a good lungeing just after we'd left Kowanyama, aye.

So then we gets to Mungana. The pub was still going then, so we has a few beers there to celebrate the end of the trip, then we rides on to Chillagoe and I'm on this mongrel horse, aye. But I didn't have me own saddle, see, and so Butler gave me one what's called a 'pig-ear-pollie'. That's because there's tiny little kneepads at the front, only about two inches. Real tiny. And this mongrel horse, every time you stood up in the irons, he'd drop his head and he'd buck and so, in the end, I had all these big black bruises down me legs. Anyrate, when we gets into Chillagoe it's around four o'clock in the afternoon and we can smell this beautiful bread being baked, so we says, 'Oh, we've gotta get inta this beautiful fresh bread.'

Okay, so I'm still on this mongrel horse, aye. So Butler goes in and he brings out this loaf of bread and it's wrapped up in paper. Anyway, he says, 'Here Goldie. Catch.' And as he throws the bread up to me, the paper frightens the horse, and it bolts. So here I am, I've got this loaf of fresh bread tucked under me arm, I'm hanging on to it for dear life, and the horse's bolting down the street and I can hear Butler singing out at the top of his lungs, 'Don't drop the bread!'

But with the way things was, I couldn't lengthen the reins to pull this thing up. So he's bolting along and there's a little side road and only about twenty yards on there's a gate and I just knew what this mongrel horse was thinking. He's thinking, Can I take this gate? Can I get over it? Anyhow, lucky for me, right at the last moment, he thinks the better of it and he pulls up just in front of the gate. But with this bread being so fresh, see, when the horse pulls up, there it is, the whole loaf's squashed under me arm to about half an inch thick. Yeah, like a pancake. So that's how tight I was holding on to it, aye.

Anyhow, after we're all paid off, I goes up to Georgetown. Like, I'm on the way back to Normanton to pick up me little truck and head back down to the Towers to start courting Edith. So I goes into the bar of the Georgetown Hotel and I'm having a chat to George Dickson, the publican. 'George,' I says, 'I've got a cheque here fer a hundred quid. Can yer cash it in 'n' give me a fiver 'n' keep the rest in the safe because I'm goin' down ter the Towers ter get on with a woman there.'

So George says, 'Good on yer Goldie. Here's five quid. I'll keep the rest of it in the safe for yer.'

And there was a young feller who'd just come to town. Nobody knew much about him. He had his swag, his saddle, his whip and everything, and I'm drinking away and it'd been a while since I'd had a few so it didn't take much to get a bit under the weather. Then this feller sidles up to me and we have a chat and when the bar closes I'm going downstairs to what's called the 'dungeons'. The dungeons was a rough-looking place at the pub where the ringers generally camp because it's cheap, whereas managers and travelling salesmen and them generally camp upstairs. Anyhow, I was pretty drunk and I vaguely remember this young feller helping me down to the dungeons. I already had me swag down there so he didn't have to help but he did for some reason or other, then he went and camped upstairs.

Next morning I'm tonguing for a drink, aye, to get meself back right again. So I gets up and I has a leak. Now I've got two belts: one's me normal belt that's already on around me jeans. But the second belt I couldn't find. That's the one with all me knives and me watches and things and a lovely big horseshoe buckle on it. So I looked around and I looked around and I says to meself, 'Oh I musta dropped it on the way down from the bar last night.' So I tracks back to the bar and I just can't find it. Anyway, I says to George Dickson, I says, 'George, have yer seen me belt anywhere, mate?'

'No.'

I says, 'Well I've lost it 'n' that belt means a lot to me.'

Then I remembers, see, so I says to George, 'George, that young feller upstairs, well, he helped me down the dungeons last night, didn't he?'

George says, 'Yes he did.'

Anyrate, later on, when the young feller comes down to the bar to have a drink, I says, 'Look mate, when yer took me down the dungeons last night, did yer happen ter see me belt anywhere?'

'No, sorry, I didn't see a belt.'

And just by the tone of it, I knew that this bloke had knocked it off, aye, so I goes over and I says to George, 'Look, I reckon that bloke's stole me belt so I'm gonna sort him out.'

George says, 'Don't, Goldie. I like yer, mate, but every time yer come ter town yer put on a bit of a stir.' He says, 'Look, I'll go up 'n' see the copper.'

I says, 'But I can sort this out meself.'

He says, 'No, I'll get Hillard.' That's the same copper feller with Georgie Buk Chung.

Anyway, so Hillard comes down. He says, 'What's goin' on, Goldie?'

I says, 'I reckon that feller upstairs's knocked me belt off. I've had it fer years. It means a lot to me. It's got a big horseshoe buckle 'n' everything's on it, like me watch 'n' me castrating knives 'n' all that.'

He says, 'Okay then, I'll go 'n' have a yarn ter him.'

This young feller's gone back upstairs, see. So I'm in the bar having a drink and Hillard comes down and he hands me a belt and he says, 'Is this it?'

'You betcha life it's it,' I says. 'By the livin' Harry I'll sort this feller out.'

Hillard says, 'Goldie,' he says, 'yer've got yer belt back.' He says, 'I don't want any strife. Just let him go. Promise me, don't do nothin' to him.'

I says, 'Righto, mate, I've got everythin' back so I won't.'

Then, later on, this young feller, very sheepishly, comes down to the bar and he's over in the corner. George Dickson goes over and he gives him a beer and I'll never forget what George said – he leans over to this feller and says, 'Look mate,' he says, 'I want yer ter roll yer swag 'n' I want yer ter leave town right now, okay.' Then George says, 'Because we don't do those sorts of things up here. It's unheard of, so just roll yer swag 'n' go.'

And he did. This young feller, he went straight upstairs, he rolled up his swag and he left. And to my dying day I'll never forget those words George said, 'We don't do those things up here. It's unheard of.' And that George Dickson, I tell you, he was a man among men he was. I reckon, if ever a man deserves to have eternal life in the kingdom, it's George Dickson. So there.

Anyrate, so I'm there at the pub the rest of that day. I'm there the next day and I done the ninety-five quid I had. I done the whole lot in a game of two-up. It took me two months to get that hundred quid and I done it in fifteen minutes. Everything I was going to take down to the Towers and start courting Edith with, I done the whole lot in a game of two-up. See, I wanted to show her a real good time and now I could show her nothing. But, there's an old saying that goes: 'If you lose by losing, then you haven't lost at all', and since then I've never gambled, aye. I've never, ever gambled.

36

So here I am, I've done all me dough, aye. Skint, yeah, and Edith's wanting to know why I'm not coming to Charters Towers and, by the way she's asking it, I'm getting the feeling she might be losing her patience, just like that New Zealand piece, Janet Wilson, had done. Anyhow, just before I'd left from Kowanyama with Butler, taking that mob down to Mungana, the head stockman from Rutland Plains, Malcolm Boota – a half-caste he was – well, he'd come to me on the quiet and he'd said, 'Goldie, I could use a feller like you so, if yer ever need a job, there's one here, if yer'd like it.'

So I got in touch with this Malcolm Boota and asked if there was still a job going.

'Too right,' he says. 'It'll be good ter have yer.'

Well, Rutland Plains Station's up on the west coast of the Cape York Peninsula, about 180 mile north of Normanton. It's about 1600 square mile, bordering on Kowanyama. So I goes back to Normanton and the night before I goes out to Rutland I'm in the bottom pub, aye, and Sam Henry the copper arrives. 'G'day, Goldie,' he says. 'Keepin' outa strife?'

'Always,' I says, but, of course, Sam has a bit of a smile, aye.

He says, 'What're yer up ter?'

'I'm off ter Rutland Plains fer the muster.'

He says, 'Well, I've got some good news fer yer. That court case with Hewetson, it's been dropped. Lack'a evidence or somethin'.'

So that Hewetson, he really must've had a good solicitor, aye. Remember he said he'd got that big-gun feller from Cairns who'd once got a bloke off a rape charge after he pleaded guilty and there was five witnesses to the fact. So now things are looking up a bit, aye. Well, sort of – you know, the court case's been dropped and I've got a good job on wages for the mustering season. So I writes to Edith telling her how I'll be coming down to the Towers as soon as the muster's over and then I heads out to Rutland Plains. That's right, I think Jack Treewick, the manager, even come and got me because I left me truck over with the Caseys. So I settles in out at Rutland but see, during that droving trip with Butler, down to Mungana, one of me molars had started to niggle a bit. Like, not enough to mention it but just a sort of dull ache on and off.

Anyhow, I starts out at Rutland and the molar seemed okay. But after about a month or so the toothache comes back and it's getting worse and worse till, eventually, I had this huge swollen jaw. By then we're at a mustering camp about fifteen mile from the Rutland homestead, named One Mile. Well, it was called that because it's one mile from the Kowanyama boundary, aye. And, you know, with all the pain, you try everything from putting tobacco in the thing or if you drink enough brandy or whisky that deadens it sometimes, and cloves, they're good, too, sometimes. Anyrate, it got so bad that Jack Treewick said me best chance was to catch up with the Flying Doctor on his next monthly clinic visit to Kowanyama Aboriginal Settlement.

'Okay,' I says. 'Good.' So, on the day, I rode into Rutland homestead and Jack Treewick drives me the twenty mile or so over to Kowanyama to meet the Flying Doctor. It was just on dark when we got there and the doctor, an Irish feller named Tim O'Leary, well, he had all these Murries all lined up, giving them injections and checking them over, doing his clinic. Now Tim was a great feller and a very well-known and liked doctor with the Royal Flying Doctor Service. So then, after he'd finished treating all the Murries, Jack Treewick says to him, 'Tim, I've got a white stockman here, Jack Goldsmith, aged twenty-four. He's got a jaw like a lumpy jaw bullock.' Lumpy jaw's a disease that bullocks get.

'So you're Jack Goldsmith,' Tim O'Leary says.

I says, 'Yeah, so what've yer heard?'

And he gives a sort of grin and says, 'Oh, only rumours. Just rumours.' Then it's, 'Okay, let's have a look at this tooth.' And after he had a bit of a poke around he said, 'Well, I shouldn't even attempt to pull that molar. It's got a real bad abscess on it.'

I says, 'Well I'm not leavin' here till it's out.' And fair dinkum, I wasn't going to budge an inch till that molar was gone.

Anyrate, he says, 'Okay then, I'll give it a go. Sit on that box.' And, see, there's this wooden box alongside a post in the building, that they used to put butter into. Tim says, 'Take yer belt off.'

Like, I didn't know what he was on about but, anyway, I took me belt off. I give it to him. Then he got the belt and he tied me head to the post, by the forehead, so I couldn't move and then he starts on the tooth with this huge pair of pliers, under the light of the dull globe, hanging down from the ceiling. And he pushed and he pulled and he yanked it this way and he yanked it that way. I can't remember just now if he even used anaesthetic but, if he did, it did nothing to help the pain. With all this pulling and yanking and going on I'm soon starting to feel pretty faint with it all. But still the molar wouldn't budge, aye.

There was some Murries there, keenly watching all this going on, and all of them with big smirks on their dials. But see, I had to put on a brave face, aye, because I had a big rep up in that country, what with all the scrapping and fighting and milling I'd done and all that. So all these Murries expected me to be real tough, except I wasn't, aye, especially not with Tim getting stuck into me with the pliers. Oh, mate, he was huffing and puffing and pulling it this way and that and then I felt a crunching in me jaw. Now, I don't know if you can go numb with pain but I reckon I did. But by now I'm sweating all over and going from pale to paler and all I could see was all these Murries grinning at me like they're enjoying every minute of it. Anyhow, eventually, Tim got it out. And I tell you what, I can still remember it – there he was, Doctor Tim O'Leary, standing there with this huge, bloodied molar in his pliers, holding it up to the dull light and saying, 'No wonder it was so difficult ter get out. Look,' he said, 'the roots are crossed.'

Now, apparently, when the roots are crossed, half your jaw or something comes out with the molar. That's what it felt like, anyway. So there's Tim, looking very proud of himself, then he turns around to me and he says, 'And what's more, that's only the second tooth I've ever pulled.'

'Well, keep it fer a souvenir, then,' I says, the best I could, and I reckon he might've too because for the life of me I never saw it again after that so I reckon he might've taken me word for it and kept it as a souvenir, aye.

But Rutland Plains Station was a very interesting place to work. A pretty wild sort of place. Like, this's '58 and the Kalala blacks was still spearing the whites right up till 1949, aye. True, on Rutland, down at the horse yard, there's two graves and it's got: 'So-and-so and so-and-so, speared by blacks – 1949.' As late as that. But it worked both ways. See, back in the early 1900s there was a copper, Bowman, up on Rutland and he used to go out with the station owner and shoot the blacks for sport. Yeah, true, just for sport. And he'd also play up with the gins something terrible, aye. Anyrate, the story goes there was a young Murri named Splinter and this Splinter made a special spear just to get Bowman. The first two foot was made out of a heavy redwood and the other six foot was whitewood and he'd sing over this spear like blackfellas do over special things.

Then one day Splinter set a trap, see, and when Bowman comes along on his horse, this Splinter's got this pretty young gin, about fourteen, to bait him. So when Bowman sees her, he thinks this gin's a pretty sure thing, aye, so he trots over with big intentions. But, as he does, the young gin just keeps moving away from him, leading him, like, deeper into the grass. So Bowman gets off his horse and he follows her. But Splinter's waiting in the taller grass, see, and, when he gives the call of a bird, the gin drops down and Splinter jumps up out of the grass and he threw the spear and it went right through Bowman's forehead and come out about eight inches the other side. And that's true. Fair dinkum, Bowman's grave's still there. I've got a photo of it. And there's lots of those untold stories, and they're stories that should be told.

Anyhow, that's a bit of a story on the side, aye, just to demonstrate, and so, yeah, while I'm on Rutland one of the ringers, well, his girlfriend worked at the Normanton Hospital and she tells this ringer to pass on the news how I'm now the father of a baby girl. Yeah, to Gladys. And Gladys called the little baby girl Cynthia and, I tell you, that was a very funny feeling I had inside me when I heard that. Yeah, Cynthia. Beautiful name, aye, Cynthia.

Okay, so now it's only a few weeks before muster's over. Everything's being scaled down and Jack Treewick gives me and Malcolm Boota's younger brother a big heap of matches to go and set fire to about 120 square mile of open country. Well, with the long grass, you burn it off and, when the first rains come all these beautiful shoots come up and the stock go in there and have a real good feed on it. Yeah, so we takes the matches, a couple of packs and our swags and we ride out and we camp at a waterhole about twenty mile from the homestead. Next day, as we go along towards the beach we drop matches here, there and everywhere. Now, before you get to the beach, right in these big patches of sand, there's about half an acre of all these lovely rainforesty trees and beautiful vines and shade and that, and in the middle of that there's some old blackfellas' waterholes, from right back in the early, early days. And there's what you call bailer's shells that you pick up on the beach. Well, I'd say there'd be a good gallon in each scoop full. So the blackfellas would get a bailer's shell and they'd dip it down one of these waterholes – not very big, only about two foot across and two foot deep – and so we had a great big gutful of this beautiful crisp, clear, cool water that'd been there all over that time. Amazing, aye.

Then a bit further on, there's all these shells laying around where the beach used to be and, I tell you, oh, it'd be a shell collector's paradise. Oh, there was just rows and rows of millions of all these beautiful-looking shells. Okay, so now we're riding along the beach. We're in the Gulf so there's not much surf, but it's still really nice, and we see all this sand being thrown up between the water and the first sand dune. So we goes over and there's this great big goanna, aye. He's got his head down the hole and his tail's just hanging out top and he's found where a turtle's laid all her eggs. So we pulls him out by the tail and we fills up our saddlebags with turtle eggs to take back to the station to give to old Ivy Wheeler, the cook. Well, Ivy could do anything with them, aye: biscuits, cakes, anything. Actually, dear old Ivy was pretty keen on me, really. Like, she'd go to town and buy me clothes and everything. Poor old Ivy. A yella piece she was. Okay, so we do that, but then, when we get back to our camp, we discover that the fire we'd lit was not only on its way to burning out a great big swag of open country but, along its way, it'd burnt our camp out as well. Burnt our swags, pack saddles, everything.

'Geez, we're in big strife here,' I says. Then when we got back to Jack Treewick we tell him what'd happened and I says, 'Mate, if yer feel like sackin' us, we'll truly understand.' But, he didn't and so I stayed there on Rutland till after the muster and by then I'd gotten a big enough cheque to go down to the Towers and start courting this Edith. Oh yeah, she was still pretty keen, yeah, even after all them times I had to make up things about why I couldn't get down there sooner.

Okay, so when I finished up, Jack Treewick drove me into Normanton and, when I gets there, other than to pick up me truck and leave town, I was also hoping I might be able to see Gladys and get to see me little daughter, Cynthia. And I did get to see them, but, well, sort of – yes and no. Well, see, I was standing on the verandah of the bottom pub and from there you can see right over to Henry Boota's sister-in-law's house and I saw Gladys over there with the little baby in her arms and, mate, how I just longed and I longed and wanted to go over there and nurse it and hold it and it's always been one of me great regrets how I didn't marry Gladys, even if it was just to give my own daughter a name. But anyway, it didn't come to that, aye.

So I got me truck and I'm ready to leave the Gulf and the only person I went and said goodbye to was Sam Henry, the copper. Yeah, Sam's the only one. I says, 'Sam, I'm leavin' this country now. I'm goin' down to the Towers. I've got a woman down there.'

And Sam sort of nods his head down the street to where Gladys lives and he says, 'So what about what yer leavin' behind here?'

See, Sam knew everything about everyone around Normanton even if they didn't know it themselves, so it wasn't much use trying to fool him, aye, so I says, 'I gotta leave Sam. It breaks me in two, mate, but if I stay here I'm only gonna be doin' the same sorts of things like duffin' 'n' fightin' 'n' all that fer the rest of me life 'n' I'll be goin' nowhere. What I really need's a good clean break 'n' to start fresh all over again.'

And he says, 'Well, all the best to yer Goldie but yer wanta watch that truck, it's unregistered 'n' the other copper in town's a transport bloke.'

I says, 'Well, then, I'd better leave right away, aye.'

He said, 'Best'a luck, mate.'

And yeah, so that was that. I left Normanton.

37

So I burns all me bridges, aye, and I goes down to Charters Towers in the little International truck to get on with this Edith Combridge. And, oh yeah, me and Edith, we got on well, real well, but, see, I still had to find a job, you know. But then, pretty soon the news got around: 'Oh, there's a ringer from the Gulf here.' See, ringers from the Gulf, they was pretty much sought-after down that way because they'd worked with wild cattle, throwing them and all that. Anyway, they're all looking for men, so a cattle buyer gets on to me, a feller named Joe Downey, and Joe says, 'Look,' he says, 'they want a ringer out at Egera Station, up the Cape River country.'

See, the turn-up there was that anybody who wanted anything went to Joe Downey. He was that sort of feller. If you wanted a ringer, you went to Joe. If you wanted a camp cook, you went to Joe. If you wanted a fencer, you went to Joe. Joe was the buyer for Swift's Meatworks so he was well known; a bit too well known to some people's liking, because he also had the rep as being a bit of a one with the women. Well, one story goes along the lines of an owner feller of one of the big stations out there had around seven hundred bullocks out on camp waiting to be sold to Swift's. Now Swift's had two local buyers – one was Tiger Nelson and the other was Joe Downey – and this owner feller didn't know which one was going to turn up that day to go out and take a look at his cattle. So the owner feller's just about to get on his horse to go out to the camp where the bullocks are waiting and he says to his ten-year-old son, he says: 'Son, now if Tiger Nelson comes out, tell yer mother ter give him a couple'a nips'a rum 'cause Tiger always likes ter have his nip'a rum. But if that Joe Downey comes out, son, I want yer ter just go and sit on yer mother's lap 'n' don't move till he's gone.'

So yeah, that was Joe Downey and he got me the job out at Egera. Egera wasn't far from the Towers, about sixty mile or so, and Joe and me became good mates. Very good. So I goes out and they give me the horse breaking in job there for a while and when the muster started I went out in the stock camp. Actually, Egera belonged to an elderly lady in England and she had a feller named Fred Brown in as manager. They called Fred 'Sovereign Mouth' because he had a mouth full of gold teeth. But Fred was good to me because he'd always get me to go into town whenever we needed anything so I could catch up with Edith. And I enjoyed it out there. Oh, it was an easy life compared to ringing up in the Gulf and I got to meet some great people. One feller who became a great mate of mine was a drover by the name of Harold Lavery. There's a bit of a story there too, see, because I remember one time when Harold came out to Egera with Joe Downey to pick up a mob of bullocks and we're sitting having smoko and Harold says, 'Guess who died this morning?'

'Wouldn't have a clue,' I says.

He says, 'Gallopin' Jones.'

Now Galloping Jones was folklore up in that country. You could write a book about him. But he was a very bad alcoholic and this's a fact that I'm going to tell you. See, years before, he was in Cloncurry and he got pinched for being drunk and disorderly and so they shut him in the cell and there was a new copper out from Brisbane and he'd heard all about this Galloping Jones. Anyhow, he's got the Jones in the cell and he says to him, 'So you're the great Gallopin' Jones I hear everyone talk about.' He says, 'Well, I can't see anythin' smart or gallopin'

Goldie horse breaking on Egera station

about you so let's see how good yer are with choppin' the wood heap out the back'a the police station.' 'As a matter of fact,' he says, 'I'll even give yer a brand new axe that's never been used before. You can use that.'

Well, see, in those days, if you had ten shillings you could bail yourself out. So Galloping Jones, he's there chopping this wood and an old drover mate of his comes past. 'G'day mate, how're goin'?' says the Jones.

'G'day, mate,' says his drover mate. 'What're yer doin'?'

'Oh,' says Galloping Jones, 'just cuttin' some wood fer the police station.'

'Nice axe yer got,' says the drover.

So Galloping Jones looks at the axe and he says, 'Yer can have it fer ten bob, if yer like. It's a bargain.'

'Too right it is,' says the drover and so Galloping Jones sells the axe to his drover mate for ten bob and he goes down to the court house and he bails himself out, then he pinches the police black tracker's horse and takes off out of town and he gets out to a place called Boomarra. And when he gets to Boomarra he goes into the post office there and he sends the copper a telegram along the lines of: 'To the new copper at Cloncurry. Now passing Boomarra. Best wishes, Galloping Jones.' So, yeah, that was Galloping Jones and that's how he rubbed salt in that copper's wound, aye.

So that was just a story on the side because, here I am, I'm in the Towers and I'm courting Edith, aye, and I'm breaking in horses and that out at Egera and I was just starting to get a bit of a name around town. So I'd go into town and visit Edith whenever I could, like on long weekends and that, and like I said, if Fred Brown wanted something he'd send me into the Towers. And when I'd come to town I'd stay at Edith and her mother's place, along with the younger sister, Pearl, and the two younger boys, Ben and Aubury.

Okay, so anyway, there was this horse out at Egera called Gilletto, and this thing was a man-killer. Oh, it was one of them I told you about that shows the whites of its eyes. Yeah, Gilletto they called it and, I tell you, this thing would come at you with its ears back. It's just lucky how one of the rails in the round yard had a bow in it so I could fly through there and get away from him. Anyway, previous to that, when I was up in the Gulf, there was an oil-drilling camp looking for oil. Like, they'd work something like twelve days on, then they'd have four days or something off. Whatever it was, they had very, very good conditions. They had this big marquee and they had the best of tucker. That sort of thing. All white fellers, and whenever they come to Normanton they used to drink at the bottom pub. And they never brawled. They never mouthed off or anything like that. They was well liked. Oh, you know, they'd get drunk every now and then, but that's all. Anyhow, I'm in town this time and I takes Edith to the pictures and during the interval we go down for a beer and, lo and behold, there's one of these oil-drilling fellers so I says, 'How're yer goin'?' I'd forgot what his name was. 'What're yer doin' down here?'

He says, 'G'day Goldie. Oh, I left the oil-drillin' team.'

'Oh, yeah.'

Then on the other side of the bar, see, there was two fellers sitting here and three fellers there and a couple more over there. Not over full. And one of them fellers sings out, 'Hey, Goldie, have yer struck any yang-yangs out at Egera, yet?'

A yang-yang is a bad horse, see, so I says, 'Oh yeah, have I what?' And then I'm into this great big theatrical act about how I get on this mongrel Gilletto. Anyrate, I stepped out from the bar and I've just cashed a pound note for a beer. So, yeah, I'm out from the bar, see, and I'm going through all these antics about getting on Gilletto and I'm really putting it on, aye, so I've got them really laughing. But while I'm doing all this, out from the corner of me eye, I notice this ex-oil-drilling feller. Like, he'd have a little sip, then he'd put his glass down. Have a little sip. And he's gradually getting closer and closer to me change, on the counter. Anyway, I just turned me head for split second, but not so far as I couldn't still see him, and, as quick as a flash, he dragged four bob across to his glass. Four shillings of mine. No, I never said a word. I let it be because I didn't want to go roughing him up and get blood all over me shirt. His blood, I tell you. I mean, going back inside the pictures when you're dating someone, it wouldn't look too good, aye. Anyway, I just thought to meself, Well, there you are. It only cost me four shillings to find out what a mongrel character you really are, mate.

Yeah, you wouldn't credit it, aye, just how low some people can get. But, anyway, see, I'm courting Edith and she's still doing her nurse's training up at the hospital and, when I'm in town, I'd wait for her at the nursing quarters in me truck, the D4 International 15 cwt. One day I'm waiting and Edith sings out, 'An emergency's come in. I can't get away for about another hour.'

So I thought, Well I'd just go 'n' see this feller who's a bit of a wheeler 'n' a dealer around town. You know, he buys and sells and all that. Anyhow, he had this De Soto, a 1949 model sedan. Beautiful-looking bit of gear, it was, and I was very impressed with this shiny-looking machine. Immaculate it was. And I'm looking at it and right out of the blue the wheeler-dealer feller says, 'Goldie, how's about we make an outright swap, you know, your International for my De Soto?'

'Yeah,' I said. 'Okay then, it's a deal.'

And so now, instead of waiting for Edith in me International, there I am waiting for her in this flashy De Soto, just to impress her, aye. Anyway, it didn't go down too well. Actually, both her and her family was disappointed that I sold me little truck and, when I come to think about it, so was I. You know, I even had

'Nelly' painted on the front of it. But that's how I got the De Soto. But, stupid, I should've kept me old truck because I loved that thing. I even took a photo of it.

Yeah, so other than that everything's going real smooth. Me and Edith are getting on real well. I'm making good money – very good money. Except then Edith's mother, Elma, started to take more than a normal interest in me. You know, getting a bit fresh with me. Trying it on, like, and at first I just tried to ignore her, aye. Well, I really don't know why. You know, I wasn't interested in a widow with four kids, who was old enough to be me mother. Oh, I'd says she'd been in her late forties and I was about twenty-seven or twenty-eight. And Edith, oh yeah, she could see it and she stuck by me. But then, when I refused Elma's advances, she started turning the rest of Edith's family against me. Yeah, she turned Edith's sister, Pearl, who was also doing her nurse's training with Edith, against me, even the two boys, Ben and Aubury. Edith was the eldest. And things got so bad that I couldn't stay there anymore. I had to go somewhere else. I made some sort of excuse about it and, from then on, whenever I come to town, I went and stayed at Joe Downey's place. Joe thought very highly of me.

38

Anyhow, I'd been on Egera for about four months or something and, like I said, whenever Fred Brown, the manager, wanted something from town he'd send me in there so I could catch up with Edith. So I'm in town this time and I runs into a feller, Rex Jones. Now, I'd worked with Rex out on Mount Elsie Station, back around 1956. So I knew Rex and Rex also knew what things I used to get up to when I was up in the Gulf and so Rex says to me, 'So Goldie, I hear yer out on Egera now.'

'Yeah.'

He says, 'Look, I've just taken over runnin' the camp on Mount Elsie.' And then he goes all quiet on it, see, and he says, 'Goldie, now you've been around a bit, aye, 'n', just between you 'n' me, I reckon we could both make a few quid out on Mount Elsie.'

I says, 'Yeah? How?'

He says, 'Well, I've got some pubs lined up, see, so, if yer come 'n' work with me, every now 'n' then we can take a nice fat Mount Elsie bullock, butcher it up, 'n' sell it to these pubs, on the side, like. But Goldie, I want someone I can trust. Someone like you, mate.'

But, see, I was trying to get away from all that sort of thing. But then I thought about it, aye. See, if I was on Mount Elsie I'd be closer to the Towers so I'd get to see more of Edith and, also, there'd be the extra money, too. So I said to Rex, I said, 'Look, Rex, I'm not sure it'd work. Yer just can't keep somethin' like that a secret while there's other men in the camp, especially if they're Murries. I mean, surely they'll know somethin's goin' on?'

'No, she'll be right. I'll fix it,' he says.

Anyhow, I says to Rex, 'Okay. Yeah. Why not?'

So like a stupid fool I left Egera and I went out to Mount Elsie. And I'd been happy on Egera. Really happy. Oh, they had a good camp and everything. Good tucker. And then, when I gets out to Mount Elsie, Rex says, 'Look mate, I don't think it's a goer. I don't reckon we'd be able ter get away with it. It'll surely get back to the owners.'

I says, 'Yer not too far wrong there, mate.'

So no, we didn't even start and Rex gave me the breaking in job there, on Mount Elsie. Then just before show weekend in the Towers, word came from a neighbouring property to say they'd got some Mount Elsie cattle over there. So Rex and me, we got a couple of packs and we heads over to this mustering camp and we're riding along and we're talking about this and that and I says to Rex, I says, 'Yer know mate, I could do with fifty quid. Me swag cover's torn. I need some decent clothes to go out with Edith in 'n' one thing 'n' another. I could do with fifty quid.'

He says, 'Oh, yeah', and he left it at that.

Okay, so we gets to this mustering camp and there's quite a few Mount Elsie cattle. I'd say we was there for about nine days in all and we're about to go home. Anyhow, the Mount Elsie cattle was all boxed in with the neighbour's cattle so the head stockman feller who was running the camp, him and a Murri, they're cutting out the Mount Elsie cattle for us to take home. Cutting out bullocks, cutting out steers, cutting out dry cows – that's cows without a calf. I'd say there'd be about two hundred cattle, all mixed up. Anyhow, Rex's over here, holding our Mount Elsie cattle. It's what they call 'the face of the camp'. Then I'm here, see. Anyhow, this Mount Elsie cow goes to walk out with her calf so I comes in and gets behind her to push her back over to Rex. But then this head stockman feller, he trots up and he pushes the cow and the calf back into his mob. And, like, I thought, Geez, there's somethin' fishy goin' on here.

Then we cuts a few more steers and dry cows. In the meantime, this Mount Elsie cow and her calf still wants to come back over into the Mount Elsie mob. Well, she must've had a mate over there or something. So I gets behind her again and pushes her and her calf back over. But then the head stockman feller trots up and pushes them both back in with his mob. Yeah, this's for the second time. So I'm wondering what's going on and then Rex rides over and he says to me, 'What're yer doin'?'

I says, 'What's it look like?' I says, 'Pushin' one'a our Mount Elsie cows 'n' her calf back inta our mob, where they belong.'

Rex says, 'Goldie, do yer want your fifty quid or not?'

That's when the penny dropped, aye. See, Rex'd made a deal with this head stockman feller, on the side, that he'd sell him Mount Elsie cows and calves. Cleanskins, like. Not branded, of course. And he'd sold whatever per head comes to 103 pound to this feller. No, I don't know how many cattle that'd be. So Rex says to me, 'Goldie you 'n' me, we'll go halves, but I'll keep the extra three quid 'cause I'm doin' the dealin'.'

Anyrate, so then we takes what we had back to Mount Elsie and on show day Rex comes up and he hands me fifty quid. Not long after that, the head stockman feller sees me with Edith and he says, 'Goldie, have yer seen Rex yet?'

I says, 'Yeah.'

'Good,' he says.

Yeah, so they're both in on it, aye, for sure. Then after the show weekend I goes back out to Mount Elsie. Anyhow, Frank Webb comes out every now and then to Mount Elsie just to see how things are going. Now, you might remember, Frank Webb was the husband of one of the sisters who owned the place. And I remember this in vivid detail; when we sold those cattle, somehow, and I don't know how, but rumours must've got back to Frank Webb. See, what I didn't like about that deal was that there was a Murri there at the time and I don't like Murris being involved in anything shady because, sure as eggs, they'll spill their guts.

Yeah, anyway, this Frank Webb comes out and he picks an argument with Rex Jones over something stupid and small. Oh, something like the amount of dogs Rex had. Well, Frank Webb didn't like dogs, aye, and Rex had lots of them. Anyway, he sacks Rex and gives him his marching orders. But, see, I knew what was really behind it, aye, because just a couple of days later a few of us was walking down to the ringers' quarters. Anyhow, Frank's waiting behind one of the sheds and he pulls me up and he says, 'Goldie, you wouldn't do the wrong thing by me with cattle or anythin', would yer?'

And, oh, it was hard. I says, 'No, Frank, I gave all that up when I left the Gulf. I've finished all that. I'm startin' afresh now I've met this Edith piece.'

He says, 'Okay, that's all I wanta know, mate.'

And, you know, it really got to me how I lied to him because even though Jonesy done all the dealing, the truth of it is, I still helped take those cattle off him. So Frank Webb knew about it, aye. But I tell you, another thing why I felt terrible was because one of the ladies who owned Mount Elsie, Mrs Morrison, like, I just got on so very, very well with her. Whenever I was in the Towers I'd always go around to her place and have a cup of tea with her and tell her all about the trouble I was having with Edith's mother and all that. And we'd talk about it. Just her and me. She really cared for me, that woman, she did. She was such a lovely person was Mrs Morrison, both to me and to Edith, and that's what also made me feel so bad about it.

39

So I ended up quitting Mount Elsie, aye. Well, you know, I felt guilty with the business about the cattle and they was such nice people, especially Mrs Morrison. Yeah, so I pulled the pin and I went back into the Towers and I'm staying with Joe Downey because things are too hot around at Edith's place. Well, you know, her mother was saying things about me and my character that just wasn't right, so Edith and me, we sort of kept our courting to just when we could.

Anyhow, Joe Downey said Southwick Station wanted a ringer so I went out there. Southwick's about forty mile out from the Towers so it was easy to get back in and see Edith. It was good country. The cattle was very, very quiet. And as well as sending bullocks off, they also bred stud bulls. Like, when the calves come in to be branded, if it was a good-looking bull they'd put it aside and see how it'd turn out and so, every now and then, they'd have a bull sale. Yeah, so at first they'd keep these calves around the homestead and then, when they had about eighty or so, another feller and me – actually it was Joe Downey's son, Warren – well, Warren and me, we'd take them from the little bull paddock, a good day's ride away, out to the big bull paddock. And me and Warren, we'd be riding along, aye, looking at these bulls and I'd say, 'Look at that bull there, yer couldn't keep him as a bull, could yer? He's got a black nose. He's back's not straight.' So along the way we'd pull a few down and we'd cut them – you know, castrate them – and we'd let them go.

But on Southwick, you never worked hard, aye. As I said, the cattle was very quiet. Anyhow, back a while, when I'd been on

Egera there was a feller in the camp there called George Orman and George was courting a woman by the name of Dorothy French. Dorothy's parents was doing yard building out on Egera. That's where he met her, and then just when I was leaving Egera, George had come up to me and said, 'Goldie,' he said, 'I'm gonna marry this girl Dorothy. Would yer be me best man?'

I says, 'No problem, George.'

So then, when I was out at Southwick, George sends word out to me, see. 'Goldie, I'm getting married on such and such a date in such and such a church in Charters Towers.'

The only trouble is that I'm out at the big bullock paddock, dipping cattle, see, and this unseasonal rain comes in and there's a river called the Hann, about thirty mile from the Towers, and it runs a banker. So I'm stuck, aye, and I can't even get word to George how I can't get to town. Anyhow, he told me later, there he is standing at the altar waiting to say his 'I do's and everything and he's wondering why I'm not turning up. Of course, he doesn't know the circumstances so he's waiting and waiting, and this Dorothy, well, she's waiting too. Anyhow, the priest feller finally gets all impatient about it and he tells George that he's got better things to do than to hang about all day. So in the end George races out in the street and he grabs the nearest ringer he knew – a feller called Ollingsworth – to come in and be his best man. Now this Ollingsworth, he's just landed in town in an old pair of riding boots, an old pair of jeans and a shirt he'd wore for a week or so and that's the best he can do. So George grabs him and takes him into the church to be the best man, aye.

Anyrate, see, I'm also planning to get married by then, too. Like, I'd bought Edith an engagement ring and all. Well I tricked her into getting the size of her finger and I let Wallace Bishop, in Brisbane, know and they sent the ring up. It cost twenty-two pound. That was almost a fortnight's wages back then. Yeah, so

I proposed to her outside the nurses' quarters one night after she knocked off from duty. I gave it to her then. But I tell you, it took a lot of courage for her to wear that ring because her mother, Elma, and her sister, Pearl, gave her hell over it. You know, saying about how wrong it was for Edith to marry a common ringer like me and all that. Oh yeah, they'd even bring her to tears. Edith was telling me that at one time there she got so upset she threw a jug of water over her mother. She'd had enough of her, aye. So yeah, it took a lot of courage for her to wear that engagement ring.

Anyhow, I was out there on Southwick Station, ringing and I just gave notice and I left. Yeah, pulled the pin. Well it was too quiet. You know, you don't gallop after cattle. You didn't have to throw cattle or anything and, really, I wanted to get up in the desert country. See, I'd never worked that country before. Anyway, Joe Downey's son, Warren, he left Southwick just before me so Joe Downey gets both Warren and me a job at Milray Station. The Cape River runs through Milray. It's about 120 mile south-west of Charters Towers. Well, it's about seventy mile from the Towers to Pentland, then another fifty mile from Pentland to Milray. Yeah, Pentland. A little one-pub town. I'd never seen it before. So Joe drives us out there and we go down to the ringers' quarters and the first thing Joe done, he got the mattress from my room and he got the mattress from Warren's room and he hung them both on the fence in the sun. So I says, 'What're yer doin'?'

He says, 'Yer always hang yer mattresses in the sun.' That's what he said and I later learned it's the thing to do because the ultraviolet rays of the sun sort of sterilises it a bit, aye.

But on Milray, I mean, even when you was out on the camp you didn't get out of your swag till eight o'clock of a morning and you don't go mustering and tracking and looking where the cattle are. So there's no real riding out. Nothing. All you do is wait for them to come in to drink at the water troughs or the waterholes and you pick them all up and take them to the yard and brand them. Oh, it was a real bludge. Good tucker, though. But to be truthful, on Milray, it taught you to be lazy, aye. A bloke called Gus Lawson was the manager and him and his wife had had something like seven daughters and people was always asking him, 'Are yer gonna try fer a son, Gus? Yer gonna try fer a son?' But he never got a son.

Okay, meantime things between Edith and her mother are going from bad to worse and I'd get an earful of it when I come to town to see her. Terrible it was. And, oh, that's right. It's coming back to me now. See, remember that ex-oil-driller feller I told you about who pinched me four shillings off the counter when I was telling the fellers about that bad horse, Gilletto? Well, one time Edith and me, we're up at the Excelsior Hotel in the Towers, see. Now the Excelsior's the pub where all the station managers and the station owners drink. A first-class place. Ringers don't drink there much. Ringers go down to all the dens and the pubs like the Southern Cross. Yeah, the old Blood 'n' Guts. But anyhow, see, Edith had nursed the publican's wife up at the hospital and she was always saying to Edith, 'Oh, you must bring Goldie down 'n' I'll shout you a drink to thank you for all your care while I was in hospital.'

So me and Edith, we're up there at the Excelsior Hotel, see, in the Ladies' Lounge. Mind you, this's where the barmaid comes around with a little tray and says, 'Can I get you anythin' to drink, sir?' So it's pretty posh, aye. Anyhow, lo and behold, I sees this same ex-oil-drilling feller that nicked me four bob when I was out on Egera Station.

'G'day,' he says.

I says the same, but I'm a bit cool on it. And, well, I had a lot of money at that time. You know, I'd just come in from the desert country so I had a big roll of notes. Five and ten pound

Goldie up a windmill on Milray station

notes. Okay, so when the girl with the tray comes out I order drinks for me and Edith and I just peels off a fiver or whatever to make a bit of a show of it. Like, I'm really trying to impress Edith a bit. And when this feller sees me there with all this money I notice how his eyes nearly fall out of his head, aye. Then he sidles over and he says, 'Oh, Goldie,' he says, 'if I had just twenty pound'a that,' he says, 'yer know, mate, I'd go back oil drillin' tomorra.'

And I almost said, 'Well, if yer hadn't knocked that four bob off me I'd lend yer twenty quid.' And actually I wouldn't have cared if I never got it back. Like, I would've helped him but – and this's the important part – but only if I thought he was the kind of a feller that's worth helping. You know, if I thought he had good, sound, solid character. Anyway, I just never said a word. No, not a thing because as I said, as we go through life, it sometimes costs us thousands to find out a person's real character and I found out this feller's character for just a miserable four bob. Oh yeah, he would've remembered what he'd done back then. Too right, he would've, the mongrel.

So anyway, I'm over on Milray and, with all the easy times we're having I starts sketching and I'm getting a bit of a rep in the Towers for me sketches. Like, I'd put them up at the pubs and the bars and that, then next time I come to town I'd pull them down and put fresh ones up. I used to do a lot of sketching. I really loved it. I never charged anything. I'd just give them away. But, no, I don't know where I learned it. I guess, I just picked it up. Just a little talent I didn't know I had.

But in the meantime Edith's mother's coming on extra heavy, trying to break us up because we're now engaged. So, of course, I kept it hush-hush about me having an Aboriginal daughter at this stage because I didn't want to lose Edith over it. Anyway, I only worked out on Milray Station for three months, up till January 1961, and then we planned to clear out to Sydney, the both of us. You know, elope. So she'd just passed her final nursing exams. Four years Queensland nurses' training was back then. Then Edith packed all her ports and she hid them under one of the nursing sister's beds, up at the hospital. And she had to do that real careful, too, because her sister Pearl was also nursing and Edith couldn't let her see all this going on because Pearl would be straight off to her mother Elma as sure as eggs.

I'd also sold the big, flash De Soto to one of the local dealers, which meant I didn't have a vehicle. Well, I just got what I could get for it, aye. Anyway, as the day drew nearer I lined up a mate to take us to Townsville. That was in a sedan because his wife wanted to come along too. Bill Bright his name was. He was out on Egera back when I pulled the pin there. The plan was for us to stay in Townsville that night and catch the plane to Sydney the next day. Yeah, I'd already bought the tickets and all. Trans-Australian Airlines it was.

Okay, then, on the eve before we're leaving, remember that Mrs Morrison I told you about who owned Mount Elsie? The place where Rex Jones and me sold the cattle from, well, she lived in town, aye, and I got to be good mates with her and she knew all about the plan for me and Edith to elope and, do you know what? On the eve we're going to leave the Towers she gave Edith a wonderful thing: a beautiful old brooch. And she asked Edith if she'd be so kind as to wear it on the day we got married because she'd wore it on the day she got married and her mother had wore it on the day she'd got married. So if anybody deserves a ride straight up into the kingdom, then that'd be Mrs Morrison, I'd reckon. Yeah, it was a lovely little locket that you put photos in and you just press it and it opened, aye.

And also the matron up at the Towers hospital, Elsie Moffatt, she was on Edith's side, too, see. The only trouble was, by now, Elma, the mother, is guarding Edith pretty close. Well, she'd always go up to the hospital to pick Edith up after she finished her shift and all that. Yeah, to try and keep her away from me. So then, on the day we're to elope, the matron, this Elsie Moffatt, when she wrote out the roster, she wrote out that Edith would be on a broken shift. You know, saying how Edith was starting at seven or eight in the morning and finishing at midday and then she also wrote her down to come back at four in the afternoon, then finish at, say, eight o'clock that night. That's what she had rostered up. So the old mother and the sister, Pearl, they thought Edith was going to finish at eight o'clock that night and that's when Elma planned to be waiting for her outside the hospital. But, in actual fact, the matron let Edith off at midday. And it worked like clockwork, aye. Bill Bright and his missus, they pulled up and we threw Edith's ports in the back of the car and we was out of there. Yeah, it went like clockwork and I tell you, it felt good, real good.

40

Yeah, so I makes the big mistake of going down to Sydney. Stupid, aye. Well, I should've gone up to Darwin or somewhere more 'bush' but I took Edith down to Sydney. And I knew it was a mistake the closer we got to Sydney because all them old feelings started coming back to me again. You know, about the stepmother and all that, from away back then. Amazing, aye. Anyhow, so we gets down to Sydney and we gets married. Bluey Flannigan was dead by then. He'd died back in '54, I think. So for me best man I got Frank Yateman. Frank's that feller I took off with out to Toowoomba when we was kids. I got him. He was still at the Government Printing Office, where I done that apprenticeship thing, and, oh, all that seemed like another world by then.

But in Sydney, we just couldn't get on our feet. We just could not get on our feet. Oh, we was living everywhere. Going from suburb to suburb. From flat to flat. Little dingy flats, taking up half your rent. Battling, battling, battling, and also I knew nothing about birth control or that, so it was an unplanned pregnancy. He was conceived a month after we got married and because Edith was pregnant, she couldn't work. So yeah, it was hard, real hard.

Still, I thought, Well, seeing I'm in Sydney I'd better go 'n' front the family 'n' show Edith off 'n' all this sort of thing. And my father was delighted. Overjoyed. Yeah, they still lived in Croydon. Then the stepmother was all over Edith and she'd come around to whatever flat we lived in at the time and take Edith out and one thing and another. Of course, the motive was that she knew I'd told Edith of the horrible life I went under so she was trying to gloss it over. And really, I held nothing against her. That was all gone. I just wanted everybody to be mates again. And I caught up with David, me brother. He was a sheet metal worker for Malley's but I noticed how he was a very heavy drinker. He'd married a woman who was a lot older than him and she turned out to be unfaithful. She even had a child to someone else while they was married. But in the end she left him, which was the best thing, aye.

Anyhow, I finally scores a job as a forklift driver at the CSR, loading the sugar on the trucks, in pallets. Shiftwork. So the first bloke came along and there was complications with that. See, with Edith being so little, she had to have a caesarean and I was on nightshift when I got called up to the hospital at Alexandria. Like, it's about one o'clock of a morning and I'm worried because the doctor, Dr Robinson, said there was trouble. So there I am sitting in the waiting room. The only one there. And I wasn't very good at praying or that but I prayed to God that things would turn out well. Then not long after, someone came out and said, 'Congratulations, you've got a son!' And I looked through a glass thing in the door where the maternity part was and I saw the baby – my baby – and he was all covered in white stuff. Anyrate, I never forget the midwife. A pommy piece. She says, 'Edith, put your tongue out.' So Edith sticks her tongue out and I found out later it's a thing they do to see if they're with it or not. So then the midwife takes a look at Edith's tongue and she said to me, 'She'll be alright.' She said, 'And by the way, that boy of yours has got huge shoulders. He's gonna be a big boy.'

Yeah, and Edith said, 'What're we gonna call him?'

I says, 'We'll call him Adrian.' See, I wanted to call him Adrian because it was the English name of that Aboriginal fella who stopped me from being shot by Chalkley, when I was up on Glenore that time.

'Okay,' she says, 'we'll call him Adrian then.'

Then I said, 'And I want his second name to be Tahmal', which was the first tribal name of that same Aboriginal fella, Tahmal Meenyarrawal, the 'Tahmal' meaning 'ringtail possum' and 'Meenyarrawal' meaning 'his tracks go back'.

She says, 'Oh, that's fine by me.'

So that was that and, anyhow, when I was at CSR I got friends with a feller, Warren Harvey. Warren was one of the truck drivers there and when we'd shift around Sydney he was good enough to lend me his little Ford truck and we'd use that. Like, I didn't have a New South Wales licence, but we'd shift around. Shift around. Never settled. So Edith and me, we become friends with Warren and his family. His wife's name was Wendy. Actually, one time this horse wandered into his yard. Very quiet, you could pick his feet up. So I had a look and I thought, Gee, I'll shoe this feller. And, see, Warren lived behind a railway so I'm shoeing this horse and I'd race out and shape the horseshoes on the railway line, you know, and trains'd come flying past – toot! toot! – for me to get off the track. Then, with all the interruptions of trains going past, it's starting to get dark, aye, so I brings the horse into the house and I've got him in the lounge room and I'm slapping the shoes on him. Every foot. So that's alright. I finished doing that, then I leads the horse outside and I puts him in the yard, and Warren's father-in-law was a very bad drunk. He used to come home drunk a lot so, to save the embarrassment of him using bad language and that, when he walks into the house, Warren grabs him and he takes his tie off and he takes him into the bedroom and he ties him up with his hands behind his feet and his knees bent and tied with his ankles and his wrists all together. Then he put something as a mouth gag so we can't hear him singing out and cursing.

So we has our tea and we watched a movie on TV and it's getting late and someone remembers that the old feller's been tied up for three hours or something in the bedroom, aye. So Warren says to me, 'Look, Goldie, I'll take yers back to yer flat first because I don't want yer ter be around when I untie him because it won't be a nice thing to hear.' Now, I forget where that flat was, because we had so many flats. Oh, we moved about eighteen or twenty times. It could've been anywhere. Very unsettled. Yeah, so they tied him up and we forgot about him, aye, and you can imagine his wrists and all that being numb.

But that was Warren's father-in-law and not his father, because Warren's father was an Adventist and I guess with all this unsettling going on I was trying to find some reasons for me life and I got on very well with Warren's father and we talked a lot about life and religion and all that. But anyway, Warren could see I was having trouble making ends meet so one day he said to me, 'Look,' he says, 'I've got a small block of country down at Nowra so how's about comin' in share farmin' with me 'n' we'll plough up some land 'n' put some corn in. There's good money in corn.'

I says, 'Yeah, mate, anything to get away from here.'

So I pulls the pin at CSR and we loads his Ford truck up and I goes down to Nowra with Edith and the young feller. What'd he be, now? Nine months or something. And the horse I told you about, well we took him down too, in the back of this truck. So we moves down there into this barn on his little farm. Yeah, like a little old slab hut sort of thing, cut out by an adze. An adze? That's an axe-type thing for shaping timber. Old-time people used it for making huts out of bush timber. Anyrate, I gets a job at the John Bull factory. They made fan belts and radiator hoses for cars, and Warren let me use his truck to go to work and that. But the problem was, there's nothing being done about ploughing or anything. Like, he's always saying, 'Goldie, I wanta get some corn in. We'll get some corn in', and I'm saying, 'Alright, so when're we gonna start?'

But nothing's happening. So I broke in two horses for him and then there was some cattle roaming free in the hills, so we'd go and muster them. Like, nobody owned them so we thought we may as well own them. And I taught him how to castrate and how to pull bulls down. Then on the little Ford he had, we built a crate to take the cattle into the Homebush saleyards. Of course, the law was that you're supposed to have a waybill and a permit to carry cattle on the road. But we never got that so when I'd go up to Homebush I'd go the long way around via Kiama because, on the main road, inspectors checked trucks at random. And I had to climb this great big steep hill. Like, I'd have to get it right down into low gear and you'd hear it going up, you'd imagine, from a fair way away. Anyhow, the inspector feller he'd always see me coming back down the main road with an empty crate and he'd wonder how I got up to Sydney without him seeing me. Then one night when I gets up on top of this hill, it's pouring rain and, oh, I had a bad bull, aye. I had his head tied because he was goring the other cattle, see. But, when I gets to the bottom of the hill, there's this feller waiting for me. Anyway, he's got a torch and he's going all round the truck and he says, 'What's wrong with that bull?'

So I told him and, as I said, I had no waybill or nothing, so when I gets to Homebush saleyard the stock squad's waiting for me, aye. Anyhow, I didn't hide anything from them. I said, 'These belong to the Harveys down at Nowra.' Warren's parents were more or else involved in it, too.

So then they're all looking under this truck, looking to see if I had anything under there I could've used to cover me tracks with. See, that's what cattle stealers do when they steal cattle. But as far as I was concerned I wasn't stealing the cattle because they was just roaming free in the hills, you know. Anyway, after they looked at the truck I was loading the cattle onto a ramp and one jumped out. So I up and pulled him down by the tail, aye, and I spun him around on his H-bone and got him to stand up, then I guided him into the yard and this stock squad feller's real impressed, aye. He says, 'Gee mate, you've been around cattle a long time, haven't yer?'

And I said, 'Yeah, sort of, on and off a bit.'

Anyhow, that's about the last time I was involved in it. I'd say we sent about three loads up, then there wasn't many more wandering in the hills. But, see, there's still nothing happening on this place and the rings in the tractor are shot. Like, you'd use about a gallon of oil every time you started the thing up. But there's no hint of anything going to happen and I was giving them a little bit of money every payday for all the corn we're going to plant and all that. Anyway, in the end, I said to Edith, I says, 'We're not doin' any good here. I think it's time we moved on.'

So the next time I'm in Sydney, a feller I was with in the army, Fred Lathline, well, his mate, Laurie Croft, had a panel van. So I lines Laurie up to the date I'm going to finish at John Bull's then I went over to Wendy, Warren Harvey's wife, and I said, 'Wendy, we're goin'. Can I have the money I gave Warren ter pay for things?'

And she gave it back. No, there was no trouble there. So we loaded our gear in Laurie's panel van and a trailer and we took it up to Springwood, which was another big mistake. But anyhow, the whole saga is this: we was really battling and we never got on our feet so things weren't looking too good, aye. Yeah, it was like we was sort of drowning, but real slow. Yeah, that was the feeling.

41

So now we're at Springwood, back where it all started. But I just don't know what could've been in me head, aye, because it's bringing up things all about me childhood. So it was hard, real hard, and also by now Edith's pregnant with the second feller. Anyhow, because I had a good rep as a forklift driver with CSR, they put me straight back on. But then I had to travel all the way down to Pyrmont, in Sydney, so I bought a little Hillman from a caryard in Springwood for forty quid. Ten pound down and I paid it off at five pound per week. But, yeah, it was all too much, especially on Edith, so I thought I'd better get a daytime job. So I pulls the pin at CSR, see, and I'm drinking with a feller at a bar and there's this big heavy from the Printers' Union drinking alongside us so I says, 'Mate, I'm lookin' fer a daytime job.'

He said, 'Go round ter Trades Hall tomorra 'n' tell this bloke I sent yer.' I forget what the bloke's name was, just now.

So I goes around there and the bloke says, 'Are you a tradesman?'

'Yeah', which I wasn't.

He says, 'Have yer got yer ticket?'

'Yeah', which I didn't so, when he stuck his hand out for me to show him me tradesman's ticket, I just grabs hold of his hand and shakes it real hard and says real quick, 'Oh, thanks very much, mate. I really need this job.'

Anyway, maybe the bloke could see I was a bit desperate because, then he says, 'Have yer worked a guillotine before?'

'Oh, yeah, yeah.' Like, I didn't have a clue how to work a

guillotine so I goes down to this box factory in Redfern and a feller there shows me the place and I'm looking at this guillotine thing, that cuts cardboard, cuts paper, cuts everything. A big long thing, like this. Big blade as sharp as a razor, and I'm acting like I know all about it. Then on the first day I gets there at the crack of dawn and I'm looking at the previous feller on the guillotine, just to see how it works. Yeah, that's how I learned all about it. So then we moved to Sydney, to a little farm out at Castle Hill. I still had the little Hillman but I wasn't too sure in the traffic, so each morning I'd walk up this big hill to catch a bus into Pennant Hills, then I caught the train into Redfern.

Okay, so then the second son comes along and it must've been four weeks or more after he was born that I still hadn't registered him. See, I wanted his first name to be something special but I couldn't think of a name. Anyhow, the Births, Deaths and Marriages, they're writing me letters: 'Under paragraph so-and-so, clause so-and-so, paragraph 3, amendment 32' or something, 'you have to register your child after fourteen days.' But, see, I didn't know what to call him. So I'm working in this tin-pot box factory, working the guillotine – but that's beside the point – and I'm over the pub on a Friday after pay. I'm standing there with this feller who works with me, drinking a schooner, and there's a bloke standing beside us who's a bit wobbly on his feet. He's sort of drunk. Then the feller I'm with, he sees a mate of his over the other side of the bar, see, and he calls out, 'How yer goin', son?'

So the feller comes around and it turns out he knows the drunk bloke beside us and he says to me and the feller I'm with, 'Oh, don't worry about Ray' or whoever it was: 'his wife's just had a baby 'n' he's wettin' the baby's head.'

Then my mate says, 'Oh, Goldie's wife's just had a baby a month ago, too, but he doesn't know what to call it.'

Anyrate, this drunk bloke, he hears all this and he says, 'Call the kid Mark. That way, they can't add nothin' onto it 'n' they can't shorten it.'

So then, when I gets home, I says to Edith, 'Guess what? I've got a name fer the kid.'

She says, 'What?'

I says, 'Mark.'

'Oh, that sounds nice,' she says. 'When did you think to name him that?'

I said, 'I didn't. Some drunk in the pub named him.' So that's how the second feller got his name, Mark. Then I added the second name of the Aboriginal fella from on Glenore, Meenyarrawal, and I claim to be the only white person since the landing of the First Fleet that's named their two sons after the tribal name of an Aboriginal.

Yeah, so we had the first one, Adrian, one year and Mark, the next year. And soon after that Edith started working, with her nursing. Well, I looked after them when I could, and also there was a childcare centre close by. Then if Edith was on nightshift she could handle them during the day as well, just as long as she got her five hours' sleep or whatever. But oh, it knocked her around. Like, she was doing casual nursing. See, that's a lot more money. Well, what she done was, she went to what's called a nurses' club and when a hospital wants a nurse they contact the club and say, 'I want a nurse for three weeks to take the place of someone who's goin' on holidays.'

And there was this person from the nurses' club, Margaret Dunlop, and when she saw how Edith was such a good nurse, she'd ring up and say, 'Edith, look, will you go out to so-and-so hospital for three weeks? It's nightshift.'

'Yes, all right.'

So I'd find out where the hospital was and take Edith out there and I'd wait while she went inside to see if everything was okay. Then after she sorted out whatever she had to sort out, she'd just give me a wave to say how everything was okay. And she was such a good worker that, after a while, a lot of the hospitals especially asked, 'Can we have that Edith Goldsmith?'

But, see, I wasn't doing so good. Well, I was only on sixteen or seventeen quid a week, cutting cardboard and I'm at a bit of a loose end. Then I read in the *Reader's Digest*, 'What does Bible prophecy say will happen in 1975?' So I sent away for it and it's saying about all the seven last plagues and how a plague's going to fall on the Earth in 1975 and all this. And that got me ploughing into the bible and I loved it, aye. So then I studied the Jehovah's Witness and I studied the Christadelphians and I was studying with Armstrong. But, see, I was never satisfied because their teachings wasn't scriptural.

Anyhow, while all this's going on, I chucked the job in at the box factory and I went around to Trades Hall and I got a job at the *Sun-Herald* newspaper. Well, twenty-seven pound a week, aye, and you start at nine o'clock in the morning and you finish the last edition at half past three. Then, believe it or not, there's an hour and fifty for dinner and an hour and fifty between editions. Five weeks annual leave a year, broke up in two weeks and then three weeks. Unlimited sick pay. They had their own hospital fund; four shillings a week, taken out of your wages. So for the first time in years I'm really starting to save, aye.

Then, with all the scripture study, see, because Warren Harvey's father was an Adventist I said to Edith, 'I'll just check these fellers out, to see what they say,' and that's when I realised I was on the right track. So I started studies with the Seventh Day Adventist Church and I studied and I studied and an Adventist minister by the name of Herbert Bryant, he come around to Edith and me and he explained all the prophecies in Daniel seven and eight and nine and that's what convinced me that the Adventist Church was the prophetic church, aye. Oh, this pastor Bryant, I tell you, he was a marvel with scripture and church history and things like that.

Because, see, I'd always wondered, why in the dickens they kept Saturday as the Sabbath when Sunday's the seventh day, the day of rest. Then I was delving into church history and, see, way back when the papal power rose, around the year 350, they changed it from the Saturday to the Sunday. I tell you, tens and tens of thousands of people was put to the stake and burned alive just because they wouldn't bow down to Rome; just because they wouldn't keep Sunday. That's true. Fair dinkum. I found all this out in the studies. So yeah, I'd found what I wanted. I found the church I loved and wanted to serve and it got me closer to God. And this Hubert Bryant, he encouraged me. He said, 'Look Goldie,' he said, 'all the things you done – all your cattle duffing, your brawling, even your Aboriginal child, Cynthia – it's all nailed to the cross. You haven't got to worry about all that. You've got a brand new life now, a life to serve the church.'

Then through this Herbert Bryant I met the secretary of an ex-Labor premier of New South Wales and the ex-Labor feller, he owned a house over near North Sydney, and the secretary got us that house for only five quid a week, fully furnished and all. I forget her name just now but her husband was a retired policeman. And the owner feller, he still had his Labor principles – you know, helping the battler and all that. In the meanwhile, both Edith and me, we got baptised at the Adventist Church in Ashfield and, from that day on, I've never drunk a drop of alcohol and I've never let a swear word pass my lips. That's the dead truth. So me whole life started to turn itself around and we saved and saved and we saved four hundred pound – might've even been five hundred.

Then because the Sabbath starts sunset Friday, and I worked on Friday nights, I decided to leave the *Sun-Herald*. Actually, if

I'd stayed there a couple of months longer I could've got the Friday night off. But anyway, I didn't because I said to meself, 'Goldie, with all the things yer've done, when the creator of the universe comes down here 'n' gets nailed up on a cross 'n' says to you, "Your slate's clean, now. I'll take the rap."', I'll tell you what, mate, you'd be mad not to take advantage of it, aye, see, because the one gift we've been given is freedom of choice. We can't help being what we are, but we need to correct ourself if we know we're doing wrong, and all through me wild days as a young feller, if I went to a town cold, broke and hungry, well, I copped it, aye. I can proudly look God in the eye, you might say, and say I never, ever thieved or stole money when I was broke. And He knows that. Never. No, I went without, rather than thieved off another human being because, see, a person isn't judged on what he knows, he's judged on what he does with what he knows. That's a Christian, and my only real regret in life is that I didn't marry Gladys, just to give me baby, Cynthia, a name. I wouldn't have stayed with Gladys, mind you, and she didn't expect I would, but that's me only one regret.

Anyhow, then the Hillman blew up so I bought a little seventeen-year-old Austin A70. I've got heaps of photos of it here. And I knew this new life wasn't there in Sydney. I'm not cut out for the city. And I don't bible bash nobody but, see, my mother died when I was three and me brother finished up bad with the grog and he hated religion and so one of us had to be there. One of us had to make a difference. And I just couldn't let me mother down. She was only twenty-seven when she died and she really loved me. She really loved me, aye. So I come home one day and I says to Edith, 'Let's get outa here.'

So I packs up Edith and the kids and we drives out of Sydney in this old Austin, towing a little trailer full of our worldly possessions. We had 303 pound in our pockets and I'm off to Darwin to give studies to anyone and everyone who requests them. But, oh, I was on fire, mate. I'm full of the spirit, aye, to overflowing, and so I'm off to convert the world overnight. It was as crystal clear as anything I'd ever done. You know, it was like, all me life, I was meant to deliver the word. You could say I'd got me calling in life, so to speak. Yeah, that's what you could say, aye.

Goldie's two boys Adrian and Mark and the old Austin on the road to Darwin – the end of one life, the beginning of another